PIRACY IN THE
ANCIENT WORLD

PIRACY IN THE ANCIENT WORLD

AN ESSAY IN MEDITERRANEAN HISTORY

BY

HENRY A. ORMEROD

Εἰς 'Ρόδον εἰ πλεύσει τις 'Ολυμπικὸν ἦλθεν ἐρωτῶν
τὸν μάντιν, καὶ πῶς πλεύσεται ἀσφαλέως.
Χώ μάντις, Πρῶτον μὲν, ἔφη, Καινὴν ἔχε τὴν ναῦν
καὶ μὴ χειμῶνος τοῦ δὲ θέρους ἀνάγου.
Τοῦτο γὰρ ἂν ποιῇς, ἥξεις κἀκεῖσε καὶ ὧδε,
ἂν μὴ πειρατὴς ἐν πελάγει σε λάβῃ.
Anth. Pal , xi 162.

THE JOHNS HOPKINS UNIVERSITY PRESS
BALTIMORE, MARYLAND

DC
61
.P5
G76
1997
may 1999

Originally published as a hardcover edition in 1924 by the University of Liverpool Press
Johns Hopkins Paperbacks edition, 1997
06 05 04 03 02 01 00 99 98 97   5 4 3 2 1

The Johns Hopkins University Press
2715 North Charles Street
Baltimore, Maryland 21218-4319
The Johns Hopkins Press Ltd., London

Library of Congress Cataloging-in-Publication Data

Ormerod, Henry Arderne, 1886–1964.
   Piracy in the ancient world : an essay in Mediterranean history / by Henry A. Ormerod.
       p.   cm.
   "Originally published as a hardcover edition in 1924 by the University of Liverpool Press"—T.p. verso.
   Includes bibliographical references and index.
   ISBN 0-8018-5505-5 (pbk : alk. paper)
   1. Mediterranean Region—History.   2. Pirates—Mediterranean Region—History.   I. Title.
DC61.P5076   1997
910´.9163´8—dc20   96-44837
                                                                      CIP

Printed in the United States of America on acid-free paper

CONTENTS

primitive seaman—piracy and war—cattle-raiding and reprisals—traces of early conventions against piracy.

The thalassocracy of Minos—Thucydides' account of Cretan police—piracy on the southern coasts of Asia Minor—The Lukki of the Tell-el-Amarna letters—the sea-raiders in the Egyptian records— many of the raiders drawn from Asia Minor, with Aegean peoples participating—echoes of these raids in the Homeric poems—resemblance to the movements of the third century after Christ—both foreshadow the great migrations.

Greek marauders in the Levant—voyages to the West—the character of early Greek commercial ventures—growth of a higher morality—the influence of Delphi and the religious leagues—the continuance of piracy fostered by commercial rivalries—Samos— trading leagues—the effects of the Persian advance— migrations to the West and confusion in the Aegean.

The police measures undertaken by the Athenians— the effects of the Peloponnesian war—privateering on both sides—serious outbreak of piracy after the war—the second Athenian confederacy—Athenian claims to be the guardian of the seas during the fourth century—the effects of the Social and Macedonian wars—conduct of the belligerents— conditions in the eastern Mediterranean during Alexander's war with Persia—his attempt to clear the seas—conditions after Alexander—pirates and mercenaries—Italian marauders in the Aegean—the

PREFACE

THE present work has grown out of a lecture delivered in Liverpool and published in *The Annals of Archaeology and Anthropology*, vol. VIII (1921). The subject seemed to be of sufficient interest to warrant a larger essay. Sestier's book, *La Piraterie dans l'Antiquité* (Paris, 1880), still remains the largest treatise on the subject, but is uncritical and contains many inaccuracies. Of other works, Lecrivain's article, *Pirata*, in Daremberg and Saglio, is an admirable collection of sources, which is supplemented by Kroll's *Seeraub* in Pauly-Wissowa. The best study of the subject is that by Paul Stein, *Ueber Piraterie im Altertum* (Cöthen, 1891), and *Zur Geschichte der Piraterie im Altertum* (Bernburg, 1894), which forms the second part. Both these articles were difficult to obtain, but contain an extremely valuable discussion of the evidence. A paper by Miss Churchill Semple, *Pirate Coasts of the Mediterranean Sea* (*The Geographical Review*, August, 1916) is a general study of piracy in the Mediterranean from the point of view of the geographer. I have failed to obtain a copy of a dissertation by Herold (Erlangen, 1914). My own interest in the ancient pirates goes back to the Rev. E. M. Walker's lectures in Oxford, and to the chapters in Bérard's *Les Phéniciens et l'Odyssée*, which first showed me how the subject should be approached.

5

My obligations to friends, with whom I have discussed problems arising in the book, are great. Professor J. D. I. Hughes has been kind enough to read the second chapter in proof, and has rescued me from many pitfalls of the law. My greatest debt is to Professor W. R. Halliday, who has read the whole book in proof. It was largely owing to his help and encouragement that the book came to be written, and he has generously placed at my disposal a great deal of information that he had himself collected. My debt to Mr. M. N. Tod is also a large one. If the collection of epigraphical material is in any way complete, it is entirely due to the notes which he has sent me. Miss Muriel Joynt, B.A., has given me valuable help in preparing the book for press. The preparation of the maps was undertaken by Mr. A. J. Sifton, F.R.G.S.

LEEDS, *July*, 1924.

PIRACY IN THE
ANCIENT WORLD

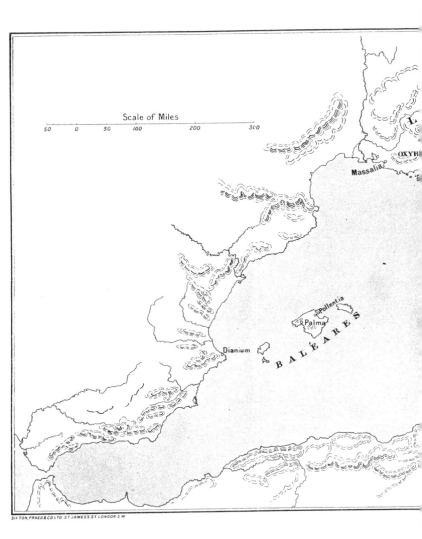

Scale of Miles

50   0   50   100   200   300

OXYB

Massalia

Pollentia

Palma

Dianium

B A L É A R E S

SIFTON, PRAED & CO LTD. ST JAMES S ST LONDON S W

MAP I

THE WESTERN MEDITERRANEAN

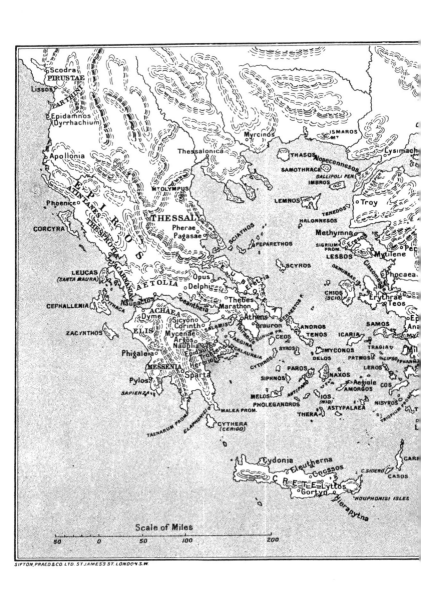

Scodra
PIRUSTAE
Lissos
PARTHINI
Epidamnos
(Dyrrhachium)

Apollonia

Phoenice
CORCYRA
E P I R U S
ATINTANES
THESPROTIA

LEUCAS
(SANTA MAURA)
ACARNANIA
ITHACA
CEPHALLENIA
Naupactus
Oeantheia
AETOLIA
Delphi
ACHAEA
Dyme
ELIS
ZACYNTHOS
Sicyon
Corinth
Mycenae
Argos
Nauplia
Phigalea
MESSENIA
Epidaurus
Hermione
TROEZEN
CALAURIA
Pylos
Sparta
SAPIENZA
MALEA PROM.
TAENARUM PROM.
ELAPHONISI
CYTHERA
(CERIGO)

Myrcinos
ISMAROS
MT

Thessalonica
THASOS
Nopeconnesos
SAMOTHRACE
GALLIPOLI PEN.
IMBROS
LEMNOS
Troy
TENEDOS
HALONNESOS
Methymna
SIGRIUM
PROM.
CRESOS
LESBOS
Mytilene

Mt OLYMPUS

THESSALY
Pherae
Pagasae
SCIATHOS
PEPARETHOS
SCYROS
Phocaea
CHIOS
(SCIO)
Erythrae
Teos

Lysimach

EUBOEA

Opus
Thebes
Marathon
Athens
Brauron
SUNIUM PR.
CEOS
ANDROS
TENOS
ICARIA
SAMOS

Eretria

Ep
Ana
MY

Tragia
Mi

OENUSSAE

PATMOS
LEROS

AEGINA
SALAMIS
SYROS
MYCONOS
DELOS

Ep
CYTHNOS
PAROS
NAXOS
SIPHNOS
Aegiale
AMORGOS
COS

MELOS
ANTIPAROS
IOS
(NIO)
ASTYPALAEA
NISYROS
T

PHOLEGANDROS
THERA
TRIOPIUM PR.
L

CAR

Cydonia
Eleutherna
C.SIDERO
CASOS
C R E T E
Cnossos
Lyttos
Gortyn
KOUPHONISI ISLES
Hierapytna

Scale of Miles
50   0   50   100   200

SIFTON, PRAED & CO. LTD. ST JAMES'S ST. LONDON S.W.

MAP II

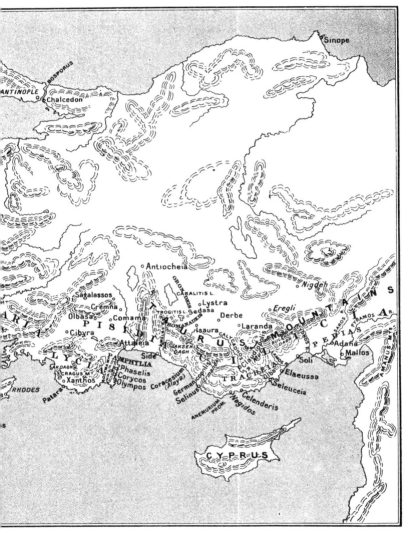

GREECE AND ASIA MINOR

CHAPTER I

THROUGHOUT its history the Mediterranean has
witnessed a constant struggle between the civilised
peoples dwelling on its coasts and the barbarians,
between the peaceful trader using its highways and
the pirate who infested the routes that he must
follow.   At different stages of their history most
of the maritime peoples have belonged now to one
class and now to the other.   From the time when
men first went down to the sea in ships, piracy
and robbery have been regarded only as one of the
means of livelihood that the sea offered.   The
earliest literature of Greece shows us the Homeric
pirate pursuing a mode of life at sea almost
identical with that of the Frankish corsairs ; in
our records of early Crete we can see the first
attempts of a civilised state to cope with the evils
of piracy and protect its sea-borne commerce.
Only at rare intervals has a complete suppression
been achieved.   Perhaps the only times when the
whole Mediterranean area has been free have been
during the early centuries of the Roman empire
and in our own day.   The Romans succeeded by
the disarmament of the barbarian communities,
and still more by the spread of civilisation.
In our own times an organised sea-police and the
introduction of steam, for the time at any rate,
have proved too strong for the Mediterranean

pirate. But it is worth remembering that as late as the Crimean war, British ships were patrolling the Cyclades on the look-out for pirate-craft, one of which had contrived to rob a boat in sight of the harbour of Syra[1]. The coast of northern Africa is still said to be dangerous to sailing vessels,[2] and quite recently a suit was brought in the King's Bench to decide whether the seizure of a Greek motor-schooner by a Turkish brigand of the Black Sea coast, tolerated by the Kemalists, constituted an act of piracy or an act of war.[3] If we remember that piracy was for centuries a normal feature of Mediterranean life, it will be realised how great has been the influence which it exercised on the life of the ancient world.

The coasts of the Mediterranean are peculiarly favourable to the development of piracy. Much of the shore line is rocky and barren, and unable to support a large population. We shall from time to time have to refer to particular localities, such as the Cilician, Ligurian and Illyrian coasts, where piracy was endemic. When the inhabitants took to the sea, navigation came easily to them on the land-locked bays and creeks of their native shore. By land, the poverty of the soil had forced them to become hunters and brigands rather than

1. Newton, *Travels and Discoveries in the Levant*, I, p. 264. For the prevalence of piracy in the Archipelago see pp. 218, 284, 326; II, p. 229.

2. Koester, *Das Antike Seewesen*, pp. 235-6, quotes the German *Segelhand-buches für das Mittelmeer* (Berlin, 1905): " Segelschiffe müssen in grossem Abstand von diesem Küstenstrich (Nordafrika) bleiben, weil . . . . sie auch Angriffe der Eingeborenen befurchten müssen." The same work also contains a warning against the common use by the natives of the false flare.

3. Banque Moustaca and Carystinaka and Central Bank of Greece *v.* Motor Union Insurance Company, Limited (*The Times*, Jan. 18, 1923). The seizure took place in 1920.

agriculturalists ; the same pursuits were followed on the sea.

In addition to the natural allurements which drew the robber tribes to the sea, the features of Mediterranean lands are such as to make the pirate's business a particularly profitable one. We may leave aside for the moment the economic conditions which promoted piracy, and consider only the geographical. The structure of most Mediterranean countries has decreed that the principal lines of communication should be by sea, and that the bulk of commerce should be carried by the same routes. The interposition of mountain barriers renders the land routes difficult and dangerous ; navigable rivers are few. But the place of roads and rivers as a means of internal communication is largely taken in Greece and western Asia Minor by deep arms of the sea running far inland, while islands lying off the coast provide a natural breakwater and shelter for small coasting vessels.[1] But if the sea invites, it also imposes certain limitations. In early days of navigation the shipper is forced to hug the shores, creeping round the coasts,[2] often becalmed or driven back by contrary winds, and lying-to for the night.[3] If he endeavours to cross the sea, he is compelled to follow fixed routes, by which

---

1. On the naves orariae see Pliny, Ep., X, 15, who writes from Ephesos : Nunc destino partim orariis navibus, partim vehiculis provinciam [Bithynia] petere.

2. Strabo, I, 48 : τοὺς ἀρχαιοτάτους πλεῖν καὶ κατὰ λῃστείαν ἢ ἐμπορίαν, μὴ πελαγίζειν δὲ ἀλλὰ παρὰ γῆν.

3. The night-voyages of the Phoenicians (ἀπὸ τῆς λογιστικῆς ἀρξάμενοι καὶ τῆς νυκτιπλοίας) were unusual (Strabo, XVI, 757). For the general objection to night-voyaging see Homer, Od., XII, 284-287, although we hear of voyages by night, where local conditions are favourable or secrecy is necessary (II, 382-434 ; XIII, 35 ; XV, 296).

alone he can keep in sight of land, threading his way between islands and following well-known channels. There can be little concealment of his movements ; the prevailing winds at certain seasons of the year tend to drive commerce in definite directions. The corsair knows this and like the Cretan in Homer[1] will make use of the favourable five days' passage from Crete to raid the Egyptian coast, or waylay the merchantmen who are following the same route. The French traveller D'Arvieux, in 1658, watched a corsair lying in wait for the merchantmen on their return journey from Egypt : " Nous apperçûmes un Vaisseau à la mer que nous jugeâmes sans peines être un Corsaire de Malte, c'est-à-dire, qui en avoit pris la Banniere : car les Chevaliers sont bien éloignez de ces sortes de brigandages. Il mouilla quelque tems après entre le Mont-Carmel et Caifa, pour attendre les Saiques d'Egypte, parce que le vent étoit excellent pour leur faire faire cette route. En effet, nous en vîmes passer quelques-unes ausquelles il ne dit rien, parce qu'elles étoient au large et qu'elles avoient l'avantage du vent : car les voiles de ces Bâtimens sont taillées de telle maniere qu'il est impossible aux Vaisseaux de les joindre, quand ils ne se trouvent pas au vent à elles."[2]   One of the

1. *Od.*, XIV, 257 ; cf. the use of the Etesian winds made by Miltiades to raid Lemnos (Hdt., VI, 140).

2. D'Arvieux, *Mémoires*, I, 283. Compare the Greek epigram (*Anth. Pal.*, VII, 640) :

'Ριγηλὴ ναύταις ἐρίφων δύσις ἀλλὰ Πύρωνι
    πουλὺ γαληναίη χείματος ἐχθροτέρη.
νῆα γὰρ ἀπνοίῃ πεπεδημένου ἔφθασε ναύταις
    λῃστέων ταχινὴ δίκροτος ἐσσυμένη·
χεῖμα δέ μιν προφυγόντα γαληναίῳ ὑπ'ὀλέθρῳ
    ἔκτανον· ἅ λυγρῆς δειλὲ καχορμισίης.

most illuminating descriptions of the corsair's
routine that I know is the account given by the
Englishman Roberts, who was wrecked at Nio (Ios)
in 1692, captured by a "crusal," and compelled
to serve as gunner on board.[1] He tells us that the
corsairs usually wintered at Paros, Antiparos,
Melos and Ios[2] from the middle of December to
the beginning of March:

And then they go for the Furnoes,[3] and lie there under
the high Land hid,having a watch on the Hill with a little
Flag, whereby they make a Signal, if they see any Sail :
they slip out and lie athwart the Boak of Samos, and take
their Prize ; They lie in the same nature under Necaria,
and Gadronise[4], and Leppiso[5] in the Spring, and forepart
of the Summer ; Then for the middle of the Summer[6],
they ply on the Coast of Cyprus ; and if they hear the
least noise of any Algerines and Grand Turks ships at
Rhodes, away they scour for the Coast of Alexandria and

1. *A Collection of Original Voyages, Published by Captain William
Hacke* (London, 1699). *IV—Mr. Roberts his voyage to the Levant, with an
Account of his Sufferings amongst the Corsairs, their villainous Way of Living,
and his Description of the Archipelago Islands. Together with his Relation of
Taking and Retaking of Scio in the Year* 1696. (My attention was first drawn
to this book by Mr. G. E. Manwaring, of the London Library.)

2. Ios was known to the Turks, from the number of Frankish corsairs
who used the island as a rendezvous, as the *Little Malta* (Tournefort, *Relation
d'un Voyage du Levant*, I, p. 252). According to Bent, most of the churches
in the island were the pious offerings of corsairs (*Cyclades*, p. 153). The
native pilots of the island and also of Melos were much sought by the Frankish
corsairs, and were considered the best in the Levant, as they knew the coasts
of Syria and Egypt, where the best prizes were made (Tournefort, I,
pp. 149, 252).

3. The Fourni islands between Samos and Icaria. A traveller in the
early nineteenth century speaks of the great number of pirates that lurk
about them (Clark, *Travels in various Countries*, II, p. 185).

4. Gaïdaronisi (to the south of Samos), the ancient Tragia.

5. Lipso, near Patmos and Leros.

6. Cf. Ptolemy, *Phaseis*, p. 60 (Teubner), ἐτησίαι ἄρχονται πνεῖν
(July 18); p. 14, ἐτησίαι παύονται (Aug. 29). (See Pauly-Wissowa,
II, A, 1, p. 409.)

Damiata, being shole Water, well knowing the Turks
will not follow them thither. The latter part of the
Summer they come stealing on the Coast of Syria, where
they do most mischief with their Feleucca, which commonly Rows with 12 Oars, and carries 6 Sitters : For at
Night they leave the Ship, and get under the shoar before
Day, and go ashoar, where they way-lay the Turks . . . .
From hence towards the Autumn they come lurking in
about the Islands, to and fro about the Boakes again,
until they put in also to lie up in the Winter.

During the winter, navigation was practically
at an end ; with it the pirate's business was
suspended and the opportunity taken to refit.
It is only rarely that we hear of them keeping the
sea during the winter. The seamanship of the
Cilician pirates allowed it, and the Governor of
Zante, in 1603, complains of the British pirates,
who were seriously molesting Venetian commerce,
that " they keep the sea even in midwinter and
in the roughest weather thanks to the handiness of
their ships and the skill of their mariners."[1]
But the ordinary practice was a return to harbour
or to a hidden base among the islands, where the
pirate could be free from molestation.[2] When the
sailing season begins, there are many sheltered
creeks among the islands, where a pirate vessel can
lie hid and pounce upon an unsuspecting

1. *Calendar of State Papers, Venice, etc.*, IX, no. 152.

2. Compare Roberts, p. 47 : "Here (Paros) the Crusals lye up to
Winter, by reason the Turks cannot come at them, for at the Entrance of it
there is a great shole under Water ; and tho' the Crusals go thither every
Year twice or thrice, yet they have always a Boat lies on the Shoal ; so they
go in and lie in 6, 5 or 4 Fathom in Winter behind an old sunk Mold, in 3
Fathom." Bent (*op. cit.*, p. 395) speaks of a wall between Paros and
Antiparos built under water by the pirates, the passage through which was
known only to themselves.

merchantman labouring up the channel.[1]   " They
infested with their row-boats every corner of the
Cyclades and Morea and made a lawful prize
of any vessel that was too weak for resistance ; or
entered by night into the villages and dwellings
near the shore, carrying off whatever they could
find. Boats of this sort, here called *Trattas*,
abounded in every creek; they are long and narrow
like canoes ; ten, twenty or even thirty men, each
armed with a rifle and pistols, row with great
celerity, and small masts with Latine sails are also
used when the winds are favourable."[2]
The particular hunting-ground which Roberts'
friends patronised was chosen in order to catch
coasting vessels coming from the south of Asia
Minor,[3] or those working through the Cyclades
from the mainland of Greece, and sheltering from
the north wind under the lee of Icaria and Samos
on their voyage to the Ionian coast.   This, it will
be remembered, was the route followed by the

1. So the suitors waiting for Telemachus' ship (*Od.*, IV, 844) :

ἔστι δέ τις νῆσος μέσση ἁλὶ πετρήεσσα
μεσσηγὺς Ἰθάκης τε Σάμοιο τε παιπαλοέσσης,
Ἀστερίς, οὐ μεγάλη· λιμένες δ' ἐνι ναύλοχοι αὐτῇ
ἀμφίδυμοι· τῇ τόν γε μένον λοχόωντες Ἀχαιοί.

2. Morritt (1795) in Walpole, *Memoirs relating to European and Asiatic
Turkey* (2nd ed.), p. 42.

3. Cf. Hasluck, *B.S.A.*, xvii, p. 169 : " The case of Samos is the most
important instance of the depopulation and abandonment of an island
owing to piracy, as also the best documented.   The island lay directly on
the coasters' route between (Egypt and) South Asia Minor and Constantinople,
and at all unsettled periods in the Aegean, the Fourni, like the Spalmadori
(Oenussae) and Moskonisi groups, which are similarly situated with regard
to the straits of Chios and Mytilene respectively, became a recognised haunt
of the pirates who preyed on this traffic.   Samos was naturally their repair
for wood, water, and other supplies, and their exactions became so intolerable
after the middle of the fifteenth century that the Samians, who had been
migrating for some time, consented to be removed *en masse* by the Genoese
and settled in Chios."

Peloponnesian squadron in 427 B.C.[1] Strabo
describes the neighbouring Tragia, the Gadronise of
Roberts, as infested with pirates.[2] A little to the
south-east Julius Caesar was caught at Pharmacussa.[3]
Further to the north, a passage of Arrian describes
how Memnon, in the war with Alexander, posted
a part of his fleet at the Sigrium promontory in
Lesbos to catch the merchant vessels coming from
Chios, Geraestos, and Malea.[4] On the more
direct route to the Hellespont the islands of
Scyros[5] and Halonnesos[6] had a bad reputation
and, according to tradition, the " Pelasgian "
natives of Lemnos carried their cruises as far
as the coast of Attica.[7] The Gallipoli peninsula
itself was full of pirates after the Persian wars,
and was a constant source of danger in the
fourth century.[8]

One of the most dangerous passages was the
Cythera channel. It was a favourite hunting-
ground of submarines during the late war, and
at all times has had a bad reputation. Thévenot
describes the passage between Cerigo (Cythera)
and the mainland as very much quicker than
between Cerigo and Cerigotto. For this reason

1. Thuc. III, 29; and in the reverse direction by Datis and Artaphernes
in 490 B.C. (Hdt. VI, 95).

2. Strabo XIV, 635.

3. Plutarch, *Julius*, 1; Suetonius, *Julius*, 4.

4. Arrian, *Anabasis*, II, 1, 3: ἵνα ἡ προσβόλη μάλιστά ἐστι ταῖς ἀπό
τε Χίου και Γεραιστοῦ καὶ Μαλέας ὁλκάσι. For the alternative routes from
Lesbos to Geraestos, seaward of Chios or inside the island by windy Mimas,
see *Odyssey*, III, 169 seqq.

5. Plutarch, *Cimon*, 8.

6. (Demosthenes), VII.

7. Hdt., VI, 138.

8. See below, pp. 108, 117.

a Venetian *galeace* was stationed near Cerigo to guard the channel.[1] His compatriot and contemporary, D'Arvieux, was chased by a suspicious vessel when making the passage. A storm of wind nearly carried him on to the point of Cerigo. Here the dangers of shipwreck were increased by the nearness of the Mainotes, " peuple méchant, cruel, sans foi, sans humanité, en un mot Grec. . . Ils n'ont à la verité que de méchantes petites Barques qui n'osent attaquer que de très petits Bâtimens ; mais ils attendent que les tempêtes jettent les Bâtimens sur leur côtes et alors sautant de rochers en rochers comme des chévres sauvages ils viennent piller les débris des Bâtimens."[2] Small mercy was shown to their captives, Christians being sold to the Turks and Turks to Christians. Dr. Covell describes the capture of some of the crew of his ship who had landed on the island of Elaphonisi, and were sold to the Turkish galleys.[3] " These miscreant wretches lye constantly watching upon the rocks and mountains, not so much to secure themselves from the injuries of the pirates as themselves to thieve and rob whom they catch."[4] It is in accord with the general principles of Mediterranean piracy to find that the Mainotes soon advanced from the stage of kidnappers and wreckers to that of genuine pirates. Beaufort, among others, states that there was a " regularly

---

1. Thévenot, *Voyage de Levant* (3rd edition, Amsterdam, 1727), I, p. 38.

2. D'Arvieux, *Op. cit.*, I, p. 33.

3. It is amusing to hear that they afterwards sued the captain for arrears of wages.

4. Covell's Diary (1670-77), ed. Bent, *Early Voyages and Travels in the Levant* (Hakluyt Society, LXXXVII), p. 133.

organised system of absolute and general piracy among them."[1]

It was therefore not only the risks of storm that gave rise to the proverb " Round Malea and forget your home "[2] ; the risks from pirates in the Cythera channel were not less in antiquity than in the seventeenth and eighteenth centuries. At the time of the Peloponnesian war, the Spartans maintained a garrison in the island to prevent its occupation by pirates, and to give security to merchantmen coming from Libya and Egypt.[3] At an earlier date, Chilon the wise had said that it would be better for Sparta that Cythera should be sunk in the sea.[4] We shall find Malea haunted by Cretan, Illyrian, and Laconian pirates in the days of Nabis.[5]

The small islands and rocks with which the Mediterranean is studded have always been a favourite haunt of the pirate, whether as a lurking-ground to catch merchantmen, or as a base for plundering the opposite mainland. In the West the Massaliotes were driven to occupy the

1. *Caramanian Coast*, p. 227. He destroyed one of their boats, which in spite of its " contemptible appearance," was fast, " possessed a swivel " and 20 muskets, and " with the forty ferocious-looking villains who manned her might have carried the largest merchant ship in the Mediterranean." There is a good account of the Mainotes by Leake (*Morea*, I, p. 260), who preserves a local poem on the manners and customs of the inhabitants of Kakovulia (Mesa Mani), which is worth reading. According to Hasluck (*B.S.A.*, XVII, p. 173), " the Mainotes are first heard of in this connection early in the seventeenth century."

2. Strabo, VIII, 378. In its modern form
Κάβο Μαλῆα, Κάβο Μαλῆα,
βοήθα Χριστὲ καὶ Παναγιά
(as given by Wace and Hasluck, *B.S.A.*, XIV, p. 172).

3. Thuc., IV, 53.

4. Hdt., VII, 235.

5. See below, pp. 144, 149, 178, 187.

Stoichades (Isles d'Hyères), to the East of their town.[1] With these in pirate hands the land-route from Marseilles to Antipolis could be rendered as unsafe as a voyage along the coast. In the Black Sea an inscription of imperial date records the occupation of the island of Leuce at the mouth of the Danube by pirates.[2] Their object, no doubt, was to catch the traffic as it issued from the Danube. The corresponding station in the Mediterranean would be at the mouth of a gulf. Such islands were Myonnesos at the entrance to the Malian Gulf,[3] and Sciathos among the northern Sporades,[4] through which ships north-ward bound from the Euripos and from the Malian and Pagasaean gulfs would pass, and a rich booty be taken from the traffic coming southward from Thessalonica and the Thermaic gulf. The Sporades are thus described by a traveller at the beginning of the last century :

The group of isles at the entrance of the gulph of Salonica has been a principal resort of pirates, partly from the number of vessels passing this way ; partly from the facility with which they can recruit their numbers among the Albanians who come down upon the coast . . . . In this unlawful vocation large row boats are chiefly employed ; they are crowded with men, armed with pistols and cutlasses, who usually attempt to board the vessels on which their attack is made. On this coast the greater number of the pirates are said to be native Albanians . . . . It must be remarked that on this side

1. Strabo, IV, 184.

2. Wilhelm, *Beiträge*, p. 205. (Polybius, IV, 41, has some interesting remarks on the shoals at the Danube mouth, ἐφ' ἣν ἔτι πελάγιοι τρέχοντες οἱ πλέοντες τὸν Πόντον λανθάνουσι ἐποκέλλοντες νυκτὸς ἐπὶ τοὺς τόπους.)

3. Aeschines, II, 72 (cf. Strabo, IX, 435).

4. Appian, *Mithr.*, 94.

the Grecian continent every desperado is currently called
an Albanian. In the Archipelago the pirates derive
peculiar advantages from the isles which crowd its surface,
some of them uninhabited, others having a population
easily made subservient to schemes of illegal plunder.[1]

The same writer alludes to the pirates of
Meganisi on the western shore of Greece and to
the protection given to them by the authorities
of Santa Maura before the British occupation.
They were largely recruited from the brigands
expelled from the mainland by Ali Pasha of
Janina.[2] Dodwell also says that the canal of
Santa Maura was looked upon as one of the most
dangerous places for pirates, who " conceal
themselves among the rocks and islands with
which the canal is studded, and if they find
themselves in danger, escape in a few minutes
either to Leucadia or to the coast of Acarnania."[3]
The predecessors of these rascals in heroic days
were the Taphians, the typical pirates of the
Odyssey, who are located by later writers in these
islands.[4] They acted as carriers and slave-
merchants to the inhabitants of the Ionian islands,[5]
with the authorities of which they cultivated good
relations,[6] the raids of which we hear being
directed elsewhere—against Epiros, Sidon, and

1. Henry Holland, *Travels, etc.* (1812-13), pp. 336-7. It is interesting
to find the name Albanian applied to all pirates. In the Roman period
there was a similar use of the name Cilician.

2. *Ib.*, p. 59. On the pirates who infested this district in the twelfth
century, see Miller, *The Latins in the Levant*, p. 8.

3. Dodwell, *Tour through Greece*, I, pp. 44, 58.

4. Strabo, X, 459; Pliny, XXXVI, 150 (on Taphiusa, qui locus est
dextra navigantibus ex Ithaca Leucadem).

5. *Od.*, I, 184; XIV, 452.

6. *Od.*, I, 187.

Mycenae.[1] For the last exploit they and the Teleboans, who are perhaps identical with the Taphians,[2] were punished by Amphitryon. Mentes' followers in the *Odyssey* were doubtless as mixed as the Meganisi pirates at the beginning of the last century,[3] and made as good a thing out of the traffic which followed this coast.[4]

When sailing vessels hugged the shore, an equal danger was presented by promontories. The cowardly man in Theophrastus is ridiculed for thinking every promontory at sea a pirate galley,[5] but it was always possible that one was lurking there, to catch the merchantman endeavouring to round it. The emperor Julian compares the Cynics to brigands and those who occupy promontories to damage voyagers.[6] D'Arvieux speaks with satisfaction of doubling Cape Spartivento without seeing any of the corsairs who usually haunted it.[7] The same writer tells us that the point of the island of Sapienza was called La Vigie des Corsaires, " parce que c'est l'endroit où ils se mettent en embuscade pour découvrir les Vaiseaux Chrétiens qui viennent du Levant pour reconnoître le Cap et qui y achevent souvent leur voyage."[8] Cockerell had pointed out to him from Aegina the pirate boats lying off

1. *Od.*, XVI, 426; XV, 427; Hesiod, *Scut.*, 19; Apollodorus, II, 4, 6-7.

2. See Strabo, *l.c.*, and Pliny, IV, 53.

3. On Taphian affinities with the Illyrians see Allen, *The Homeric Catalogue of Ships*, p. 97.

4. As attested by *Od.*, XIV, 334.

5. Theophrastus, *Characters*, 25. A similar mistake is recorded in Hdt., VIII, 107.

6. Julian, VII, 210 A.

7. D'Arvieux, *op. cit.*, III, p. 382.

8. *Ib.*, p. 375.

Sunium, one of their favourite haunts.[1] We have already examined Memnon's ambush at Cape Sigrium. One of the best examples from antiquity is the advice given by the Milesians to the Peloponnesian privateers to lie off the Triopian promontory in order to catch the Athenian merchantmen on the voyage from Egypt.[2]

From many of the illustrations which have been given it will have been realised that much of the work in more recent times was done close in shore and with small craft. The same was undoubtedly the case in antiquity. Frequently the pirate-boats were quite small, only large enough to hold the number of ruffians required to surprise the crew of a merchantman lying-to for the night, or off their guard.[3] The boats used by the Megarian privateers for this purpose in the Peloponnesian war were small enough to be placed on a wagon.[4] In the Black Sea we hear of a special kind of boat, the *camara* of the Caucasian coasts, capable of holding twenty-five or thirty men, which was so light that it could easily be lifted from the water and hidden in the scrub.

1. Cockerell, *Travels in S. Europe and the Levant*, 1810-17, p. 42. Cf. the letter of Byron (1811), published in *B.S.A.*, XXII, p. 107: " I was nearly taken myself six weeks ago by some Mainote pirates (Lacedaemonians and be damned to them) at Cape Colonna."

2. Thuc. VIII, 35. For the difficulties experienced in bad weather by small craft when doubling the promontory (now Cape Crio) see Newton, *op. cit.*, II, p. 168. For the Capherean promontory see below, p. 79.

3. For risks of this type, see George Sandys (1610) in *Purchas, His Pilgrimes* (Glasgow; Maclehose & Sons, 1905), VIII, p. 102: " On the three and twentieth wee continued weatherbound, remooving after it grew dark unto another anchorage; a custom they held, lest observed by day from sea or shoare, they might by night be surprised." Cockerell, *op. cit.*, pp. 8-9, records the surprise and capture of a British Brig of War by a boat-load of Mainote pirates, while the captain and crew were at dinner.

4. Thuc., IV, 67. See below, p. 111.

In these craft the pirates would attack merchantmen at sea, or sail to raid the neighbouring coasts,
where the boats were left in the marshes, while the
men wandered through the district in search of
prey.[1] The sea-going ships of the Ligurian
pirates are spoken of as wretched affairs, cheaper
than rafts.[2] The inhabitants of the Baleares kept
watch from the rocks for the approach of foreign
vessels, and then assailed them with a crowd of
rafts.[3] The ease with which such craft could be
removed from the water and hidden made the task
of suppression a peculiarly difficult one in certain
localities. The authorities in the East Indies were
faced with a similar difficulty in dealing with the
Dyaks of Borneo. On an alarm, the pirates would
sink or hide their boats in creeks and rivers, and it
was only by intercepting the whole fleet on its
return from a plundering expedition that Rajah
Brooke was able to deal with them.[4]

A shallow draft was, as we saw from Roberts'
account, a necessity in the pirate boat. The
warships, which the Cilicians are said to have
built towards the end of their career, were
unusual, and date from the time when the pirates
were organised by Mithradates almost as a part
of his regular navy.[5] Normally, a light build

---

1. Strabo, XI, 495; Tacitus, *Hist.*, III, 47. See Torr, *Ancient Ships*,
p. 107. (On the cannibalistic tendencies of these pirates, see Aristotle,
Politics, VIII, 1338b. See also Diod. Sic. XX, 25). Belon, *Observations*
(Paris, 1553), p. 87 (II, x) gives much the same account of the tactics of
the Aegean pirates in the sixteenth century.

2. Diod. Sic., V, 39.

3. Florus, III, 8.

4. See S. C. Hill, *Episodes of Piracy in the Eastern Seas*, *The Indian
Antiquary*, 1920, p. 118.

5. See below, p. 222.

was preferred, as it gave the speed necessary both in attack and in flight. When pursued by the heavier warships of the maritime powers, the pirate could easily escape by entering shoal waters, or if forced ashore could often save his ship by means of a portage. Spratt recounts the loss of the British frigate *Cambrian* in 1829, while operating against pirate shipping inside Grabusa harbour off Crete, on a reef running across the harbour like a mole.[1] A Christian corsair, manned by some twenty-eight or thirty men, when pursued by Turkish galleys, ran for the isthmus of Corinth, and the boat was carried across to the other sea.[2] A similar story is told of a pirate boat dragged by sixty men across the isthmus of Athos to avoid capture.[3]

The pirate boat is nearly always distinguished from the warship, and frequently the use of the word πλοῖον enables us to realise that pirate-craft are indicated rather than the warships of a hostile power.[4] As a rule, however, we do not find that the pirates made use of any particular rig or build. Probably, in most cases, the would-be pirate was content with the first boat that came

---

1. Spratt, *op. cit.*, II, p. 226.

2. Spon and Wheler, II, p. 208.

3. Cousinéry, *Voyage dans la Macédoine* (1831), II, p. 154. It will be remembered that Torghut Reis, when blockaded by Doria at Jerbah, saved his whole fleet by similar means.

4. *I. G.*, II, 331, the πλοῖα of Glaucetas (see below, p. 124); *I. G.* XII, 3, 1291, πλοῖα μακρά of Cretan pirates; Ditt. Syll.³, 581. The mention of πλοῖα in *I. G.*, IX, 1, 683, makes it probable that pirates are intended; the πλοῖα are certainly not *naves onerariae* recovered by the Corcyraeans, as the editor suggests *ad loc.* It is probable that the πλοῖον and the ἡμιολία in the fleet of Metrophanes, the admiral of Mithradates (Appian, *Mithr.*, 29) were pirate boats and that Metrophanes was himself a pirate leader (see below, p. 220).

to hand by theft or purchase. Some types of
craft are native to, or named after particular
communities, such as the *samaina* of Samos ;
the *lembus*, *pristis* and *liburna* were originated or
developed among the tribes of the Illyrian coasts.[1]
But the latter designs were widely imitated by the
shipbuilders of the naval powers, and were much
employed in the regular navies from the third
century onwards. Even the two vessels which in
Hellenistic and Roman times are most closely
associated with the pirates, the *hemiolia* and
myoparo,[2] were widely used by others. The
hemiolia was employed by Alexander for river work,
by Philip V of Macedon, and in the Roman fleets.[3]
As no ancient representation of it has survived
we are uncertain as to its exact design and rig ;
it is usually held that it possessed one complete
and one half-bank of rowers, the upper bank
being reduced to give room for the fighting men.[4]
It is clear, however, that both the *hemioliae* and
the *myoparones* used by the Cilicians were smaller
than the two-banked vessels and triremes with

1. See below, pp. 101, 167.

2. *Hemiolia* is used in the sense of pirate-boat in its earliest mention
(Theophrastus, *Char.*, 25) ; cf. Suidas and Photius, *s.v.*, and Appian,
Mithr., 92. For the *myoparo* as a pirate-boat, see Appian, *l.c.* ; Sallust,
fr. III, 8 (Maurenbrecher) ; Cic., *Verr.*, II, 5, 89 and 97 ; Florus, III, 6.
The *myoparo* was also used in the Roman fleets (Plut., *Antonius*, 35), and for
coast defence (Cic., *Verr.*, II, 1, 86).

3. Arrian, *Anab.*, VI, 1, 1 ; Polyb., V, 101 (against the Illyrians) ;
Appian, *Pun.*, 75. Were the ἡμιολίαι used by Agathocles pirate-boats ?
(Diod. Sic., XIX, 65). The *condottiere*, Phalaecus, is also said to have used
hemioliae to escort the transports conveying his troop to Italy after the
Sacred War.

4. Mr. Torr's discussion of both the *hemiolia* and the *myoparo* (*Ancient
Ships*, pp. 15 and 118) and his collection of the evidence, make it unnecessary
to go into greater detail. (I take this opportunity of expressing my general
indebtedness to his work.)

which they were beginning to replace them.[1]
The *myoparo*, according to Mr. Torr, was broader
than the regular warship in proportion to its
length, and, we may assume, more suitable for
stowing loot. Both vessels were sea-going ships,
the *myoparo*, at any rate, possessing a mast and
sails, as well as oars.[2]

For their in-shore work at Pylos the Messenian
privateers were using a thirty-oared vessel
(τριακόντορος) and a *celes*, a small vessel built for
speed, and used as a despatch-boat with the Greek
navies.[3] Although the *celes* is not often mentioned
in connection with pirates,[4] it is probable that its
speed and size made it a convenient craft for this
kind of work, and a derivative, the ἐπακτροκέλης
is used by Aeschines, just as Theophrastus speaks
of the *hemiolia*, as the typical pirate-boat of
his day.[5]

It goes without saying that the seamanship of
the pirates was of the highest order. Their
safety, as well as their success, depended on it
as well as on a thorough knowledge of the coasts
where they operated. When inexperienced lands-
men took to piracy, their end was swift. In the

1. Appian, *l.c.* οἳ τὸ μὲν πρῶτον ὀλίγοις σκάφεσι καὶ μικροῖς οἷα
λῃσταὶ περιπλέοντες ἐλύπουν, ὡς δὲ ὁ πόλεμος ἐμηκύνετο, πλέονες ἐγίγνοντο
καὶ ναυσὶ μεγάλαις ἐπέπλεον . . . . μυοπάρωσι πρῶτον καὶ
ἡμιολίαις, εἶτα δικρότοις καὶ τριήρεσι κατὰ μέρη περιπλέοντες.

2. The *myoparo* is represented in the Althiburus mosaic (*Mon. et Mém.
Piot*, XII (1905), p. 127, fig. 16 ; fig. 7 represents the κέλης or *celox* mentioned
in the next paragraph). Illustrations of these two craft from the mosaic
will be found also in Stuart Jones, *Companion to Roman History*, fig. 54, 57.

3. Hdt., VIII, 94 ; Xen., *Hell.*, I, 6, 36.

4. See, however, Livy, XXXVIII, 27, piraticas celoces et lembos (at
the Ionian Myonnesos). It is possible that piraticis celetibus should be
read (with Ruhnken) in Velleius, II, 73.

5. Aeschines, I, 191. Theophrastus, *Char.*, 25.

Jewish wars with Rome a number of refugees
seized Joppa, and building ships, endeavoured to
plunder the trade route from Syria and Phoenicia
to Egypt. When Vespasian sent to attack them,
they fled on board their boats, but were soon
caught by a squall (the *Melamboreion*), driven
ashore, and destroyed.[1]

So far, we have considered only one aspect of
the pirate's activity, his attacks on ships, at sea or
sheltering. There is a still more sinister side to
his work, the plundering raids on shore and
constant kidnappings of individuals. It was this
that made him most feared and has had the
greatest effect on Mediterranean life. When
piracy was active, there could be little or no
security for inhabitants of the coast ; if ransom
was not forthcoming for the victim, his inevitable
lot was slavery.

The passage from Roberts has already indicated
in what way this kidnapping was carried on.
A small party would put into the shore at night
and carry off anyone whom they met. Certain
localities were particularly dangerous. The
difficult road along the coast from Megara to
Corinth by the Scironian rocks bore in the seventeenth century the name of *Kake Skala*, from the
frequency of the corsairs' visits. The Turks, in

1. Josephus, *Bell. Jud.*, III, 9, 2. It is curious that, outside the Odyssey,
we hear little of piracy on this coast, although in the sixteenth and seventeenth
centuries it was one of the corsair's favourite hunting-grounds. Strabo
(XVI, 759) mentions Joppa and Carmel as dangerous, and Dio Cassius,
XXXIX, 59, says there was a serious outbreak during Gabinius' governorship
of Syria. At an earlier date we hear of a raid made by Dionysius of Phocaea
on the Phoenician shipping (Hdt., VI, 17), but it is probable that, as a rule,
the coast was too well-guarded by the Phoenician navy.

consequence, were afraid to use it.[1]   Though the robber Sciron in the Greek legend is a brigand rather than a pirate, the story may nevertheless have arisen from similar descents from the sea on travellers using this path.   The lonely traveller carried off by pirates was a familiar figure in Greek story.   " I was carried off by Taphian pirates as I was returning from the fields."[2] " Did hostile men take you with their ships, as you were alone with the sheep or kine ? "[3] Normally a ransom would be accepted by the pirates.[4]   Julius Caesar was ransomed for the sum of fifty talents[5] ; Clodius on the other hand nursed a hatred against Ptolemy Auletes, because he had considered a subscription of two talents sufficient.[6]

We have, unfortunately, little information as to how these matters were arranged in antiquity, and how the pirates were approached, but the transaction probably differed little from the scene attending the redemption of Stackelberg by his friend Haller.   Stackelberg had been caught while

---

1.   Spon et Wheler, *Voyage d'Italie, de Dalmatie, de Grèce et du Levant, fait aux années 1675 et 1676* (Amsterdam, 1679), III, p. 223.   Cf. Chandler, *Travels in Asia Minor and Greece*, II, p. 223.   In Alciphron, III, 34, there is an allusion to Megarian λῃσταί οἱ περὶ τὰς Σκειρωνίδας τοῖς ὁδοιπόροις ἐνεδρεύουσι.

2.   *Od.*, XV, 427.

3.   *Ib.*, 386.   Compare the kidnappings in the *Homeric Hymns*, II, 123 ; VII, 1-12 ; and Hdt., I, 1-3 ; II, 54.

4.   Dittenberger, *Sylloge*[3], 263, 520, 521.

5.   See below, p. 232.

6.   Appian, *B.C.*, II, 23.   D'Arvieux has an amusing story of Algiers " On dit qu'un Espagnol ayant entendu qu'on l'avoit donné pour cent piastres, demanda tout bouffi de colere à celui qui le menoit, si on le prenoit pour une bourique, et si un homme de sa façon n'étoit estimé qu'à ce prix." (*Op. cit.*, V, 268).

crossing the gulf of Volo, and it fell to Haller to arrange the matter with the help of the Armenian Acob, who acted as intermediary. A sum of 60,000 piastres had been demanded : "The conference was opened by Acob with singular address : he represented himself as the captain of a privateer in those seas, assured the pirates that they were mistaken in supposing their prisoner was a man of fortune since he was merely an artist labouring for his bread, whose prospects they had injured by the destruction of his drawings ; that if they rejected the offers he now made he should depart satisfied with having done his duty, and finally he represented to them that a Turkish man of war was on the coast, as really was the case, to the commander of which, if they continued obstinate, he should leave their punishment."[1] Acob then offered 10,000 piastres, which the pirates refused. After an offer by Haller to take Stackelberg's place they retire, but are roused in the night by one of the pirates, offering to come down to 20,000 and finally 15,000 piastres. " Acob, however, conjecturing that they were in some alarm, remained steady to his former determination, which in the course of an hour brought the chief himself to their lodging, where the bargain was at last concluded for 10,000 piastres with an additional present of 1,000. A shake by the hand was the seal of this negotia-tion, as sacred and valid as the firman of the sultan." The ransom was paid next day by Haller in person. " Baron Stackelberg was then shaved

---

1. There is a story in Polyaenus (VI, 54), which shows how easily the pirate could be bluffed on occasion, but the ruse took a different form.

by one of the gang, a ceremony which they never omit on these occasions, and handed over to his friends. They were all pressed very much to stay and partake of a roasted lamb and an entertainment about to be prepared . . . . The robbers then wished them a good journey and expressed their hopes of capturing them again at some future time."[1]

Dodwell, speaking of the pirates of Santa Maura, says that " one of the thieves takes a letter to the prisoner's friends demanding a certain sum for his liberty. If the sum demanded can be paid, a person accompanies the thief to the place appointed ; and on his depositing the money, the prisoner is set at liberty. They never fail in their engagement when the sum is delivered ; and the person who takes it risks nothing, as a deficiency of mutual confidence would ruin the trade."[2]

In antiquity, the Black Sea pirates, according to Strabo, used to send word of their captures to the victim's friends and then took a ransom ; the inhabitants of Bosporus not only provided them with an anchorage but also with the means of disposing of their plunder.[3] The same was often the case in the Mediterranean, when control was

1. Hughes, *Travels in Sicily, Greece and Albania*, I, p. 278.

2. Dodwell, *op. cit.*, p. 58. Polybius has an amusing story about the Aetolian ambassadors sent to Rome in 189 B.C. They were captured by an Epirote pirate or privateer and handed over to the Government. A ransom of five talents was asked, but the sum was reduced to three, as the Epirotes were anxious to get the money before their Roman allies heard of the business. All the ambassadors consented and were released, with the exception of Alexander, who was the richest man in Greece. In the end he was the only one to escape for nothing, as the expected despatch soon arrived from Rome ordering his release. (Polyb., XXI, 26).

3. Strabo, XI, 496. The letter from the pirates or their victim to his relations figures prominently in Seneca and Quintilian. (See below, p. 264).

lax. The Cilicians openly frequented the slave-market of Delos, and the people of Side in Pamphylia were in league with them, as were also the Phaselites in Lycia. The complicity of local authorities has, of course, been one of the pirate's chief advantages. The well-known inscription of Teos contains imprecations against magistrates who harbour pirates.[1] The Venetian despatches are full of complaints against the Turkish author-ities for abetting the English pirates.[2] Frankish corsairs disposed of most of their booty through the so-called consuls.[3] Doubtless a handsome profit was made both by consul and Turkish official, but frequently the authorities were compelled to come to terms in order to recover stolen goods. D'Arvieux gives the following description of the methods followed on the Syrian coast. The captures made by the corsairs off Carmel were taken to Caiffa :

Ils exposent alors un pavillon blanc et si le Soubachi est d'humeur de traiter avec eux, il en expose un de même couleur sur la muraille. (The corsairs are not allowed to land but the business is carried on in boats.)

1. See below, p. 107.

2. *Calendar of State Papers, Venice, etc.*, X, no. 681 : " The Turks are in league with the English pirates with whom they share the plunder." Only the closing of the Turkish ports against the English will end their piracies (A.D. 1606). Cf. VIII, 1003 ; X, 53, 71, 85 (cf. 170), 103. In a deciphered despatch from the Venetian ambassador in Constantinople to the Doge and Senate (A.D. 1603) : " The Ambassador asks the Capudan Pasha to punish the English pirates and their abettors. The Capudan gives a dissertation on the difference between the Turkish and the Venetian Galleys " (X, 92).

3. Tavernier, *The six voyages . . . . made English by J. P.* (1678-84), I, p. 121 : " As for the islands of *Sifante* and *Miconoa*, in regard there is nothing of Trade in either but only with the Pirates, who sometimes touch there, if there be any Consuls that live there, it is only to buy their stol'n Goods." Cf. *State Papers*, X, 47 ; Thévenot, *op. cit.*, I, p. 332.

Puis on ploye les pavillons et on devient aussi ennemis qu'avant le traité.[1]

In his kidnapping raids the pirate was quick to make use of the opportunities which chance might offer ; one of the most favourable would be the celebration of a festival in the country or near the seashore, attended only by women or unarmed men. In Crete, Spratt heard the story of an event which was supposed to have happened some centuries earlier at the Chapel of St. Nikolas. When it was crowded with pilgrims on the eve of a *festa*, the fires lighted by the visitors were seen by a cruising corsair, who landed his crew, and stealing up to the sacred cave locked the door on the Christians. But the Saint showed a miraculous way of escape through the rock.[2] Similar attempts were common in antiquity. Herodotus describes how the Pelasgians of Lemnos " knowing well the festivals of the Athenians," lay in wait for the women celebrating the feast of Artemis at Brauron.[3] An inscription of the second century B.C. tells of a descent made by pirates on the territory of the Ephesians and the capture of a number of persons from the shrine of Artemis Munychia.[4] The Chian refugees after the battle of Lade were similarly thought by the Ephesians to be pirates come to carry off women

1. D'Arvieux, *Op. cit.*, II, p. 11.   Roberts, p. 9, gives a similar account.

2. Spratt, *op. cit.*, I, p. 343.

3. Hdt., VI, 138. Solon is said by Plutarch (*Sol.*, 8, cf. Polyaenus, I, 20) to have played a trick on the Megarians, inducing them to attack Cape Colias to carry off the women sacrificing to Demeter. Some beardless youths were dressed to act the part of the women.

4. *I. G.*, XII, 3, 171.

on the occasion of the Thesmophoria, and were at once attacked and killed by the population.[1]

Mistakes of this character were always liable to happen. In a story preserved by Apollodorus, Catreus, landing in Rhodes in search of his son, was mistaken for a pirate and killed, because his explanations could not be heard owing to the barking of the dogs.[2] At sea, honest men were often mistaken for pirates. Peter Mundy, off Cape St. Vincent in 1608, nearly got into trouble through mistaking the King of Spain's fleet for " Turkish Pyrats," " there being notice of twenty-six saile lyeinge about the Straights mouth . . . but God bee praised we parted friends."[3] Conversely, the pirate would pose as an ordinary trader. In the seventeenth century, the Turkish authorities did not allow Christians to come up the gulf of Corinth, through fear that the corsairs of Malta would get in under the guise of merchant-ships loading currants at Corinth,[4] and the Venetians in 1491 were compelled to increase the

1. Hdt., VI, 16. Professor Halliday reminds me of the former Turkish practice of locking the Christians into their quarter on Fridays through fear of attack. Cf. Lucas, *Voyage dans la Grèce, L'Asie Mineure, etc.*, I, 243 : " Elle (Adalia) est separée en trois parties, qui composent comme trois differentes villes : du moins voit-on à chacune ses murailles de separation et de bonnes portes de fer . . . . Tous les Vendredis on ferme toutes les portes de Satalie depuis midi jusqu'à une heure . . . . L'on me dit que les habitans ont une prophetie suivant laquelle les Chrétiens doivent prendre leur ville un vendredi entre midi et une heure." Was the observance at the festival of the *Magophonia* (Hdt., III, 79) due to a similar cause ?

2. Apollodorus, III, 2, 2. Diod. Sic. (V, 59) tells the same story, but without the picturesque detail of the dogs. The alarm was often given in this way. Chandler (*op. cit.*, II, p. 220) says that the people of Megara were accustomed to hide their goods and run away on seeing a boat approach by day, or hearing the dogs bark at night. (There are some interesting remarks in Plutarch, *Aratus*, 7, 8, and 24, on the subject of dogs.)

3. Hakluyt Society, New Series, II, 17 ; Vol. I, p. 16.

4. Spon and Wheler, *op. cit.*, I, p. 109.

duty on the export of wines from Candia, because
the pirates were in the habit of going there to
load wines, and on their way back captured and
plundered merchant-ships.[1] The pirate posing
as trader is as old as Homer ; Strabo's account of
the Corycian trick shows that when admitted to
harbour the pirate could acquire much information that was useful to him.[2]

Frequently, however, the pirate would boldly
enter port without disguise and attack the shipping
lying there. An inscription of Aegiale in Amorgos
gives an account of an episode of this character.[3]
When he was strong enough for this, there was
no need for petty subterfuges, nor were his attacks
limited to the kidnapping of women or single
travellers. The shores of the Mediterranean still
bear traces of the effect which the continued
descents of the pirates have wrought.

In his account of early conditions in Greece,
Thucydides lays stress on the fact that the oldest
inhabited sites, both on the mainland and in the
islands, lay at a distance from the sea owing to the
prevalence of piracy. It was only with the
development of the Greek marine and increased
wealth from trade, that more recent foundations
could be planted on the shore and fortified by
walls.[4] We need only call to mind the earliest
settlement on the hill of Cnossos, four miles from
the sea, primitive Athens on the Acropolis inland,

1. *Calendar of State Papers, Venice, etc.*, I, no. 609. Cf. X, no. 53 :
Caution Money exacted from English ships in Zante before sailing.

2. See below, p. 205.

3. Ditt., *Syll.*[3], 521. See below, p. 139.

4. Thuc., I, 7.

and the first settlements on the Acrocorinthos, to
which in the seventeenth century the inhabitants
were again forced to return, when no village could
exist on the isthmus.[1] Outside Greece the
difference, which Thucydides notes between the
ancient and more recent sites, has an important
bearing on the history of Greek colonisation.
The colonists found the best sites round the
Mediterranean coast for the most part unoccupied
at a time when they themselves had grown strong
enough to occupy and fortify them.[2] What
Thucydides observes of primitive Greece has
been the case all over the Mediterranean. Until
the middle of the last century it was normal to
find the principal towns or villages at some distance
from the sea, and often hidden from it. The
town was served by a *skala* on the shore, consisting
only of one or two houses. On the Catalan coast
the equivalent of the Greek *skala* is the *grau*.[3]
In the Cornice, and also on the coast of Calabria,
villages and ruined castles may be seen built
high up on the cliffs to give protection against
the Barbary pirates.[4] Even on the Mainote coast
of the Peloponnese the villages were built inland.[5]
The practice may best be illustrated from the
Aegean islands. Thus in Leros, Nisyros and
Telos, the principal villages are hidden from the
sea and lie about half-a-mile from it.[6] In Cos,

1. Spon and Wheler, III, pp. 226, 230.

2. Cf. Appian, *B. C.*, IV, 108, the Thracian coast.

3. See the translator's note in the Hakluyt Society's edition of Muntaner
(Series II, nos. 47, 50), Vol. I, p. 200.

4. Symonds, *Sketches in Italy and Greece* (1879), p. 3.

5. Cockerell, *op. cit.*, p. 82.

6. *B.S.A.*, XII, p. 159.

as Professor Halliday[1] tells me, the village of
Antimachia was situated inside the circuit of an
old castle of the Knights of Rhodes, on a hill some
forty minutes from the sea. It was inhabited
until the Crimean War, but the inhabitants have
now dispersed to form villages round. In contrast
to this modern *dioicismos*, it is interesting to notice
that the motive for the *synoicismos* of Attica
was said by an ancient writer to have been the
" Carian " descents from the sea and Boeotian
raids by land.[2] Though we need not believe this
to have been the case in Attica, the cause which
Philochorus suggests may well have been the real
one in other cases. The increased protection
thereby offered was a strong motive for the
inhabitants of a number of villages to combine
and occupy a single fortified site. Thévenot
records it of Scio, and says that all over the island
groups of two or three villages had thus been
united.[3] In his day also there was only one
village in Pholegandros, consisting of about
100 houses, three miles from the sea and
approached by a rocky valley. There were no
other houses in the island.[4] The village, according
to Tournefort, was of the usual semi-fortified
type ; there was no surrounding wall, but the
houses on the outside of the town faced inwards

---

1. In his lectures on *The Growth of the City State*, p. 41, he quotes the
case of Syra : " The town beside the sea is purely modern, the older settlements, both the Catholic and Orthodox, are perched on the hills behind."
(See also Newton, *op. cit.*, pp. 262-4 ; Bent, pp. 305, 308-9. There is an
interesting view of the Catholic settlement in Tournefort, I, p. 321.)

2. Philochorus in Strabo, IX, 379.

3. Thévenot, *op. cit.*, I, p. 306.

4. *Ib.*, p. 340.

and were joined to form a continuous blank wall
at the exposed points.[1] The more wealthy
inhabitants might, in some cases, possess fortified
houses of their own, such as are recorded in Andros
by Paul Lucas,[2] but where no fortified refuges
existed, the islands became uninhabitable. There
was no fortress in Myconos in the seventeenth
century and, consequently, no Turk would live
there through fear of the Christian corsairs.[3]

An interesting relic of one method of protection
adopted by the Ancients survives in the numerous
Towers, which are to be found in the Aegean
islands. One of them has recently been described
in detail by Professor Droop[4] and a short general
account is given by Messrs. Dawkins and Wace,[5]
who record them in Astypalaea, Andros, Ceos,
Cythnos, Seriphos (2), Siphnos ("about a dozen")[6]

1. Tournefort, *op. cit.*, I, p. 259; see Appendix A (p. 56).

2. Lucas, *op. cit.*, I, 225-6. He says that all persons of any
consideration (cf. Bent *op. cit.*, p. 274) live in high towers on account of the
corsairs : " Ce qui est de plaisant, c'est que l'on y monte par une échelle
qu'on tire après soi; de sorte que l'on demeure ensuite dans la Tour
comme dans une veritable prison." See also Newton, *op. cit.*, I, pp. 59,
79, on the Pyrgi of Mytilene and the opposite coast.

3. Spon and Wheler, *op. cit.*, I, p. 149 (see also their account of Megara,
II, p. 220). On the depopulation of the islands from this cause, see Miller,
Latins in the Levant, pp. 8-9, and Hasluck's valuable article, already quoted,
Depopulation in the Aegean Islands, in *B.S.A.*, XVII, pp. 151-175.

4. *Annals of Archaeology and Anthropology*, X, pp. 41 *seqq.*

5. *B.S.A.*, XII, p. 155 *seqq.*

6. A very much longer list of the towers in Siphnos is given by Dragatsis,
Praktika, 1920, pp. 147 *seqq.* (to which my attention was drawn by Mr.
M. N. Tod, after the above was in type), where the towers in the island
are fully described. That towers of this character, when built near the sea,
were used also as lighthouses or signalling stations is shown by an interesting
inscription of Thasos, discovered among the ruins of a round tower on the
cape at the north-east extremity of Potamia Bay, and dating from the end of
the sixth or early fifth century B.C. (Penoyre and Tod, *J. H. S.*, XXIX, p. 95):

Κηλάτο ε[ἰ]μὶ μνῆμα τὸ Φ - - ηρίδο,
κεῖμαι δὲ ἐπ' ἄκρο ναυσ[τ]άθμο σωτήριον
νηυσίν τε καὶ ναύτησιν· ἀλλὰ χάιρετε.

Sciathos (2), Scopelos (4), Amorgos (12), Leros (2).
They are round, like the Naxian example, or
square; some of them possessing a court-yard,
as at Naxos, others standing by themselves.
The towers are placed for the most part in the
more fertile parts of the islands at a distance from
a town, and, as was first pointed out by Ross,
probably served as temporary refuges in the
case of a raid, the towers sheltering the
men and the courts the flocks.[1] Some of
them were perhaps intended to serve rather
as forts to ward off attacks than as mere places
of refuge.

Forts of this kind to serve as a protection
against piratical descents were common in the
Mediterranean at all times, when the dangers of
piracy were great, and are frequently mentioned
by later travellers. Thévenot, in the seventeenth
century, says that in Scio, owing to the descents
of corsairs, towers had been built round the island
at intervals of two or three miles, each village
sending two men as guards, who gave the signal
when pirates approached.[2] On the Syrian coast,
D'Arvieux describes two towers, one square, the
other round, connected by a curtain wall and
mounted with small guns, which had been built
to prevent the landing of the corsairs who infested
this coast.[3] In Crete, Spratt speaks of a small
mediaeval fortress on a rocky eminence between
Praesos and Rhokaka with the ruins of a large
church in it, which was probably used by the

1. Ross, *Reisen auf der Gr. Inseln*, I, p. 132.

2. Thévenot, *op. cit.*, I, p. 324.

3. D'Arvieux, *op. cit.*, II, p. 99.

inhabitants of villages on the slopes of Dicte when in danger from pirates.[1]

Thévenot's description of the towers in Scio suggests that the ancient towers in the islands, in addition to being places of refuge, served also as signalling stations in the event of a raid. The signal would naturally be given by the smoke of beacons or by their flames at night.[2] This was a common warning in later days. While Thévenot was sailing from Acre to Jaffa, his ship was suddenly fired on from a fort on shore, and flares were lit all along the coast. As he approached Jaffa, the ship was again fired on, and when admitted to harbour, he found the inhabitants under arms and the women and children fled. The reason was that the boat had been mistaken for an Italian corsair operating off the coast, which had recently made a descent at Castel Pelegrino, between Acre and Jaffa.[3] Paul Lucas gives us similar information regarding Tripoli in Syria : " Quand on voit quelque vaisseau en mer qu'on croit être corsaire, on allume des feux dans ces tours pour avertir les Bâtiments du pays de venir dans le Port."[4] The flare was a recognised signal in antiquity in such emergencies. During Verres' government of Sicily, the news of the approach of the pirate

1. Spratt, *op. cit.*, I, p. 173.

2. Compare George Sandys (1610) in *Purchas, His Pilgrimes*, VIII, p. 98 : " The coast [of Scio], especially towards the South, is set with small Watch-towers, which with smoake by day, and fire by night, doe give knowledge unto one another (and so to the up-land) of suspected enemies." Thévenot, II, 906, also mentions smoke-signals at Capri " pour avertir la côte."

3. Thevénot, *op. cit.*, II, pp. 712-720.

4. Paul Lucas, *Voyage du Levant*, I, p. 144.

squadron that had destroyed the guardships was flashed to Syracuse as much by the flames of the burning Sicilian vessels as by the fires of the regular beacons : Non enim, sicut erat semper antea consuetudo, praedonum adventum significavit ignis e specula sublatus aut tumulo, sed flamma ex ipso incendio.[1]

The fires which Odysseus saw burning in Ithaca were probably beacons of this kind. After leaving the island of Aeolus, he sailed for nine days and nights with a favouring breeze,

$$τῇ δεκάτῃ δ'ἤδη ἀνεφαίνετο πατρὶς ἄρουρα$$
$$καὶ δὴ πυρπολέοντας ἐλεύσσομεν ἐγγὺς ἐόντες.[2]$$

The explanation usually given is that the fires were the watchfires of the shepherds, or that it was a fire lighted to guide the ship in, or merely a fire on the farm " introduced into the picture to show how near they had come to their home." Spratt speaks of an Hellenic watch-tower called Palaeokastro, above Poro bay in Crete, on which the coast-guard in his day lit a signal fire at sunset, if any ship was in sight, as a warning against

1. Cicero, *Verrines*, II, 5, 93. It is interesting to note that the custom still lasted in Sicily down to the beginning of the last century. On the coast-road from Palma to Alicata every mile and a half were towers or, failing these, huts for the coast-guard to give warning of the approach of the Barbary corsairs (Cockerell, *Travels in S. Europe and the Levant*, 1810-1817 p. 209). Dr. Mackail tells me that one of the most striking features on the north-east coast of Corsica is a series of similar towers at intervals of two or three miles. Col. Kitson Clark says that similar towers are to be seen in Sardinia. Flares, of course, were used by the pirate or his accomplices on shore. Beaufort (*op. cit.*, p. 227), having captured a Mainote pirate in a creek of Hermonisi off Astypalaea, was prevented from capturing its consort by the warning flares raised from the top of the island.

2. *Od.*, X, 29-30. For the explanations usually offered, see Merry and Riddell, *ad. loc.* Euripides, *Helena*, 767, uses πυρπολήματα of the flares used by Nauplius.

smugglers or pirates.[1] This is obviously the case in the Homeric picture. Odysseus has been away for ten years, and his vessels are not recognised as Ithacan ships returning from Troy. As they draw near to the land, they are seen by the look-out men posted on the heights, and the warning beacons are fired.[2]

To return to the towers—it is hardly to be expected that we should find much allusion to them in literature, but a series of inscriptions from the Southern Sporades contains interesting information regarding them, at a time when Rhodes was at war with certain of the Cretan states, and a Cretan attack on her allies and her dependants was expected.[3]

The first inscription (no. 567, from Calymnos) sums up the character of the war as waged by the Hierapytnians of Crete. The Cretans were noted corsairs, and their raids on this occasion differed

1. Spratt, op. cit., I, p. 140 ; see also II, p. 3.

2. For the watchers on the heights, compare Newton's account of Calymnos (Op. cit., I, p. 296) : " In the old times, when the Archipelago swarmed with pirates, the Calymniotes dwelt in a fortified city perched on the top of a steep rock, as the inhabitants of Astypalaea do to this day. Sentinels were perpetually stationed on the hills to give a signal in case of the approach of pirates. This custom is curiously commemorated in the names of two of the highest mountains in the island, one of which is called *Vigli*, ' the watch,' the other *Mero Vigli* (ἡμερόβλιγι), ' the day-watch.' " It is interesting to find the name *Hemeroscopeion* used in antiquity for a similar reason ; cf. Strabo's account of the Dianium in Spain : Ἡμεροσκοπεῖον ἐπὶ τῇ ἄκρᾳ τῆς Ἐφεσίας Ἀρτέμιδος ἱερὸν σφοδρὰ τιμώμενον, ᾧ ἐχρήσατο Σερτώριος ὁρμητηρίῳ κατὰ θάλατταν · ἐρυμνὸν γάρ ἐστι καὶ λῃστρικόν, κάτοπτον δὲ ἐκ πολλοῦ τοῖς πλέουσι. (III, 159.)

Further information regarding the use of flares as warning signals against pirates will be found in *Annals of Archaeology and Anthropology*, XI, p. 33, but I am inclined to withdraw the suggestions there put forward regarding the Homeric simile in *Iliad*, XIX, 375.

3. Dittenberger, *Sylloge*³, 567-570. The historical bearing of these inscriptions is fully discussed by Herzog in *Klio*, II, p. 317 seqq. They belong to the war of c. 204-201 B.C. between Rhodes and Crete, which was fomented by Philip V of Macedon. See below, p. 148.

little from those of the ordinary pirate. Information was received regarding an impending attack, which was met by the Rhodian admiral off the promontory Laceter in Cos (Antimachia Point), a Calymniote especially distinguishing himself in the action.

The second inscription (no. 568, from Halasarna in Cos) records that a certain Diocles, having made arrangements with the commander of a Rhodian ship (or squadron) to land light-armed troops, held up the enemy at the *peripolion* (the reading is not certain[1]) and prevented them from doing damage to the countryside.

The third (no. 569, also from Halasarna) gives an account of the measures taken by Theucles, probably one of the Coan *strategi*,[2] for the defence of the countryside. Realising that the most exposed districts of the island lacked protection, he arranged for the hurried fortification of the *peripolion*, so as to ensure the safety of the inhabitants of Halasarna with their wives and children; foreseeing also the enemy's attacks and the extent of the danger, he provided sufficient money for the walls ($\tau\epsilon\iota\chi\eta$) to be put into a state of defence, but with an eye to the future arranged that the capital sum devoted to the *peripolia* should remain untouched. When the enemy attack was made on the city and countryside, he caused the country-folk to be released from service in the town garrison of Cos, thinking that they ought to remain in their own district to guard the forts. Without failing to

---

1. παρακατέσχε τὸς ἐ[ναντίος ὑπὸ (?) τὸ περιπ]όλιον.
2. So Herzog, *op. cit.*, p. 325.

make adequate provision for the defence of the capital, he displayed the greatest care for the *peripolion*, increasing the number of guards and their pay. When the country was overrun, he arranged for a covering force of cavalry and infantry, giving special instructions regarding the Halasarna district. As the weapons of the country-folk were inadequate or wanting, he also provided money for the proper arming of those entrusted with the duty of guarding the *peripolion*.

The fourth inscription (no. 570, from Potidaea in Carpathos), the beginning of which is mutilated, narrates that Pamphilidas so encouraged his (?) men that the enemies' attacks were beaten off, and " We in danger with our wives and children found safety," while the *peripolion* was held for the people.

The last inscription clearly deals with an attack on the *peripolion* itself, in which the natives of Potidaea had taken refuge with their families. The valour of Pamphilidas (or possibly his timely arrival with a relieving force) had driven off the enemy and saved the spot. In the Halasarna inscriptions it is not clear whether a *peripolion* already existed but had fallen into disrepair, or whether Theucles caused a new one to be built to meet the emergency. In any case, it was ready to receive the country-folk when the danger arrived. If the reading of the first of the two Halasarna texts can be trusted, it was not actually assaulted, the enemy attack being stopped at or below the *peripolion* with the help of troops landed from the fleet. It is clear that the *peripolia* on occasions of this kind, when the islands were attacked by enemies or marauders, served not only as refuges, but as strong-points, from which troops could operate to protect the countryside.

In the *peripolia* of these inscriptions we have something that exactly answers the purpose for which Ross conjectured that the towers in the islands were intended. The word[1] is rightly explained by the editor as meaning not a " suburb " (a later use of the word) but a station for *peripoloi*, a guard-house. This exactly suits the character of the towers which we find in the Greek islands, the single towers being more in the nature of a fort, where only a few persons could take refuge, the towers with a surrounding or adjacent courtyard offering protection to a greater number. The fort at Halasarna would appear to have been of the latter type. A distinction is made in the inscription between the *peripolion* and the τείχη and it is probable that by the τείχη are meant the outer walls of the courtyard. Another small detail in the Halasarna inscriptions is not without significance. Among the services of Theucles it is stated that as the available supplies of wood had been used by the Coans in general for making a *stoa*, which in this case is a covered gallery inside the defences, Theucles found it necessary to provide additional sums of money for wood at Halasarna, presumably for the same purpose. It is natural that in the case of a fort provided with a courtyard, a wooden gallery or penthouse should be fixed along the inner face of the courtyard walls, which would give protection against missiles to men or cattle

1. περιπόλιον.

collected within.   In some of the surviving Greek towers the courtyard does not surround the tower, as in the Naxian example, but is adjacent to it.[1] It cannot in such cases have been an outer line of defence to the tower itself, but only an additional place of refuge.

As the result of this general insecurity and continued harrying of the coasts, wide tracts of country passed out of cultivation.[2]   At the same time, the existence of fortified villages and strong-points inland gave a peculiar character to the pirates' descents, which may best be illustrated by a passage in the Odyssey :—

The wind bearing me from Ilios brought me to the Cicones, to Ismaros ; there I sacked a city and slew the men, and taking from the city their wives and many possessions we divided them, that no man for me might depart deprived of an equal share. Then, indeed, I ordered that we should fly with nimble foot, but they, fools that they were, obeyed not.   But much wine was drunk, and many sheep they slew by the shore and shambling, crook-horned kine.   Meantime Cicones going called unto Cicones, who were their neighbours, far more numerous and warlike, dwelling inland, knowing well to fight with

1.   See the plans published in *B.S.A.* of the tower at Vathy, Astypalaea (fig. 3).   The photograph of the tower at Haghia Triadha, Amorgos, shows a similar arrangement.

2.   Cf. Gonzalez de Clavijo, *Life and Acts of the Great Tamerlane*, 1403, (Hakluyt Society, 1859, ed. Clements Markham) : p. 8, " Between the sea and the town [Terracina] there were fruit gardens and tall trees and between these gardens and the town there was a monastery which was once occupied by nuns, but they had all been carried off by the Moors of Barbary." Coryat (1612), in *Purchas, His Pilgrimes*, Vol. X, p. 413 : " The ground [valley opposite Tenedos] being as fruitfull to produce all manner of Commodities as any plot of ground under the sunne, but by reason that the inhabitants of the countrey are oftentimes infested by pirats and men of warre, which take away from them what they list, they cannot find any secure place of habitation in all that tract : by means whereof it commeth to passe that there are few dwelling-houses there, and so consequently the coast is more untilled and onmannured then otherwise it would bee."

men from chariots and on foot when need be. They came then, in number like the leaves and flowers in their season, in the morning. Then did an evil doom come upon us ill-fated.[1]

The whole passage has been carefully examined by Bérard[2] and illustrated with a wealth of quotation from the journals of travellers of the seventeenth century. He notes that the wide coastal plains of Thrace, equally with the lands of the Egyptian Delta, have always been the most exposed to the corsairs' raids. To his illustrations may be added what Polybius says about the exposed character of Elis and Messenia at the time of the Illyrian piracies : " The expedition began by making a descent on Elis and Messenia, lands which the Illyrians had always been in the habit of pillaging, because, owing to the extent of their sea-board and owing to the principal cities being in the interior, help against their raids was distant and slow in arriving ; so that they could always overrun and plunder those countries unmolested."[3]

The "city" which Odysseus and his companions sacked was therefore a small and unprotected site on the coast, which the captain was anxious to leave before the Cicones of the interior, " far more numerous and war-like," could rally to the assault. To " flee with nimble foot " was the corsair's regular practice, as soon as the spoils lying ready to his hand had been collected. Muntaner thus describes a raid by Roger di Luria in Provence : " The pursuit lasted to within

1. *Od.*, IX, 39-52.
2. *Les Phéniciens et l'Odyssée*, II, p. 3 *seqq.*
3. Polybius, II, 5 (Trans. Paton).

a league of Beziers, but it was vesper-time and the admiral feared that they would not be able to return to the galleys by daylight, and they were on the worst beach that there is, East or West."[1] But Odysseus' men disobeyed the order to embark before night, and fell to carousing on the shore.[2] The miseries of the corsair's life at sea, of which Roberts and Thévenot,[3] who also was captured, give ample illustrations, were sufficient inducement to run the risk ; much wine was drunk and cattle devoured, and in the morning the inhabitants, rallying from the interior, came down on them.

There are a few minor points in the description of this raid which Bérard remarks. He notes that here, as on other occasions,[4] the spoils are equally divided among the crew, but contrasts the practice of the Franks, among whom the ordinary members of the crew got nothing. The difference, however, is only superficial ; the crew of the Frankish corsair was divided into fighting men and those who worked the ship. The latter, in some cases, were actually slaves, or more usually men enticed

1. Muntaner, *op. cit.*, II, p. 379.

2. Bérard quotes the *Mémoires* of a certain de Sauméry (I, pp. 34-6), who had fallen in with some Maltese pirates at Sapienza : " Je mangeai tellement de ces viandes demicuites qu'à peine pus-je respirer pendant vingt-quatres heures." I have been unable to obtain a copy of the works of this interesting rascal.

3. Of the " miserable life of a poor Saylor here," Roberts says (p. 4) : " I am sure that nothing can parallel it for the Badness thereof." The work was hard and the food bad. Except for occasional sardines there was only bread at sea, and when cattle were captured on shore, the crew only got the meat when it had become too foul for the captain and volunteers. But food was frequently shoat all round. The advent of the Frankish prisoners, according to Thévenot (II, p. 66), was a serious matter to their captors, who were already short of food and water.

4. E.g. *Od.*, IX, 547.

or pressed on board at Italian ports. There was little chance of escape ; if any succeeded in leaving the boat, Greek priests were captured on shore and forced to raise the natives to search. The fighting men on Roberts' ship consisted of about forty " Voluntiers," all ruffians guilty of crimes at home and without motive to return ; they spy on the crew, and if a mutiny takes place, on board, it is " for want of Compliment of these Hell-hounds." They get all the plunder that there is, but there are fixed perquisites belonging to the senior officers. Roberts, when promoted to be gunner, found that his ἐξαιρετὸν δώρημα consisted of the *patereroes*. The same principle prevailed among the British pirates of the Western seas, whose " articles," if we can trust the account given by Captain Chas. Johnson, contained a fixed system for the disposal of loot.[1]

The priest figures also in the epilogue to the Ismaros raid. The wine with which Odysseus drugged the Cyclops is said to have been given to him by Maron, the priest of Apollo at Ismaros.[2] It is possible that the priest Maron, as Bérard hints, was in league with the corsairs, or was utilised by them, in much the same way as Roberts' men employed the *papadhes* of the islands, to guide them to what they wanted. Spon and Wheler mention the case of a priest at Corinth, whose brother was a pirate and had turned Turk when in danger of capture. The *papas* himself, when drunk, had let fall that he had seen three

1. *General History of the Pyrates*, pp. 230, 352. An interesting account of the tariff of the Mediterranean pirates of the thirteenth century will be found in Miller, *Latins in the Levant*, p. 156 (from Sanudo).

2. *Od.*, IX, 200.

pirates in a house and when this was reported to the *Vaivode* he was bastinadoed and sentenced to the galleys. This effected his own conversion.[1] Hughes was warned against the *papas* at Delphi, who was reported to be in league with the *Clephts*, and quotes an earlier traveller's statement that a gang of robbers or boat of pirates was seldom without its chaplain.[2] The case of Maron, however, is somewhat different. His life is spared, but his " gifts " to Odysseus, in addition to the twelve jars of wine, consisted of seven talents of gold and a silver bowl. The pirates' " reverence " for the priest did not prevent them from acquiring most of his substance, although no personal violence was offered to him or his family.

It is never easy to comprehend the part which superstition played in the pirate's life.[3] Stackelberg gave an amusing description of the religious views of his captors, which is of considerable interest : They were mostly Turks, " but with the most imperfect knowledge of the Mussulman faith : in the hours of danger they had recourse to all kinds of superstition, but when secure they indulged in the most horrid blasphemies. In their bark a light was always kept burning before a picture of the Virgin, and in storms they vowed the dedication of wax tapers to St. Nicholas . . . . in a church dedicated to that saint upon an island which they sometimes visited ; these vows they religiously performed."[4]

1. Spon and Wheler, *op. cit.*, III, p. 232.
2. Hughes, *op. cit.*, I, p. 278, quoting Douglas, *Dissertation upon Ancient and Modern Greece*, p. 361.
3. There are some good remarks on this point in Bérard, *l.c.*
4. In Hughes, *op. cit.*, I, p. 361.

Plutarch alludes to the strange sacrifices and secret rites practised by the pirates of Cilicia; but it would be obviously unwise to build much on his statement that the worship of Mithras was first disseminated by them.[1]

Methods of dealing with these miscreants, when captured, have varied little in different parts of the world, the object in most cases being to ensure that the punishment should, so far as possible, fit the crime, and by its publicity act as a deterrent to others.   In sixteenth century England it is said that " the punishment for corsairs is to hang them in such a way that their toes well nigh touch the water ; so they are generally hanged on the banks of rivers and on the sea-shore."[2]   The later performances at Execution Dock were of a similar character, and Roman law provided that the punishment of brigands and pirates should be carried out as openly as possible : Famosos latrones in his locis, ubi grassati sunt, furca figendos compluribus placuit ut et conspectu deterreantur alii ab isdem facinoribus.[3]   A public execution was no doubt a gratifying spectacle to those who had to fear the corsair's crimes. Cicero, at any rate, is insistent on the disappointment felt by the Syracusans, when deprived by Verres of the iucundissimum spectaculum of seeing the arch-pirate executed.[4]   Little mercy was shown to the pirate when he fell into his victims'

1. Plutarch, *Pompeius*, 24.

2. Barbaro's report on England in 1551 (*Cal. State Papers, Venice, etc.*, V, no. 703).

3. Digest, IX, ii, 28, §15.

4. Cic., *Verr.*, II, 5, 65-66.

hands. Miller quotes the case of a Turkish corsair who was driven ashore at Melos and slowly roasted for three hours by the populace about the year 1500,[1] and burning seems to have been the usual penalty inflicted by the Turkish and Syrian peasantry.[2] The official punishments of the Romans, however, were beheading,[3] crucifixion[4] and exposure to the beasts.[5] Since pirates were regarded in Roman law as communes hostes gentium,[6] it was the duty of every provincial governor to proceed against them.[7] The individual also was empowered to take the necessary measures of self-defence against pirates and brigands,[8] but how far Julius Caesar was justified in ordering the crucifixion of his captors, in defiance of the governor of Asia, is doubtful.

We have little information regarding Greek law on the subject of piracy. It is probable enough that full provisions were made in the Rhodian code, if we may argue from one of the few fragments of it that have survived.[9] An inscription

1. Miller, *op. cit.*, p. 618.

2. Thévenot, II, pp. 665, 722. It was also practised officially. The Pasha of the Morea arrived at Lepanto with orders to burn all corsairs using the Adriatic (Spon and Wheler, II, p. 22).

3. Cic., *Verr.*, II, 5, 71 ; 78-9.

4. Plut., *Julius*, 1 ; Velleius, II, 42.

5. Digest, *l.c.*

6. Cic., *Verr.*, II, 5, 76 ; cf. 4, 21 ; *de off.*, III, 107; and Digest, quoted below, p. 60.

7. Digest, I, xviii, 3 : Nam et in mandatis principum est ut curet is, qui provinciae praeest, malis hominibus provinciam purgare nec distinguuntur unde sint.

8. *Ib.*, IX, ii, 4.

9. Digest, XIV, ii, 3 : Si navis a piratis redempta, Servius Ofilius Labeo omnes conferre debere aiunt : quod vero praedones abstulerunt, eum perdere cuius fuerint nec conferendum ei qui suas merces redemerint (Lex Rhodia de iactu).

from Ephesos tells us that captured pirates were dealt with in a " manner that befitted their villainy " ;[1] but having examined some of the methods favoured in the Mediterranean, we may perhaps refrain from further inquiries. There is, however, one interesting monument, figured as the frontispiece to this volume,[2] which shows us that the practice of keel-hauling, beloved of the pirates of the Western seas, was known also to the ancients. But there is, unfortunately, nothing to show whether the patient on this occasion is the pirate or his captive.

APPENDIX A. (Chapter I, p. 41)

Considerable architectural interest attaches to many of the fortified villages of the Greek Archipelago, and I am indebted to Professor R. M. Dawkins for the following information regarding them : The best preserved is to be found in Cimolos (visited in 1907), where the village is of

1. *I. G.*, XII, 3, 171, ἀξίως τῆς ἐαυτῶν (sic), μ[οχθηρίας.

2. The drawing has been made for me from the original in Athens by Miss E. Tankard, to whom my best thanks are due. The vase in question is figured also in Dumont and Chaplain, *Céramique de la Grèce propre*, p. 385, pl. xxiii, where the scene is similarly explained.

I have to thank Mr. A. M. Woodward, Director of the British School at Athens, for the following description : " Athens, National Museum, 1st Vase Room, Case 14, Museum No. 487. Found at Pikrodaphni in Attica. Ht. ·28m; lekythos with black paint on a white ground, paint nearly all flaked off or burnt to a pale brown; broken into many pieces, but carefully mended."

My best thanks are due to the Ephor in charge and to the Director of the National Museum (Dr. Kastriotes and Dr. Kourouniotes) for permission to reproduce the vase, and to Mr. Woodward for obtaining this permission.

I cannot help feeling that the story in Hdt., IV, 154, contains a reminiscence of the practice of keel-hauling, although on this occasion it was done on a lady.

quadrangular form, each side of the square measuring some seventy paces. The outer walls are formed by the backs of houses, which face inwards only and are joined together so as to present a continuous blank wall to the outside. Remains of two round towers are preserved at the north-west and south-west angles, and entrance is afforded only by gateways on the south side and to the north-east. On this outer line the houses are built one deep, and usually consist of a single room.

The middle of the village is occupied by the church, surrounded by a second quadrangle formed by houses built back to back, which touch the church on its south and east sides. The inner square thus formed is pierced for gates to the north-east and south-west, and a broad passage-way runs between the houses forming the inner and outer squares. (My description is given from the notes and sketch-plan kindly sent by Professor Dawkins.)[1]

The Pholegandros example mentioned by Tournefort shows one half of the Cimolos plan, as it is built on the edge of a precipice above the sea (cf. also Bent, *Cyclades*, p. 198). The Sicinos example described by Bent (*op. cit.*, p. 173) is constructed on the same plan, but is not so well-preserved, or so accurately set out. There is also said to be a good square *castro* of this type in Antiparos. Professor Dawkins adds : " The principle of building houses to form an enclosure

---

1. It is stated by Thévenot, *op. cit.*, I, p. 343, that the village of Cimolos was burnt by corsairs in 1638. The plan of the village described above may have been laid out soon after that date.

so that they themselves make the wall of the castle is common and natural ; generally the construction is on a rock, and so follows the shape of the rock ; the square plan only comes out when it is built on a flat space. The best example of the rock type is in Astypalaea. The nucleus of the old village of Apeiranthos on Naxos is a knot of houses built in such a way that, if one lane is closed, they cannot be reached, but an invader is faced by the almost unpierced pack-walls ; this is a rudimentary *castro*, and is at the highest point of the village, but is so small and so much built up that one does not notice it unless one walks into it. The Chora of Naxos is big, but the old part, which is irregularly shaped, crowns its hill in much the same way. The invariable principle is that the houses all have their backs outwards and the back wall of the houses makes the wall of the castle ; there is no separate wall apart from the houses themselves."

CHAPTER II

PIRACY, PRIVATEERING AND REPRISALS

Καὶ αὐτὸν ὁ Παπινιανὸς ὁ ἔπαρχος ἀνήρετο Διὰ
τι ἐλήστευσας ; καὶ αὐτὸς ἀπεκρίνατο Διὰ τί σὺ
ἔπαρχος εἶ ; (Dio Cass., LXXVI, 10 on the trial of
Felix Bulla.)

Πειρατοῦ δὲ καταδραμόντος τὴν χώραν και ὡς ἑάλω
λέγοντος ὅτι Τροφὴν οὐκ εἶχον τοῖς στρατιώταις
παρέχειν, πρὸς τοὺς ἔχοντας οὖν ἑκοντὶ δ' οὐκ ἂν δόντας
βίᾳ ληψόμενος ἦλθον · ἔφη, Σύντομος ἡ πονηρία.
(*Apophtheg. Lac.*, p. 223D.)

THE English word pirate is derived through the
Latin *pirata* from the Greek πειρατής, which is
explained by Liddell and Scott as one who makes
attempts or attacks (πεῖραι) on ships.[1] The word
is of comparatively late date in Greece and is not
found before the third or fourth century B.C., the
ordinary word before that date being λῃστής.[2]

---

1. An alternative derivation is given in the *Thesaurus* from περᾶν :
"quoniam mare semper pererrant et navigantibus invadunt : quam ob
causam et περιδίνους nominari" (Plato, *Legg.*, VI, 777 ; cf. Athenaeus,
VI, 264 ; but these are rather *footpads*).

2. Duris of Samos (*temp.* Theophrastus) *ap.* Schol. Eurip., *Hecuba*, 933,
uses πειρατεύειν, which implies the existence of the word πειρατής. πειρατής
first appears in inscriptions during the third century B.C. (Dittenberger,
Syll.[3], 521), although λῃστής is still more commonly used. (*I. G.*, XII,
3, 1291 ; IX, 1, 1291 ; Dittenberger, *Syll.*[3], 581 ; 1225). Both words occur
in a second century decree of Ephesos (*I. G.*, XII, 3, 171). From the
beginning of the next century πειρατής is the more common (e.g., *I. G.*,
IX, 1, 873 ; XII, 5, 653 ; *ib.*, 860 ; IV, 2 ; *Mon. Anc.*, XXV : θαλάσσην
πειρατευομένην.) λῃστής, however, is occasionally used in official documents
until a late date (e.g. *Arch. Ep. Mitt.*, XI, 37 ; *I. G. Rom.*, IV, 219). It is
noticeable that in a document of *c.* 200-197 B.C. πειρατεύειν is definitely
used of the action of privateers (Dittenberger, *Syll.*[3], 582), the word πειρατής
having attached to itself all the meanings of λῃστής. Cf. its use in Polybius.

Both words, however, are used in a wider sense than the word pirate as defined by English law, and throughout our discussion it will be necessary to make a careful distinction between piracy and such measures of war as would in modern times be classed as privateering. Piracy, as understood in English law, is " the commission of those acts of robbery and violence upon the sea, which, if committed upon land, would amount to felony. Pirates hold no commission or delegated authority from any sovereign or state empowering them to attack others."[1] According to a further definition it is " an act of violence done upon the ocean or unappropriated lands or within the territory of a State through descent from the sea by a body of men acting independently of any politically organised society."[2]

In the case quoted above regarding the seizure of a Greek motor schooner in the Black Sea,[3] it was argued by Counsel that in law a pirate was one who was an indiscriminate enemy of the whole human race, and not one who merely attacked persons of a particular class or a particular race. Such a definition goes back to the Roman distinction between iusti hostes and humani generis communes hostes : " Hostes sunt quibus bellum publice populus Romanus decrevit vel ipsi populo Romano : ceteri latrunculi vel praedones appellantur."[4] And in the judgement given in the case

1. Professor Batt gives me this definition from Wharton's *Law Lexicon* (ed. 1911).

2. Hall, *ap.* Barclay, *Law and Usage of War.*

3. See above, p. 14.

4. Digest, XLIX, 15, 24.

in question the claim that the brigand was holding the commission of the state to which he belonged was admitted.[1]

The difficulties of distinguishing between piracy and other forms of maritime violence are increased tenfold in any discussion of piracy in antiquity, when privateering was practised on a wide scale. Piracy and privateering were intimately connected, and the nomenclature in both cases almost identical. Moreover, the general practice of privateering in war-time gave a strong impetus to piracy of the ordinary type.[2] Closely allied to privateering is the system of reprisals and distraint as recognised in ancient law.

Privateering, that is to say, hostile action undertaken by privately owned vessels in war-time, was the inevitable concomitant of ancient war, and was practised wholesale by the citizens of belligerent states without the limitations imposed in more modern times by the granting of *letters of marque* to the individual. Its universality is perhaps to be explained by the lack of any distinction in ancient war between combatant and non-combatant.[3] The operations of the privateers in ancient warfare differed little from those of the pirate, so far as the enemy was

1. Cf. Wheaton, *Elements of International Law* (5th edition by Coleman Philippson, 1916), p. 205 : " An offence on the high seas is not piracy *iure gentium* so long as the ship on which it is committed remains subject to the authority of the state to which it belongs. An essential ingredient of piracy is throwing off this authority."

2. Cf. Andocides, *de Myst.*, 138, ἔτι δὲ πολέμου γενομένου καὶ τριηρῶν ἀεὶ κατὰ θάλατταν οὐσῶν καὶ λῃστῶν, ὑφ' ὧν πολλοὶ ληφθέντες, ἀπολέσαντες τὰ ὄντα, δουλεύοντες τὸν βίον διετέλεσαν.

3. See Maine, *Ancient Law*, p. 260, to the effect that on the outbreak of hostilities the institution of private property fell into abeyance so far as concerned the belligerents.

concerned, and in fact the activities displayed in the Peloponnesian war throw much light on the general tactics of the Aegean pirate. The operations of both privateers and pirates are described in identical terms, with the result that on occasion it is difficult to ascertain which class is intended. Nor can it be said that the laws of neutrality were always observed. The Aetolian activities are perhaps exceptional, but even in a state like Athens we find occasional breaches of neutrality. An interesting case is provided by the speech of Demosthenes against Timocrates.[1] In 355 B.C., three Athenian ambassadors, who were sailing in a warship to the court of Maussolus in Caria, fell in with a vessel from Naucratis, which they captured and brought to the Peiraeus. The Naucratite merchants appealed to Athens, but since Egypt was in revolt from Persia and the Athenians were anxious to cultivate good relations with the Great King, the ship was condemned as an enemy. The prize-money, which by law belonged to the state, had been retained by the three ambassadors.

Not less dangerous to the peace of the seas was the ancient law concerning reprisals, and here again the legal terminology differed little from that which described the pirate's doings. In the fourth century, Demosthenes states that owing to the reprisals undertaken by the Athenian captains it was impossible for an Athenian to go anywhere without a flag of truce.[2] Reprisals could be

1. Demosth., XXIV, *arg.* 1, and §§11-12. See Wayte *ad loc.*, and Schäfer, *Demosthenes*, 1, p. 330.

2. Demosth., LI, 13, διὰ τὰς ὑπὸ τούτων ἀνδροληψίας καὶ σύλας κατεσκευασμένας.

undertaken by the state, that is to say, a general permission granted to all and sundry to plunder the inhabitants and commerce of another state, just as the Lacedaemonians in 416 B.C., in reply to continued Athenian depredations carried out from Pylos, issued a general permission to their subjects to plunder Athenians, without yet declaring war.[1] There are numerous examples of similar practices in Hellenistic times, which greatly embarrassed the Romans in their endeavours to secure peace and quiet in Greece.[2]

Equally common in ancient international law was the practice of granting rights of reprisal to an individual against the citizens of a foreign

1. Thuc., V, 115, ἐκήρυξαν δὲ εἴ τις βούλεται παρὰ σφῶν Ἀθηναίους λήξεσθαι. Cf. Xen., Hell., V, 1, 2, ξυνδόξαν και τοῖς ἐφόροις ἐφίησι (Eteonicus) ληίζεσθαι τὸν βουλόμενον ἐκ τῆς Ἀττικῆς.

2. Polybius uses the phrases ῥύσια καταγγέλλειν and λάφυρον ἐπικηρύττειν. IV, 53 : The people of Eleutherna τὸ μὲν πρῶτον ῥύσια κατήγγειλαν τοῖς Ῥοδίοις (in revenge for a supposed injury) μετὰ δὲ ταῦτα πόλεμον ἐξήνεγκαν. XXII, 4 : on the Boeotians failing to carry out an agreement with the Achaeans, Philopoemen ἀπέδωκε τοῖς αἰτουμένοις τὰ ῥύσια κατὰ τῶν Βοιωτῶν. There is an interesting case of ῥύσια in XXXII, 7. In XXII, 4, it is a case of limited reprisals granted to individuals rather than a general permission to all Achaeans ; cf. also the use of συλᾶν discussed below, and the use of ῥυσιάζειν in Dittenberger, Syll.³, 629 (Aetolian league and Eumenes II) μηθένα ἄγειν μηδὲ ῥυσ[ιάζειν τινὰ] ἐντὸς τῶν ὁρίων (of the temple of Athene Nikephoros at Pergamon) εἰ δέ τίς κα ἄγῃ ἢ ῥυσιάξῃ ἢ ἀποβιάξαιτο ἢ διεγγυάσῃ κ. τ. λ. The earliest use of the word ῥύσιον is in Il. XI, 674, ῥύσι' ἐλαυνόμενος, denoting the plunder taken from Elis by way of reprisals for an earlier raid by the Eleians (see below, p. 73), cf. Et. Mag., s.v. ἀντὶ τοῦ ἐνέχυρα τὰ ἀντί τινων ἑλκόμενα ἅπερ ἀντὶ τῶν ἡρπασμένων ἁρπάζονται. But the phrase κατὰ ῥύσιον is applied to pirates (κακοῦργα πλοῖα) in I. G., XII, 5, 653. The phrase λάφυρον ἐπικηρύττειν is similarly used by Polybius (IV, 26 ; 36) ; λάφυρον ἀποδιδόναι occurs in Dittenberger, Syll.³, 535, with the same meaning as σύλας διδόναι (see below). The word λάφυρον also is frequently used, without any technical sense, with the meaning of spoil taken in war or by pirates (e.g. Xen., Hell., V, 1, 24 ; Dittenberger, Syll.³, 521, ὅπως . . . . μηθεὶς ἄχθει ἐπ[ὶ] τὸ λάφυρον, on the occasion of a pirate raid; cf. the λαφυροπώλια of the pirates at Side (Strabo, XIV, 664). On the Aetolian λάφυρον ἀπὸ λαφύρου (see below, p. 141).

state. Demosthenes alludes more than once to
the practice known as ἀνδροληψία.   In the speech
against Aristocrates a law is quoted to the effect
that if any Athenian citizen died a violent death
abroad, the relatives of the deceased might be
granted the right of seizing the persons of not
more than three citizens of the state concerned,
until justice was promised or the guilty surrendered.[1] The abuses to which this rough and
ready system of obtaining justice gave rise, even
when regulated by Attic law, are emphasised by
the orator in another speech.[2] Similar rights of
distraint on the property of individuals were
granted in the event of a commercial dispute with
citizens of a foreign state, the ordinary word in
the fifth and fourth centuries for the exercise of
such reprisals being σνλᾶν, which denotes the
act of self-help which in early times would be the
only means of obtaining justice from a foreigner.[3]
It is noticeable that the ordinary word for
plundering and pillaging is thus used in a
specialised sense to denote the seizure of a pledge

1. Demosth., XXI, 82. If the text of the law quoted is not genuine, it[3]
substance is clearly given by the orator himself in the following section. See
also §218.   There is an interesting case of self-help in Pausanias, IV, 4, where
the Messenian Euaephnus, failing to get justice from the Spartan authorities
for the murder of his son, undertook to murder any Spartan whom he could
catch.   Glotz, *La Solidarité de la Famille*, p. 213, sees in the story of the
death of Androgeos and the tribute of seven Attic youths and maidens an
early attempt to limit the exercise of universal reprisals (Plutarch, *Theseus*, 15 ;
Diod. Sic., IV, 61.)

2. LI, 13 (see above, p. 117).

3. There are some interesting remarks on theft considered as a private
rather than a public wrong (even between citizens), and on methods of
redress in Vinogradoff, *Historical Jurisprudence*, I, p. 356. See his derivation
of the word *ransack*, to search for stolen goods (cf. Murray, *New Engl. Dict.*,
s.v.). See Appendix B (p. 74).

to enforce payment of a claim.[1] Action of this kind was doubtless at one time universal, but was gradually limited by intermunicipal agreements, the συμβολαί of Greek international law being directed to the purpose of securing justice between citizens of different states without recourse to violence.[2] Nevertheless, even when such conventions were in existence, we find cases where, the legal guarantee having failed, it was necessary for the citizen of one state to apply for rights of reprisal against another state, the granting of such rights being analogous to the modern grant of *letters of marque* in its original significance.[3] Such rights might be granted to one citizen

1. In inscriptions the word generally has the technical meaning given above, but in Dittenberger, *Syll.*³, 372, it is used of pirates landing in Samothrace to plunder the temple offerings. In two cases, it is doubtful whether συλᾶν, σύλη are to be interpreted in the technical sense or not (See below, pp. 76, 101).

2. See the convention between Lyttos and Malla (*G. D. I.*, 5100). On the agreement between Oeantheia and Chaleion, see below, p. 76. It is impossible to enter here into the series of agreements guaranteeing ἀσυλία to communities or individuals. Among the most interesting are the decrees of the Delphic Amphictyony (*I. G.*, II, 551) guaranteeing immunity to the Athenian theatre artists, except in the case of debt : μὴ ἐξέστω δὲ μηδενὶ ἄγειν τὸν τ[εχνίταν μήτε] πολέμου μήτε εἰρήνας μηδὲ συλᾶν [πλὴν ἐὰν χρέ]ος ἔχων πόλει ἢ ὑπόχρεως καὶ ἐὰν ἰδ[ίᾳ ἢ ἰδιώτ]ου ὑπόχρεος ὁ τεχνίτας. Cf. *Ins. Jurid. Gr.*, I, p. 148, εἶναι δέ αὐτῶι ἀσυλίαν ἐργαζομένωι τὰ πρὸς τὴν πόλιν . . . . καὶ αὐτῶι καὶ τοῖς μετὰ Χαιρεφάνους ἐργαζομένοις ἅπασιν . . . . πλὴν εἴ τις σῦλον κατὰ τῆς πόλεως ἔχει · τούτω[ι δὲ μὴ ἐξεῖναι συλᾶν τοὺς μετὰ] Χαιρεφάνους πρὶν ἂν διαλύσωνται πρὸς τὴν πόλιν πάντ]α. (Chaerephanes was engaged in draining a marsh for the Eretrians.) Among the ἀσυλίαι inscriptions of Teos (*G. D. I* 5165-80; Michel, 51-68), Michel, no. 58, states that a violation of the agreement was punishable by reprisals on the guilty which might be undertaken by any Teian present : εἴ τινες τῶν ὁρμιομένων Ἀρκάδων ἀδικήσωντί τινα Τηΐων ἢ κοινᾶι ἢ ἰδίαι παρ τὸ γραφὲν δόγμα περὶ τὰς ἀσυλίας ὑπὸ τῆς πόλιος τᾶς Ἀρκάδων ἐξέστω τῶι παραγενομένωι Τηΐων ἐπιλαβέσθαι καὶ τῶν σωμάτων καὶ χρημάτων, αἴ τίς κα ἄγηι.

3. Wharton, *op. cit.*, *s.v.*, defines *letters of marque*, according to the earliest use of the phrase, as a " commission for extraordinary reprisals to merchants taken and despoiled by strangers at sea, grantable by the Secretaries of State with the approbation of the Sovereign and Council and usually in

against an individual belonging to a foreign state, or against the whole body of its citizens[1]; or in certain cases, as we have seen, the right of carrying out reprisals would be granted to the whole body of citizens of the injured state.[2] It is unnecessary to discuss the exact procedure by which these transactions were governed in the state to which the offended party belonged.[3] What principally concerns our present subject is the fact that even among the more advanced states of Greece reprisals and violent seizures of persons and of

time of war." This is an earlier use than the *letters of marque* granted to owners of private vessels for the purpose of privateering.

For the phrase σύλας or σῦλα διδόναι, see Demosth., XXXV, 23 and 26. Wayte, on Demosth., XXIV, *arg.* II, endeavours to draw a distinction between σῦλα and σῦλαι, the latter, in his view, denoting rights of seizure, the former the prize or captured property. But the distinction is impossible to maintain. τὸ σῦλον in Hicks and Hill, 44 is certainly used of the object seized, but in Dittenberger *Syll.*³, 10, ἡ σύλη is used with this significance. The distinction again breaks down in *Ins. Jurid. Gr.*, I, p. 148 (quoted above), and in (Arist.) *Oec.*, II, 1347b (see below). Cf. *I. G.*, XII, 5, 24 ἐσσύλωι ἀσυλίαν. (In *C. I. G.*, 2557 = Michel, 41, we should probably read περὶ τῶ σύλω rather than περὶ τῶσύλω.) A somewhat similar attempt has been made to draw a distinction between ἀνδροληψιον, the *right* (Pollux, VIII, 41; 50) and ἀνδροληψία (Demosthenes, *l.c.*; Pollux, VIII, 51, ἀνδροληψία κεχρημένος), the *practice*. (See Philippson, *International Law and Custom of ancient Greece and Rome*, II, p. 350). But it is not easy to maintain in view of the similar usage of συμβολή, σύμβολον, of which Hitzig (*Altgriech. Staatsverträge*, p. 31) states that σύμβολον is merely a later usage than συμβολή, the former being used universally after 177 B.C.

1. Cf. (Arist.) *Oec.*, *l.c.* (at Chalcedon) εἴ τις τῶν πολιτῶν ἢ μετοίκων σῦλον ἔχει κατὰ πόλεως ἢ ἰδιώτου.

2. See above, p. 63. Lysias, XXX, 22 : Βοιωτους δὲ σύλας ποιουμένους ὅτι οὐ δυνάμεθα δύο τάλαντα ἀποδοῦναι. (Here σῦλαι are exercised to recover a public debt.) In Demosth., XXXV, 23, ὅπου ἂν μὴ σῦλαι ὦσιν Ἀθηναίοις, it is obvious that the whole body of citizens on either side is concerned, although it is uncertain whether the Athenians have to fear reprisals or have the right to exercise them. In Demosthenes, VIII, 25, where foreigners are said to purchase exemption from Athenian generals, it is uncertain whether general reprisals are being carried out, or whether Athenian officers are acting on behalf of individuals who are their friends. In view of LI, 13, perhaps the latter is more probable.

3. On the whole subject, see Philippson, *op. cit.*, II, pp. 349 *seqq*; Gilbert, *Gr. Staatsaltertümer*, II, p. 381 *seqq*.; Hitzig, *op. cit.*, pp. 39 *seqq*.

goods continued till a late date, under the guise of lawful transactions, alongside the admittedly illegal plunderings of the pirate. While depredations of the one kind were permitted by law, it was obviously difficult to restrain activities of the other sort.[1]

It is equally difficult to apply the modern conception of the " politically organised society " to early conditions of ancient life.[2] It was only as the result of a long process of development that the ancient world came to distinguish between foreigner and enemy, piracy and privateering, lawful trade and kidnapping. To the Roman representations regarding the piracies carried out by her subjects Queen Teuta replied that it was not the habit of their kings to interfere with the normal pursuits of the Illyrians at sea.[3] Even in sixth century Greece we find Polycrates of Samos, according to Herodotus,[4] carrying on a piracy business directed against all users of the Aegean. A reputed law of Solon seems to have recognised similar proceedings

1. It is interesting to notice the attempt made by the Persian government, in 491 B.C., to enforce peace in Ionia, by compelling the states to adopt a system of δωσιδικία and lay aside their endless disputes (Hdt., VI, 42, συνθήκας σφίσι αὐτοῖσι τοὺς Ἴωνας ἠνάγκασε (Artaphernes) ποιεῖσθαι, ἵνα δωσίδικοι εἶεν καὶ μὴ ἀλλήλους φέροιέν τε καὶ ἄγοιεν.)

2. The doctrine, however, is clearly stated by Cicero, de Rep., I, 39 : Est igitur respublica res populi, populus autem non omnis hominum coetus quoquo modo congregatus, sed coetus multitudinis iuris consensu et utilitatis communione sociatus. But it is obvious that difficulties would arise in practical application. The Greek distinction between Hellene and Barbarian (expressed in its crudest form by Plato, Rep., V, 470c, and Aristotle, Politics, I, 1252b) evoked a strong protest even from the Greeks themselves, at any rate in post-Alexandrian times (cf. Eratosthenes ap. Strabo, I, 66, βέλτιον εἶναί φησιν ἀρετῇ καὶ κακίᾳ διαιρεῖν ταῦτα, πολλοὺς γὰρ καὶ τῶν Ἑλλήνων εἶναι κακοὺς καὶ τῶν βαρβάρων ἀστείους).

3. See below, p. 172.

4. See below, p. 104.

among the Athenians.[1] The plundering of neighbours was to the primitive inhabitant of the
Mediterranean area a form of production, which
was sanctioned and encouraged by the community, so long as it was directed against the
people of a different tribe.
The best description of such conditions is that
given by Thucydides :

For the Grecians in old time, and of the barbarians
both those on the continent who lived near the sea, and
all who inhabited islands, after they began to cross over
more commonly to one another in ships, turned to piracy,
under the conduct of their most powerful men, with a
view both to their own gain, and to maintenance for the
needy, and falling upon towns that were unfortified, and
inhabited like villages, they rifled them, and made most
of their livelihood by this means ; as this employment
did not yet involve any disgrace, but rather brought
with it somewhat of glory. This is shown by some that
dwell on the continent even at the present day, with
whom it is an honour to perform this cleverly ;[2] and by
the ancient poets, who introduce men asking the question
of such as sail to their coasts, in all cases alike, whether
they are pirates :[3] as though neither those of whom they

1. Gaius, in Digest, XLVII, 22, 4. Sed haec lex videtur ex lege Solonis
tralata esse. Nam illuc ita est : ἐὰν δὲ δῆμος ἢ φράτορες ἢ ἱερῶν ὀργίων
ἢ ναῦται ἢ σύσσιτοι ἢ ὁμόταφοι ἢ θιασῶται ἢ ἐπὶ λείαν οἰχόμενοι ἢ εἰς
ἐμπορίαν ὅτι ἂν τούτων διαθῶνται πρὸς ἀλλήλους κύριον εἶναι ἐὰν μὴ
ἀπαγορεύσῃ δημόσια γράμματα.
There is nothing to show that ἐπὶ λείαν refers to reprisals, as Dareste
assumes (Rev. Et. Gr., 1889, p. 311).

2. Compare Xenophon, Anab., VI, 1, 7-8, on the armed dance of the
Aenianes and Magnetes called the Carpaia : Ὁ δὲ τρόπος τῆς ὀρχήσεως
ἦν ὅδε · ὁ μὲν παραθέμενος τὰ ὅπλα σπείρει καὶ ζευγηλατεῖ, πυκνὰ
μεταστρεφόμενος, ὡς φοβούμενος · λῃστὴς δὲ προσέρχεται · ὁ δ', ἐπειδὰν
προΐδηται, ἀπαντᾷ ἁρπάσας τὰ ὅπλα, καὶ μάχεται πρὸ τοῦ ζεύγους · καὶ
οὗτοι ταῦτ' ἐποίουν ἐν ῥυθμῷ πρὸς τὸν αὐλόν · καὶ τέλος ὁ λῃστὴς δήσας τὸν
ἄνδρα καὶ τὸ ζεῦγος ἀπάγει · ἐνίοτε δὲ καὶ ὁ ζευγηλάτης τὸν λῃστήν.

3. Od., III, 71 ; IX, 252.

inquire, disowned the employment; nor those who were interested in knowing, reproached them with it. They also robbed one another on the continent; and to this day many of the Greeks live after the old fashion; as the Locri Ozolae, the Aetolians and Acarnanians, and those in that part of the continent.[1] And the fashion of wearing arms has continued amongst these continental states from their old trade of piracy.[2]

Piracy and brigandage are here regarded as a means of production, and were so classified by Aristotle :

Others support themselves by hunting, which is of different kinds. Some, for example, are brigands, others, who dwell by lakes or marshes or rivers or a sea in which there are fish, are fishermen and others live by the pursuit of birds or wild beasts."[3]

The life of the hunter precedes the life of the agriculturalist, and will be of longer duration in countries where cultivation is difficult and the soil barren. Where the country is narrow, or game scarce, the primitive inhabitant will take early to the sea. His pursuits will be fishing, trade, where trade is possible, or hunting, but the creatures hunted will be his fellow-men, who may be caught, like the beasts[4] on land, in the chase or in traps.

One of the most interesting figures of Greek legend is Nauplius, whose profession of wrecker,

1. See Appendix C (p. 76).

2. Thuc., I, 5 (Tr. Dale).

3. Arist., *Politics*, *I*, 1256a (tr. Jowett). Cf. Plato, *Legg.*, VII, 823 : " Let not any desire of catching men and piracy by sea enter into your souls and make you cruel and lawless hunters " (Jowett).

4. I had written " wild beasts," but see Plato, *Sophistes*, 222c : Ἀλλ' ἡμᾶς τε ἡμερον, ὦ ξένε, ἡγοῦμαι ζῷον, θήραν τε ἀνθρώπων εἶναι λέγω.

slaver and pirate may be regarded as typical of the early inhabitants of the Mediterranean coast. On shore he is a wrecker, accustomed to lure sailors to their death by means of false flares.[1] At sea, as slaver and pirate, he fills the part of the robbers in the *Babes in the Wood*, and to him unwanted children and naughty ladies are entrusted to be drowned or otherwise disposed of. A certain Catreus, king of Crete, gave him his two daughters, Aerope and Clymene, with instructions to sell them into foreign lands. Aerope was sold by Nauplius, but Clymene was retained as his wife.[2] Auge, daughter of Aleos, was similarly handed over for destruction after her liaison with Heracles, and disposed of to a crew of Carian pirates.[3] His name means simply " sailor " (as the first sailor he is credited with the discovery of the Great Bear[4]), and his conduct probably differed little from that of all early seamen in the Mediterranean.[5] We have already examined the practices of the Mainotes, who were wreckers and pirates in the seventeenth and eighteenth centuries, and of the Tauri in the Black Sea ; we hear of other communities who made a livelihood by such means, where the character of the coast-line was favourable.[6]

1. Apollodorus, *Bibl.*, II, 1, 5, οὗτος μακρόβιος γενόμενος, πλέων τὴν θάλασσαν, τοῖς ἐμπίπτουσι ἐπὶ θανάτῳ ἐπυρσοφόρει, συνέβη οὖν καὶ αὐτὸν τελευτῆσαι ἐκείνῳ τῷ θανάτῳ.

2. *Ib.*, III, 2, 2 ; Sophocles, Ajax, 1295.

3. Apollodorus, II, 7, 4 ; III, 9, 1 ; Diod. Sic., IV, 33.

4. *Schol.* Aratus, *Phaen.*, 27. Two of his sons are Oeax and Nausimedon. (Apollodorus, II, 1, 5).

5. See Appendix D (p. 77).

6. The inhabitants of the Iapygian promontory (Hdt., III, 138) ; the Nasamones of the Syrtes (Lucan, IX, 438 ; Silius Italicus, III, 30) ; Zimmern

Wrecking, then, is one form of production from which the community as a whole may derive benefit. Similar views were held by primitive peoples regarding war. " In one point of view the art of war is a natural art of acquisition." War of this kind is classed by Aristotle with farming, piracy, fishing and hunting as producing sustenance without the media of exchange and trade.[1] Similarly Thucydides, as we saw, notes that the motives which inspired piracy were private gain and the maintenance of the weaker members of the family or tribe.[2] When men are organised on a tribal basis the two things, war and piracy, are almost indistinguishable.[3] The

(*Greek Commonwealth*,[3] p. 33) has an interesting note on the Myrmex rock near Scyros (Hdt., VII, 183). See also Petronius, 114. The worst wreckers were in the Black Sea, where, besides the Tauri, the Thracians of Salmydessos, μήτρυια νεῶν, developed an organised system of plundering wrecked ships (Xenophon, *Anab.*, VII, 5, 12 ; see also VI, 2, 2, on other wreckers).

For Roman penalties against wreckers, see Digest, XLVII, ix, 4 : Divus Antoninus de his qui praedam ex naufragio diripuissent ita rescripsit : Quod de naufragiis navis et ratis scripsisti mihi, eo pertinet, ut explores, qua poena adficiendos eos putem, qui diripuisse aliqua ex illo probantur et facile, ut opinor, constitui potest : nam plurimum interest, peritura collegerint an quae servari possint flagitiose invaserint. Ideoque si gravior praeda vi adpetita videbitur, liberos quidem fustibus caesos in triennium relegabis aut, si sordidiores sunt, in opus publicum eiusdem temporis dabis : servos flagellis caesos in metallum damnabis. Si non magnae pecuniae res fuerint, liberos fustibus, servos flagellis caesos dimittere poteris.

1. Aristotle, *Politics*, 1256b (Jowett): διὸ καὶ ἡ πολεμικὴ φύσει κτητική πως ἔσται.

2. Thuc., I, 5 : κέρδους τοῦ σφετέρου αὐτῶν ἕνεκα καὶ τοῖς ἀσθενέσι τροφῆς.

3. See on this point Francotte, *L'Industrie dans la Grece*, p. 270. There are some valuable remarks in Wallon, *Histoire de l'Esclavage* (2nd edition), pp. 161 *seqq.* In historical times, piracy and war were the principal sources of slaves for Greece, the one perennial, the latter only intermittent ; (cf. Beauchet, *Droit Privé*, II, 411 : " La guerre n'était qu'un mode de recrutement intermittant de l'esclavage, mais la piraterie y subvenait d'une façon continue.) Cf. Dio Chrys., XV, 242 : τοὺς γὰρ πρώτους δούλους οὐκ εἰκὸς ἐκ δούλων φῦναι τὴν ἀρχὴν ἀλλὰ ὑπὸ λῃστείας ἢ πολέμου κρατηθέντας οὕτως ἀναγκασθῆναι δουλεύειν τοῖς λάβουσι, and Aristotle, *Politics*, VII,

proceeds of both are derived from outside, and it is only within the unit that theft is forbidden. Theft, whether armed or not, is no disgrace, if committed at the expense of an enemy or foreign people. Autolycus the thief was under the special protection of Hermes, but it is to be presumed that his gift was not exercised at home.[1]

It is clear, therefore, that the ambiguous terminology which existed in the historical period regarding piracy, reprisals and captures in war was an inheritance from an earlier date when little distinction was made between the various processes of acquisition. Odysseus uses the word λήίσσομαι, when he proposes to recover his losses from the suitors,[2] the word which is elsewhere used both of captures made in war[3] and of the plunderings of pirates, λήίστηρες. λήΐς[4] in the epic is used of plunder in general, whether taken by armies in the field[5] or by pirates[6], but also in a narrower sense to denote the especial object of plundering forays, the form of property by which the ancients set most store, namely cattle.[7]

1333b-34a, who justifies wars undertaken for raising slaves among barbarians. In the first century B.C., the Cilician pirates were the chief purveyors of slaves to the Roman world (see below, p. 207).

1. *Od.*, XIX, 395 ; *Il.*, X, 265.

2. *Od.*, XXIII, 357.

3. *Il.*, IX, 406 ; XVIII, 28 ; *Od.*, I, 398.

4. *Od.*, III, 7 ; XVI, 424 ; XVII, 425, λήίστηρες πολύπλαγκτοι ; XVI, 427, Τάφιοι λήίστορες ἄνδρες.

5. Of the booty at Troy, *Il.*, IX, 138, 280 ; XVIII, 327 ; *Od.*, III, 106 ; V, 40 ; X, 41 ; XIII, 262.

6. *Od.*, XIV, 86.

7. Plundered cattle : *Il.*, XI, 677 ; Hymn, *Hermes*, 330 (cf. 335). In Hesiod, *Theog.*, 444, the word is used absolutely of " stock." The words λήΐζομαι, λήΐς, etc., come from a root λαϜ, which gives us also ἀπολαύειν and the Latin lu-crum. See Curtius, *Principles of Gk. Etymology* (E.T., 1886),

It is, therefore, not surprising that the oldest Greek legends consist largely of the exploits of the heroes engaged in inter-tribal cattle-raids. The war against Thebes is said by Hesiod to have been waged for the sake of the flocks of Oedipodes.[1] The Trojan war began as reprisals for the rape of a woman and in its course consisted largely of cattle-driving.[2] The liveliest picture of warfare of this type is given by Nestor.[3] A debt of old standing had been owed by the Eleians to the men of Pylos, since the days when the Epeians of Elis had profited by the weakness of the Pylians to raid their country. Now the debt is recovered by the valour of young Nestor, and the spoils divided among all who had suffered from the Eleian depredations. But on the third day all the Epeians came and a new battle took place. Was the question settled by the victory won by Nestor's men or did the Epeians make another attempt ?

Nevertheless, just as the feud within the tribe was beginning to give way to settlement in court,[4] so the inter-tribal feuds were already in the *Odyssey* being settled by mutual agreement.

I, p. 439, quoted by Glotz, *op. cit.*, p. 200, and Boisacq, *Dict. Etymol*². *s. vv.* ἀπολαύειν, λεία. Cf. Vinogradoff, *op. cit.*, I, p. 357 : " It is at least characteristic that some of the expressions referring to ownership in Indo-European language go back to the notion of conquest, the taking of booty. The Italian *roba*, meaning chattels, goods, is nothing but the Teutonic *Raub*, the produce of robbery, and the Latin *praedium*, estate, is related to *praeda*, booty."

1. Hesiod, *Erg.*, 163. One of the most famous cattle raids was that carried out by the Dioscuri and Apharidae, *Cypria*, XI (Oxford text), Apollodorus, III, 11, 2. For the rape of women and reprisals, see *Cypria*, X, Hellanicus *fr.* 74 (*F. H. G.*, I, p. 55.)

2. *Il.*, III, 106 ; VI, 421 ; cf. the scene on the shield, *Il.*, XVIII, 520 *seqq.*

3. *Il.*, XI, 670-761.

4. *Il.*, XVIII, 488 *seqq.*

Odysseus in his youth was sent by his father and
the elders on an embassy to Messenia, to recover
a debt which all the people owed ; for men of
Messenia had raided Ithaca and carried off
three hundred sheep and their shepherds.[1] Instead
of immediate reprisals, the Ithacans first attempt
diplomatic methods, and we may suppose that the
matter was settled by agreement, and that no
more raiding took place. A similar agreement
had been reached between the Ithacans and the
Thesprotians.[2] Eupeithes, who had violated it
by joining a band of Taphian pirates in a descent
on the Thesprotian coast, only escaped the wrath
of the people of Ithaca through the protection
which Odysseus granted to him. There are
glimpses, then, in the Odyssey of a distinction
between the politically organised society and the
barbarian beyond the pale, and we have in this
story perhaps an echo of the earliest attempts
among the Greeks to combine for mutual protection against the dangers of piracy which threatened
them at the hands of the barbarian communities.

APPENDIX B (Chapter II, p. 64)

An interesting case of reprisals of this character
is to be found in an Egyptian papyrus of the reign
of Ramses XII (c. 1118-1090 B.C.), containing the
report of the voyage of Wen-Amon (Pap. Golénischeff, Breasted, *Ancient Records* IV, §§ 558 *seqq.*
whose versions I follow in this and the next

1. *Od.*, XXI, 15 *seqq.*
2. *Od.*, XVI, 424-430, οἱ δ' ἡμῖν ἄρθμιοι ἦσαν.

chapter): The Egyptian envoy, having been robbed at Dor of the Thekel (on the Syrian coast) of 5 *deben* of gold and 31 *deben* of silver, claimed that it should be repaid by the king of Dor. The king refused on the ground that it was one of Wen-Amon's own men who had stolen the money (§ 566). In the course of his voyage from Dor, Wen-Amon seems to have fallen in with a Thekel ship . . . . " I found 30 *deben* of silver therein. I seized [it, saying to them : ' I will take] your money, it shall remain with me until ye find [my money. Was it not a man of Thekel] who stole it, and no thief of ours ? I will take it ' . . . ." (§ 568).

Naturally, this high-handed action produced retaliation. As Wen-Amon tells us, while he was at Byblos negotiating for the timber which he had been sent to purchase, " I went to the shore of the sea, to the place where the timbers lay ; I spied eleven ships coming from the sea, belonging to the Thekel, saying : Arrest him ! let not a ship of his pass to Egypt . . . . (§ 588)

" Morning came and the king of Byblos called unto his [————]. He stood in their midst and said to the Thekel : ' Why have ye come ? ' They said to him : ' We have come after the stove-up ships which thou sendest to Egypt with our [————] comrades.' He said to them : ' I cannot arrest a messenger of Amon in my land, let me send him away, and ye shall pursue him to arrest him ' " (§ 590).

The last paragraph offers a close parallel to the Locrian τὰ ξενικὰ ἐ θαλάσας ἤγεν ἄσυλον πλὰν ἐ λιμένος τô κατὰ πόλιν. (see *App. C*).

APPENDIX C (Chap. II, p. 69)

In view of what Thucydides says regarding the backward conditions prevailing in this part of the Greek world, it is difficult to decide whether συλεῖν of the Oeantheia-Chaleion agreement (*I. G.*, IX, 3, 333 ; Hicks and Hill, 44 ; Michel, 3 ; Buck, *Greek Dialects*, 56) is to be interpreted in the technical sense (see above), or as simple plundering. According to the second interpretation, the freebooters of Chaleion are not to interfere with the game of the Oeantheians in the harbour of the latter town and *vice versa*, but foreign shipping (the pilgrim traffic to Delphi) may be plundered at sea by the mariners of either town (as is suggested by Zimmern, *Greek Commonwealth*[3], pp. 315-316). But in view of similar agreements between other states it is wiser to give the technical sense of seizure by way of reprisals to συλεῖν on the present occasion. Cf. *G. D. I.*, 5100 (Lyttos and Malla), μὴ ἐξέστω δὲ συλεῖν [μήτε] τὸν Λυττίον ἐν τᾶι τῶν Μαλλαίων μήτε τ[ὸν Μαλ]λαῖον ἐν τᾶι τῶν Λυττίων · αἰ δέ τίς κα συ[λάσηι], ἀποτεινύτω τό τε χρέος ὅ κα συλάση[ι], where the mention of τὸ χρέος makes it certain that we have to do with seizure as reprisals ; *Ins. Jurid. Gr.*, II, p. 319 (Gortyn and Rhizon) ἐνεχυραστὰν δὲ μὲ παρέρπεν Γορτύνιον ἐς τὸ Ῥιττενίο, " Le Gortynien ne viendra pas faire de saisies-gages (à Rhizène) contre le Rhizénien." (*Edd.*)

In the one case the Lyttian may not be subjected to reprisals in the territory of Malla (and *vice versa*), in the other the Gortynian may not visit the territory of Rhizon for the purpose of executing reprisals on a Rhizonian. The Locrian agreement, however, reveals a more advanced stage than either of these, and is concerned with the exercise of reprisals against foreigners using the port of one of the two states, where they might be liable to reprisals from a citizen of the other. The insertion of τὸν ξένον which is found in neither of the two agreements quoted above is no mere accident, as Riezler (*Finanzen*, p. 79, approved by Zimmern, *l.c.*) seems to suppose, when he renders : " Niemand sollte im Gebiet der einen einen Bürger der anderen Stadt berauben dürfen." The ξένος is a member of neither state. Reprisals may be exercised at his expense on the open sea, but with the growing responsibilities of the two towns, reprisals carried out against foreigners by citizens of either of the two contracting states had to be prevented in home waters, since, if exercised, *e.g.* by a Chaleian at Oeantheia, they might violate an existing convention between Oeantheia and a third party. (On the whole question see Meyer, *Forschungen*, I, pp. 307 *seqq.*)

APPENDIX D (Chap. II, p. 70)

The account which I have given in the text is probably the original version of the Nauplius story ; much confusion was caused by his introduction into the Trojan saga, where the prince of wreckers encompasses the destruction of the Greek fleet, to avenge his son Palamedes (full

refs. in Frazer's *Apollodorus*, vol. II, p. 247).
It is noticeable that this version is not Homeric.
Again, Nauplius, the καταποντιστής, to punish
Odysseus, attempts the drowning of Penelope, and
is further credited with the corruption of the
Achaean ladies on a voyage specially undertaken
for the purpose (refs. in Pearson, *Fragments of
Sophocles*, II, p. 82). He is also brought into the
Argonaut story as the successor of Tiphys the
helmsman (Ap. Rhod. II, 896). The longevity
with which he is credited (see Apollodorus, II, i, 5)
is, no doubt, a reply to such criticisms as that of
Strabo (VIII, 368) to the effect that Nauplius,
the son of Poseidon and Amymone, cannot have
been alive at the time of the Trojan war. Other
writers accordingly distinguished this Nauplius,
the founder of Nauplia (Paus. II, 38, 2), from
Nauplius the son of Clytoneus, fifth in descent
from Nauplius I (refs. in Roscher).

Of the two plays by Sophocles, Ναύπλιος
Πυρκαεύς and Ναύπλιος Καταπλέων, the Πυρκαεύς
clearly dealt with the later figure of the legend,
the Nauplius who wrecked the Greek fleet off
Caphereus (see Pearson, *op. cit.*, p. 80). It is hard
to believe that the Nauplius Καταπλέων, Nauplius
landing or returning home, can have been other
than the pirate and wrecker who met the fate of
the hero of the *Inchcape Rock*. (See Geffcken,
Hermes, XXVI, pp. 38-39, quoted by Pearson,
p. 83).

It may well be doubted whether the connection
of Nauplius with Caphereus was original and not
due to the later story. The statement in Steph.
Byz. *s.v.* Καφηρεύς that the Euboeans were noted

wreckers, rests partly on a false etymology, partly on the localisation of Nauplius in Euboea in accordance with the later story. On the other hand, the risks from pirates in the d'Oro channel were proverbial in the Middle Ages (see Miller, pp. 156, 580), and as late as 1797 the Capherean promontory was regarded with particular aversion. See Hawkins (1797), in Walpole, *Travels in the East*, p. 285 : " Here ships are not unfrequently stopped by adverse winds and constantly assailed by currents of air which blow round Cavo d'Oro [the Capherean promontory]. This, in fact, is regarded by the Levant sailors as the most dangerous part of their navigation ; for there is no sheltered retreat at hand, and the horrors of shipwreck are heightened by the inhospitable character of the natives of this mountainous promontory. Numerous stories are related of their rapacity upon these occasions ; and the life of a shipwrecked mariner is said to be little regarded if it be an obstacle to its gratification." Chandler, *Travels in Asia Minor and Greece* (1764-1766), II, p. 4, speaks of the existence of a small fort near Caphereus on a rocky eminence, where there was the ruin of a *pharos* erected by a corsair for signalling and to facilitate his entering in the dark.

CHAPTER III

Καὶ μὲν δυσμενέες καὶ ἀνάρσιοι, οἵ τ᾽ἐπὶ γαίης
ἀλλοτρίης βῶσιν καί σφι Ζεὺς ληΐδα δώῃ
πλησάμενοι δέ τε νῆας ἔβαν οἰκόνδε νέεσθαι,
καὶ μὲν τοῖς ὄπιδος κρατερὸν δέος ἐν φρεσὶ πίπτει.
(Homer, *Odyss.* xiv, 85.)

THE earliest attempts to clear the Aegean of
pirates were made, according to Greek tradition,
by the rulers of the first state to attain to any
degree of civilisation and to develop maritime
power. Minos of Crete, according to Thucydides,
was the first to acquire a fleet, control the seas,
and rule the Cyclades. He cleared the sea of
pirates so far as he was able, in order that his
revenues might come in.[1] The truth of
Thucydides' account has been abundantly proved
by excavation. Unwalled cities possessing the
wealth which has been revealed in Crete could never
have existed, unless the inhabitants had been able
to rely on a powerful navy to keep marauders from
the island. The constant intercourse with Egypt
which the excavations have shown to have existed
would have been equally impossible without the
control of the sea-routes that Thucydides postu-

1. Thuc., I, 4. (There is a curious story in Plutarch, *Theseus*, 19, from
Cleidemus, regarding police work done by Jason in the Argo.)

lates. Cretan domination of the Cyclades is also proved by the character of the later Cycladic civilisation. During the first two periods of the Late Minoan Age Cycladic art is almost wholly dependent on Crete.[1] It is true that a risk of occasional raids remained, as is shown by the fact that the rulers of Cnossos found it necessary to fortify the northern approaches to the palace.[2] Such a measure may have been purely precautionary, but the precaution was a necessary one, while the robber tribes of southern Asia Minor were still unsubdued. It is not, indeed, until a somewhat later date that we have definite evidence of the overseas activities of these peoples, but their later history shows that piracy and brigandage were always among their principal occupations. The district which they inhabited was eminently suited to be a base for pirating expeditions, and, as the Romans later discovered, was extremely difficult to control. It is not without significance that in the disturbances which followed the fall of Cnossos (*c.* 1400 B.C.) many of the principal raiders, as recorded by the Egyptian monuments, can be identified with the inhabitants of this coast.

The first mention of piracy on the part of these peoples is to be found in one of the Tell-el-Amarna letters, where the king of Alašia, in answer to a complaint from the Pharaoh that his subjects are joining with men of the land Lukki to plunder Egypt, replies that the Lukki are every year

1. See *B.S.A.*, XVII, pp. 11 *seqq.*

2. Evans, *The Palace of Minos at Knossos*, I, p. 398 ; see also Burrows *The Discoveries in Crete*, p. 17.

capturing some small town in his own country.[1]
The men of the land Lukki mentioned in this
tablet are to be identified with the inhabitants of
Lycia,[2] whose career of crime is known from the
Egyptian monuments to have lasted for some
hundred and fifty years. We hear of Luka as
members of a great confederacy of Anatolian and
Syrian peoples whose southward advance through
Syria was checked by Ramses II (c. 1292-1225) at
the battle of Kadesh. Besides the Luka and
Hittites, many of the confederate tribes would
appear to have been of Anatolian origin, and it is
probable that the Hittite army consisted to a large
extent of mercenary contingents raised among their
neighbours in Asia Minor, who fought under their
own leaders.[3]

No charge of piracy can be brought against the
Luka on this occasion, but they figure again in the

1. Knudtzon, *Die El-Amarna Tafeln*, I, no. 38. The depredations in
Alašia are clearly pirates' work, not that of regular invaders. The Pharaoh
in question is probably Ikhnaton (c. 1375-1358); see Knudtzon, *op. cit.*,
no. 33, 9-11. On the probable locality of Alašia in Northern Syria, see
Wainwright, Klio, XIV, pp. 1 seqq. Hall, in *Anatolian Studies*, p. 178,
inclines to the view that it may be the later Elaeussa off the coast of Cilicia
Tracheia.

2. Knudtzon, II, p. 1084; Meyer, *Geschichte des Altertums*, I, 2, § 515.

3. See Breasted, *Ancient Records*, III, p. 129, note b, with special
reference to the conclusion of §306 : " He left not silver nor gold in his land,
(but) he plundered it of all its possessions and gave to every country in order
to bring them with him to battle." Of the various identifications proposed,
Luka and Kelekesh (I have kept Breasted's rendering of the names throughout
this section) may fairly certainly be regarded as Lycians and Cilicians (see
Hall, *B.S.A.*, VIII, p. 178). The other names are more doubtful; Pedes
may be Pisidians or men of Pedasos in Caria (Hall, *l.c.*; cf. Hdt., I, 175;
VI, 20; VIII, 104). In the Derden it is possible that we have the Dardanoi
of the Troad. The others are even more doubtful. Mesa or Masa have been
taken for Mysians. For Breasted's Erwenet, Hall—following Petrie—suggests
Ari-wen-na = Oroanda. Other suggestions are Maeonians (Maunna) or
men of Ilion (Iliunna). (I much regret that I have been unable to use
Dr. Hall's careful discussion of the names of the " Peoples of the Sea " in
the *Cambridge Ancient History*, vol. II, chap. xii.)

war which Merneptah (*c.* 1225-1215), the successor of Ramses II, waged in the fifth year of
his reign against invaders from Libya who had
been joined by " Northerners coming from all
lands,"[1] Ekwesh " of the countries of the sea,"[2]
Teresh, Luka, Sherden, and Shekelesh.[3] Besides
the Anatolian names of Luka and possibly
Shekelesh, and the doubtful Teresh and Sherden,
it is generally agreed that in the Ekwesh of these
inscriptions we have a mention of the Greek
Achaioi ('Aχαιϝοί), with whom, as their own
records show, raids on the Egyptian Delta were
a favourite pastime both now and at a later date.
The Pharaoh seems to have believed that Hittites
were included among the raiders, or at any rate
that the raids were undertaken with Hittite
complicity,[4] but from the general character of
these raids on the Delta it is more natural to
suppose that the invading Libyans were joined by
independent bands of pirates, who happened to be
cruising off the Egyptian coasts and made use of
the disturbances caused by the Libyan invasion.

The sea-raiders on this occasion were but the
forerunners of a more serious movement that
threatened Egypt a few years later. In the fifth
year of Ramses III (*c.* 1198-1167) fresh hordes of
Libyans invaded the kingdom, accompanied as
before by bands of sea-rovers. " The northern
countries are unquiet in their limbs, even the
Peleset, the Thekel who devastate the land . . . .

1. Breasted, III, § 574.
2. *Ib.*, §§ 588, 601.
3. *Ib.*, §§ 574, 579.
4. See Breasted's notes to §§ 580 and 617.

They were warriors upon land and also in the sea."[1] Only two tribes of Northerners are named on this occasion, but the same two peoples figure prominently among the invaders of the next war, and it is probably right to regard the Peleset and Thekel allies of the Libyans as the advance guard of the peoples whose main body was met by the Egyptians three years later on the Syrian coast. " The [Northerners] in their isles were disturbed. . . . . Not one stood before their hands from Kheta, Kode, Carchemish, Arvad, Alasa, they were wasted. [Th]ey [⌈set up⌉] a camp in Amor. . . . . They came with fire prepared before them, forward to Egypt. Their main support was Peleset, Thekel, Shekelesh, Denyen and Weshwesh. (These) lands were united."[2] The invaders were met and defeated on land, and their fleets destroyed off the Syrian coast.[3]

Three of the tribes mentioned in the list given by Ramses III are known to us from other sources. The Peleset are generally admitted to be identical with the Philistines of the Palestinian coast. The Thekel are found at a later date at Dor,[4] and the Denyen (D'-y-n-yw) are probably identical with the Danuna of the Tell-el-Amarna letters, who appear to have been a tribe of northern Syria.[5] It might, therefore, be held

1. *Ib.*, IV, § 44.

2. *Ib.*, § 64.

3. See Breasted, IV, p. 33.

4. Breasted, IV, § 565 (Golénischeff Papyrus): " I arrived at Dor a city of Thekel."

5. Knudtzon, *op. cit.*, I, no. 151 (letter of Abimilki of Tyre): " The king, my lord, wrote to me : 'What thou hearest from Kinaḫna (Canaan), that write to me.' The king of Danuna is dead and his brother is become

that the war in which Ramses was engaged was a purely local affair with Syrian tribes. The account, however, which the king gives, shows that there was a great disturbance of peoples in northern Syria, and in the Egyptian representations of the invaders the migratory character of the movement is clearly shown by the pictures of ox-carts carrying women and children, by which the land forces are accompanied.[1] Thekel and Peleset may well have reached their later homes in Palestine as the result of this migration, and the Denyen be a tribe of Northern Syria swept forward by the invaders in their advance. The movement is known to have been a two-fold one by land and sea. Peleset and Thekel ships had raided the Delta three years earlier, and an important part of Ramses' victory in Syria was the sea battle represented on the monuments.[2]

It is not easy to discover the countries from which these invaders were derived. Migratory hordes moving by land and sea are likely enough to have consisted of a mixed multitude coming from a variety of sources. Archaeological discoveries in the country later occupied by the Philistines have shown that the island of Crete exercised a considerable influence on the civilisation of the district.[3] Although we are scarcely warranted in deriving the whole of the Philistine

---

king after him." If the Danuna of this letter = Denyen, the proposed identification with the Homeric Δαναοί must be abandoned, although in Breasted, IV, § 403 (Harris papyrus) they are called " Denyen in their isles."

1. Breasted, IV, § 73; Champollion, *Monuments*, CCXX, *bis*.

2. Champollion, *Monuments*, CCXXII, CCXXIII.

3. Macalister, *Philistines*, p. 15; Evans, *Scripta Minoa*, pp. 77 *seqq*. Wainwright, *Annals of Archaeology and Anthropology*, VI, p. 72.

nation from Crete, it may well have been the case that large numbers of the inhabitants of the Aegean were concerned in this movement, just as we have already seen that the Ekwesh invaders during the reign of Merneptah are probably to be regarded as Achaeans.[1]

Fortunately, the Egyptian representations have left us accurate pictures of the appearance of these invaders. Most of them are figured with a large round shield and the high feather head-dress which Herodotus says was characteristic of the Lycians at the time of the Persian wars.[2] The same distinctive ornament appears on the sign representing a man's head on the Phaestos disk, which, though found in Crete, is pretty certainly to be regarded as of Anatolian origin.[3] The fact that the invasion of Syria took place both by land and sea would naturally incline us to look for the origin of most of these peoples among the maritime tribes of Southern Asia Minor. The Shekelesh have been identified with the inhabitants of Sagalassos in Pisidia.[4] It is possible that the Teresh, who seem to wear a high conical head-dress similar to that worn by certain of the figurines found in Hittite districts, came also

1. On the possibility of an Aegean element in the later Phoenicians, see Woolley, *Syria*, II, pp. 189, 190.

2. Hdt., VII, 92, εἶχον . . . . περὶ τῇσι κεφαλῇσι πίλους πτεροῖσι περιεστεφανωμένους. See further Max Müller, *Asien und Europa*, p. 362.

3. Evans, *Scripta Minoa*, pp. 25-27 ; *The Palace of Minos*, pp. 654 *seqq.* An excellent summary of the Anatolian characteristics of the raiders will be found in Wainwright, *op. cit.*, p. 64, n. 4. See also A. J. Reinach, *Rev. Arch.*, 1910, pp. 20 *seqq.*, and Woolley, *Annals of Arch.*, IX, pp. 53-4.

4. This identification, first proposed by Maspero (see Hall, *l.c.*), is intrinsically far more probable than that which would connect them with Σικελοί. The names of the Pisidian towns of Sagalassos (also called Selgessos, Strabo, XII, 569) and Selge may well have preserved an ancient ethnic.

from Asia Minor.[1] The origin of the Sherden who are joined with the invaders must remain doubtful. The name had been used for a long time in the Egyptian records to denote the foreign mercenaries of the Pharaohs, but it is noticeable that the invading Sherden wear a helmet exactly similar to that worn by the Sherden mercenaries in the Egyptian armies.[2] The Homeric poems

1. The representation of the captured Teresh (Champollion, *Monuments*, CCIII) is unfortunately damaged, but the head-dress appears to resemble that of the figurines published by Chantre, *Mission en Cappadoce*, pl. xxiv, fig. 2 (said, however, to have come from Carchemish), fig. 109, etc. Whether they were identical with the later Τυρσηνοί of Lemnos or Τυρρηνοί of Italy is uncertain, but see Meyer, *G.D.A.*, I, 2, § 515. It is noticeable that in this reign they are not mentioned among the invaders of the great war in the year 8, but occur with Hittites, Amorites, Thekel, Sherden, Bedwi, and Peleset in the Syrian war, probably of year 11 (Breasted, IV, § 129.)

2. Širdan are mentioned in the Tell-el-Amarna letters (temp. Ikhnaton), where they appear to have been troops in the service of the Egyptians (Knudtzon, *op. cit.*, I, nos. 81, 122, 123; see note in II, p. 1166). Sherden invaders (Š'-r'-d-n) are mentioned in the Karnak inscription of Merneptah (Breasted, III, §§ 574, 579, 588, 601, among "Northerners coming from all lands," and in the Medinet Habu inscriptions of Ramses III (Breasted, IV, § 129), as "Sherden of the sea," where the helmet of the captive Sherden (Champollion, *Monuments*, CCIII) is identical with that worn by the foreign auxiliaries of the Egyptian troops (unnamed) in Champollion, CCXIX, CCXXVIII. The crew of one of the ships of the invaders (unnamed) in these reliefs (Champollion, CCXXII, CCXXIII) have similar accoutrements except that the horned helmet does not carry the disk or ball shown in Champollion, CCIII, CCXIX, CCXXVIII. It is clear that during the XIXth and XXth dynasties (and in the XVIIIth, if the Širdan of the Tell-el-Amarna tablets are identical) Sherden was used as a general term for these foreign auxiliaries of the Pharaohs, the troop, like the Achaeans of the Odyssey (see below), being for the most part composed of the remnant of defeated invaders. Cf. Breasted, III, § 307 : "The Sherden of the captivity of his majesty from the victories of his sword" (Ramses II); cf. III, § 91, where some of them appear to have taken the part of the invaders in the reign of Merneptah (See Breasted's note c to § 491). For the Sherden auxiliaries of the reign of Ramses III, see Breasted, IV, §§ 397, 402, 410 (Harris papyrus). Though their equipment is usually shown to have been the same as that of the Sherden invaders, they were probably of mixed origin. In Champollion, CCV, the accoutrements of the auxiliaries are partly the normal accoutrements of the Sherden, partly those of the Thekel and Peleset (as shown in Champollion, CCIII, CCXX, CCXXVI, CCXXXI *bis*).

make it clear that invaders from the North, like the Norsemen of a later date, were often to be found in the service of the countries which their compatriots were in the habit of raiding. The name of the Weshwesh also shows distinct affinities with Asia Minor,[1] and it is possible that in the Thekel we have the ancestors of a royal family in Cilicia, whom we shall meet again in the last two centuries before the Christian era.[2] The state of the Aegean after the fall of Cnossos is vividly portrayed by the Homeric poems, in which additional light is thrown on the character of these raids. It is not certain whether the women brought from Sidon by Paris were the fruit of a raid on the Syrian coast or a gift from the king.[3] Menelaus cruised for seven years in the Levant and off the African coast, and gathered much substance.[4] A Taphian

The name Sherden has been connected with Sardis and also with Sardinia, but the comparisons with later Sardinian art are not very convincing. (See Max Müller, *Asien und Europa*, p. 372.)

1. W'-š'-š'. See the list of personal names Ουαοας, Ουαουας, Ουουας, Ουασις, Ουασσος, etc., from Lycia, Caria, Pisidia, Cilicia, given by Sundwall, *Einheimischen Namen der Lykier*, p. 240. For Ουασαδα in Lycaonia, see *B.S.A.*, IX, p. 266 ; *J.R.S.*, XII, p. 56.

2. For details see below, p. 195. I put this forward merely as a suggestion, but regard it as at least as probable as the common identification of the Thekel (T'-k-k'-r') with the Teucrids of Cyprus. (It is possible that the Teucrids of both Cilicia and Cyprus had a common ancestry.) It becomes more probable if Wainwright's localisation of the land of the Keftiu in Eastern Cilicia is correct (*l.c.*, pp. 33, 75). The Thekel and Peleset are closely connected in the Egyptian representations, and clearly came from the same district. (On Keftiu = Caphtor, the traditional home of the Philistines, see Macalister, *op. cit.*, pp. 5-7 ; Wainwright, p. 95. It should be noted, however, that Hall, in *Anatolian Studies*, p.182, still regards Petrie's suggested identification of the name Thekel with the modern Zakro in Crete with approval.)

3. *Il.*, VI, 290.

4. *Od.*, IV, 80-90. Roberts' ship was out nine years on her first voyage, and on the second trip had been out four (*op. cit.*, p. 9). The Maltese galleys could not stay out more than five years. Thévenot's two galleys had been out 30 and 40 months respectively (II, p. 715).

raid on the Syrian coast produced the nurse of Eumaeus.[1] We have already examined the account which Odysseus gives of his raid on the Thracian coast ; in another of his stories he gives us a graphic picture of the life of the freebooters of his day.[2] The typical pirate now boasts that he is of Cretan race ; he is the bastard son of a wealthy man, and thanks to his reputation as a warrior is married to a wealthy wife : But I loved not work nor household cares, but ships and war were my delight ; nine times before the war at Troy I raided men of another race with my ships, and my house grew great and my reputation was established among the Cretans. After the war at Troy I remained but a month at home, but then my heart bade me sail to Egypt. There follows a vivid description of the rapid gathering when the Viking arms, and of the swift voyage to Egypt with a favouring breeze.[3] On arrival in the river of Egypt, the corsair's followers, over-eager for the booty, get out of hand. Disdaining his orders to remain by their ships while scouts explored the country, they attacked the fields of the Egyptians and carried away the women and children.[4] The results were similar to Odysseus' experiences among the Cicones. Word of the raid came swiftly to the city and all the plain was

1. *Od.*, XIV, 455.

2. *Od.*, XIV, 199 *seqq.* ; with variations in *Od.*, XVI, 424 *seqq.*

3. XIV, 255, ἀλλ' ἀσκηθέες καὶ ἄνουσοι ἤμεθα. Bérard, *op. cit.*, II, p. 27, has some interesting remarks on the ravages of νόσος, usually small-pox, among the Frankish corsairs.

4. Cf. Breasted, III, § 616 : " The herds of the field are left as cattle sent forth, without herdmen, crossing (at will) the fulness of the stream. There is no uplifting of a shout in the night : ' Stop ! Behold, one comes, one comes, with the speech of strangers '." (Hymn of victory for Merneptah).

filled at dawn with foot-soldiers and chariots
and the gleam of bronze, and Zeus cast panic on
the marauders. The raiders are slain or taken
prisoner ; the leader casts himself on the mercy
of the king[1] and, like other raiders before and
since, was taken into his service,[2] in spite of the
people's wrath. For seven years he served the
king and won wealth among the Egyptians, until
a knavish Phoenician trader tempted him away to
his undoing. Forced service with the king of
Egypt and similar unhappy attempts to escape
were perhaps the lot of many of the defeated
peoples of the sea.

So far as it is possible to arrive at an exact
chronology, the raids of which we hear in the
Egyptian records belong to an earlier period than
the great migrations in Greece, which the Greeks
themselves knew as the return of the Heracleidae
and supposed to have taken place two generations
after the Trojan war.[3] The evidence of the
Homeric poems is in agreement. An important
feature of the wanderings both of Menelaus and
Odysseus is their return ; the peoples of the
Homeric world are still regarded as settled and
as yet there has been no great displacement,
although new races are pressing forward into the
Mediterranean area. Conditions in the Eastern
Mediterranean after the fall of Cnossos were in

1. Cf. Breasted, IV, § 80 : " Utterance of the vanquished of Peleset :
' Give to us the breath for our nostrils, O King, son of Amon.' "

2. *Ib.*, § 403 : " The Sherden and the Weshwesh, of the sea, they were
made as those that exist not, taken captive at one time, brought as captives
to Egypt, like the sand of the shore. I settled them in strongholds, bound
in my name. Numerous were their classes like hundred-thousands. I taxed
them all, in clothing and grain from the storehouses and granaries each year."

3. Traditionally *c.* 1200 B.C. ; e.g., Mar. Par. (*I. G.*, XII, 5, 44) 1208/7.

many respects similar to those prevailing in the
third century after Christ, when the barbarian
migrations were heralded by dangerous outbreaks
of piracy at sea, as soon as the Roman power
showed signs of weakening. The Roman fleet,
by which the police of the seas had been maintained during the first two centuries of the
empire, had fallen into decay, and special
measures against piracy were found to be necessary
in the reign of Severus Alexander (222-235 A.D.).[1]
By the middle of the century, large bands of
marauders from the Black Sea were making their
way into the Aegean, plundering on both shores,
penetrating as far south as the coasts of Lycia and
Pamphylia, and forcing their way inland as far as
Cappadocia[2]. Hitherto, these attacks, however
widely extended, had been of a predatory
character, but, as Mommsen points out, " what
had hitherto been piracy begins to form a portion
of that migratory movement of peoples to which
the advance of the Goths on the lower Danube
belongs,"[3] For some twenty years after the
death of the Emperor Decius (251 A.D.) until the
defeat of the invaders by Claudius, marauding
tribes from the Danubian lands, Goths, Heruli and
Scythians, were pressing forward by land into the
Balkan Peninsula. By sea, marauders from the
northern coasts of the Euxine, obtaining ships

1. See *I. G. Rom.*, IV, 1057, and Domaszewski, *Rhein. Museum*, LVIII,
p. 384, who states that the command conferred on Sallustius Victor, τὸν ἐπὶ
πᾶσαν θάλασσαν ἡγησάμενον εἰρήνης μετ᾽ ἐξουσίας σιδήρου, was necessitated
by the piracy which was again disturbing the Mediterranean.

2. Zosimus, I, 28 ; Ammian. Marc. XXXI, 5, 15 ; Dexippus, *fr.* 21
(*Hist. Gr. Minores*, I, p. 189, Teubner) on the siege of Side.

3. *Provinces*, I, p. 243.

from the Bosporans, were raiding the Roman
possessions in the Black Sea and in Bithynia.
Other bands, acting in conjunction with the
hordes which advanced by land, appeared in the
Aegean, ravaged the coasts of Macedonia and
Greece, and penetrated as far south as Rhodes
and Crete.[1] These movements of the second part
of the century are parallel to the later and more
serious attacks on Egypt during the reign of
Ramses III.

A remarkable feature of the Scythian and Gothic
raids is the effect which they produced upon the
southern coast of Asia Minor. Allusion has
already been made to the attack upon Side in
Pamphylia,[2] and there is evidence that Lycia was
suffering at the hands of the marauders in the
year 253.[3] At the same time, the Isaurians of
Cilicia fell back into their old predatory habits,
and broke into open revolt. A certain
Trebellianus appears to have made an attempt
at this time to set himself up as emperor, building
a palace in the Cilician hills and issuing an
independent coinage. Though he was overthrown by an officer of Gallienus, the people of
Isauria proved altogether intractable and relapsed

---

1. The authorities are Zosimus, I, 29-37; 39-45; Zonaras, XII, 25;
Orosius, VII, 22, §7; 23; Eutropius, IX, 11; *Vita Gall.*, 5-6, 12-13;
Vita Claud., 6-9.

2. Dexippus, *fr.* 23 (see above).

3. *I. G. Rom.*, III, 481, an inscription which vividly portrays the
helplessness of the Roman government to protect its subjects (See Domaszewski
op. cit., p. 227.) Compare *Or. Sib.*, XIII, 139 (quoted by Treuber, *Gesch.*
der Lykier, p. 219.)

  ὦ Λύκιοι Λύκιοι λύκος ἔρχεται αἷμα λιχμῆναι
  Σάννοι ὅταν ἔλθωσι συν Ἄρηι πτολιπόρθῳ
  Και Κάρποι πελάσωσιν ἐπ' Αὐσονίοισι μάχεσθαι.

For the Κάρποι see Zosimus, I, 31.

into barbarism.[1] Henceforward, whenever allusion is made to this district it is only to record some act of aggression on the part of its inhabitants against their neighbours.[2]

The conditions revealed by the Egyptian monuments of the XIXth and XXth dynasties and by the Homeric poems were in many respects the same. Raiders, urged perhaps by pressure from the North, were pouring from the southern coast of Asia Minor. Crete was already possessed by a mixed multitude, Dorians, Pelasgians, Achaeans and the rest,[3] some native, others the advance guard of the coming hosts of invaders, ready enough to join with other freebooters or to take service under a great captain, as he himself takes service with the Egyptian king. How the first Dorians had reached the island is unknown, but just as the Scythians and Goths in the third century found their way there by sea, the Dorians of Homeric Crete may equally have been part of a thrust from the North.[4] As the raids of the third century after Christ were the prelude to the later migrations *en masse*, so the disturbances reflected in the Egyptian records and in the *Odyssey* were symptomatic, if not a part, of the coming movements which were finally to put an end to the Bronze Age civilisation of the Aegean. These movements as a whole lie outside our present

1. *Hist. Aug.*, *Triginta Tyr.*, XXVI (Teubner, II, p. 123) : Quem cum alii archipiratam vocassent, ipse se imperatorem appellavit.

2. *Vita Probi*, 16 (Quae cum peragrasset hoc dixit : " Facilius est ab istis locis latrones arceri quam tolli."); Zosimus, I, 69; IV, 24; Migne, *Patrol. Gr.*, LXXXV, 474 *seqq.*

3. *Od.*, XIX, 172 *seqq.*

4. See Myres, *J. H. S.*, XXVII, p. 177.

subject, and such records of them as we possess are based only on a dimly remembered tradition.[1]

It might indeed be argued that much of the picture of the voyages and raids in the Odyssey is inspired rather by the earliest voyages and settlements of the Greeks in the days which followed the great migrations, and, although I for my part am not prepared to subscribe to this answer to a vexed question, it is undoubted that many of the earliest Greek adventures across the sea followed similar lines to those described in the Homeric poems. " Bronze men " from Ionia and Caria were still in the seventh century raiding the Egyptian coast, and like Odysseus entering the service of the Egyptian king.[2] The Assyrian records of the reign of Sargon (722-705 B.C.) speak of similar raids in the Levant, when the king caught marauders of the Iauna, " like fish," and " gave rest to Cilicia (Kue) and Tyre."[3] Greek marauders also were concerned in a revolt of Cilicia from Sennacherib, which took place in 698 B.C.[4] If we possessed a fuller record of the Milesian exploration of the Euxine, there would be many grim tales to tell of opposition from the natives, of raids and counter-raids on its inhospitable shores.[5] Towards the end of the

1. For a picturesque description, see Murray, *Rise of the Greek Epic*, pp. 72 *seqq.*

2. Hdt., II, 152.

3. Winckler, *Der alte Orient*, VII, 2, p. 24 ; King, *J. H. S.*, XXX, p. 331 *Cun. Inscr. West. Asia*, I, Pl. 36, l. 21).

4. King, *op. cit.*, p. 327 *seqq* ; Hall, *Anct. Hist. of Near East*, pp. 486-7 ; Olmstead, in *Anatolian Studies*, pp. 289-90.

5. The early piracies of the Lycians (*Heracleides Ponticus, fr.* 15) are explained by Treuber, *Gesch. der Lykier*, pp. 89-90, as a reminiscence of the opposition offered to the Rhodian settlements on the coast of Lycia. See also *Ib.* p. 126.

seventh century, adventurous Samians, and after them Phocaeans, were making their way into the Western Mediterranean, where the merchant Colaeus, blown out of his course for Egypt, came to the virgin market of Tartessos.[1] A tenth of the wealth which he acquired on the voyage was dedicated to the Samian Hera. We may wonder what proportion of his gains came from the usual sources that enriched the shrine.[2]

The merchant-shipper still acted with a high hand at sea and ashore. We have seen that the Taphians in the Odyssey were both slavers and merchants. The "grave Tyrian trader," the Phoenician rogue,[3] did not scruple to enslave a foreign supercargo, or to kidnap women and boys from a friendly port.[4] A passage in a foreign ship had special risks of its own. The fate which Odysseus pretends befel him on the Thesprotian vessel, but for a miracle would have been that of Arion on a ship of Corinth.[5] Robbery and murder or enslavement was a risk that must have often been faced in these early days, and with the greater demand for slaves that arose with the growth of industrialism in Greece and at the courts of the tyrants,[6] the temptations to wrong-doing were increased. Apart from wars or trade

1. Hdt., IV, 152.
2. See below, p. 100.
3. τρώκτης (Od., XIV, 416).
4. Od., XV, 440 seqq.; Hdt. I, 1; II, 54.
5. Od., XIV, 339; Hdt., I, 24.
6. See Beloch, Griech. Gesch., I², 269-70. For the work to which Polycrates set his prisoners see Hdt., III, 39. There was an increasing demand for Greek slaves at the Oriental courts (see Hdt., VII, 105, on Panionios the slaver of Chios; I, 48, Periander and the Corcyraean boys; III, 134, on the fashions at the Persian court).

with the barbarians[1], the captures of pirates and brigands were still the main source of supply.

There was still the risk of raids from barbarian communities. Herodotus has a story of an early raid by the Lemnians on the coast of Attica, and their island was still a hot-bed of piracy at the beginning of the fifth century, when the Pelasgian inhabitants were expelled by Miltiades.[2] It is possible that the first development of the Athenian navy, as represented on the Dipylon vases, was due to the raids of " Carians " and other marauders who infested the Attic coast.[3] As late as the time of Peisistratus a careful watch for pirates and a system of coast defence was being maintained.[4] We have seen that brigandage was still rife in certain parts of the mainland in the time of Thucydides.

Nevertheless, in spite of the continued existence of petty piracies round the headlands and bays of the Aegean, the activities of the principal marauders were being diminished by the navies of the mercantile states. Thucydides is emphatic on this point,[5] and apart from material considera-

1. For the sale of Thracian children, see Hdt., V, 6. For the slave-trade with the Phoenicians, Joel, III, 6.

2. Hdt., VI, 137-140.

3. See Helbig, *Les vases de Dipylon et les Naucraries, Mémoires, Ac. Inscr.* (1898), XXXVI, pt. I, pp. 387 *seqq.* He regards the scenes of naval actions on the vases of the first part of the eighth century as representing attacks of raiders on the Attic coast. This may well be the case, but his identification of the defenders with the *naucrariai* is extremely hazardous (p. 403). We know so little again of the 'Αειναῦται of Miletos (Plut., *Qu. Gr.*, 32) and possibly of Chalcis (Roehl, *I. G. Ant.*, no. 375) that it is hardly possible to accept his view that they represent an early form of sea-police.

4. Polyaenus, V, 14 (if the story is worth anything).

5. Thuc., I, 13, τὰς ναῦς κτησάμενοι τὸ λῃστικὸν καθῄρουν. (There is an opposition between νῆες and the earlier undecked boats τῷ παλαίῳ τρόπῳ

tions there are indications that indiscriminate robbery on land and sea was becoming an object of condemnation among the more civilised Greek states. There are signs of this already in the Homeric hymns,[1] and the Delphic oracle taught a higher morality in this respect both between individuals and states. Herodotus' story of the punishment of Glaucus[2] shows a considerable moral advance on the divine patronage of Autolycus. It was Delphi also that ordered reparation to be made by the people of Agylla (Caere) to the murdered Phocaeans,[3] just as the oracle at an earlier date is said to have interested itself in the doings of the Lemnians.[4] It is probable that deeper causes underlay the Sacred War and destruction of Crissa than those alleged by Aeschines,[5] but in the following century there is

λῃστικώτερον παρεσκευασμένα (I, 10).) It has been suggested that in the so-called "list of thalassocracies" (on which see Myres, *J.H.S.*, XXVI, pp. 84 *seqq.*) we have the record of early attempts to police the Aegean, but the early part of the list, at any rate, contains little more than vague tradition regarding the activities of certain peoples by sea, whether for good or evil. There is absolutely no evidence for Winckler's suggestion (*Der Alte Orient*, VII, 2, pp. 21 *seqq.*) that Midas of Phrygia was the patron of a league of sea-faring peoples, and that after his defeat by the Assyrians the official title of thalassocrat passed to the Kings of Assyria to confer or withhold. Murray, *op. cit.*, p. 336, suggests that in the Lydian and Maeonian thalassocracy we have a federation of the coastal peoples of Asia Minor for resisting the piracy of the "Carians." But as he himself points out, the Thracian control of the sea could not have amounted to more than piracy. (On Thracian raids in the Aegean, see Myres, *op. cit.*, p. 126.)

1. *Hom. Hymn, Hermes*, 334; *Apollo*, 278.

2. Hdt. VI, 86. Note especially the allusion to νόμοι οἱ Ἑλλήνων and the phrase ὅρκῳ ληίζεσθαι. Cf. Hesiod, *Erg.*, 322 (quoted by How and Wells *ad* Hdt.):

εἰ γάρ τις καὶ χερσὶ βίῃ μέγαν ὄλβον ἕληται
ἢ ὅγ' ἀπὸ γλώσσης ληίσσεται . . . .

3. Hdt., I, 167. Cf. the curious story of the placation of the ghost of the murdered sailor at Temesa (Paus., VI, 6, 8).

4. See above, p. 96.

5. III, 107. See Beloch, I², pp. 337-8.

a clear case of the interest displayed by Delphi in the extermination of the piratical communities of the Aegean, when the Athenians had the authority of the Amphictyony for expelling the pirates of Scyros.[1] How far religious leagues of this character made it a part of their policy to stamp out piracy and brigandage is uncertain. In the Calaureian league, whose members, according to Strabo, met in the temple of Poseidon in the island of Calaureia, it has been conjectured that we have a federation of maritime states under the presidency of the Sea-god, whose origin is to be traced to the period of the migrations, and whose *raison d'être* was the necessity of maintaining the police of the Saronic gulf.[2]

In spite of all, however, it is obvious that little progress was made before the Persian wars towards an organised police of the whole Aegean area. Apart from the unsubdued barbarians, the Greek world itself provided ample resources from which pirate boats could be manned. Greek love of adventure, as well as continued faction in the states, drove men abroad to serve as mercenaries, like Alcaeus' brother Antimenidas,[3] or, like Archilochus, to become freebooters.[4] A band of Samian exiles in the reign of Polycrates approached the island of Siphnos and, after an unsuccessful attempt to raise a loan, descended on the island

1. Plutarch, *Cimon*, 8.

2. Strabo, VIII, 374. See Curtius, *Hermes*, X, pp. 385-392; Wilamowitz, *Gött. Gel. Nachrichten*, 1896, p. 160; pp. 167-170.

3. Alcaeus, *fr.* 33 (Bergk). Cf. the Greek mercenaries at Abusimbel (Hicks and Hill, 3).

4. Archilochus, *fr.* 59 (See Halliday, *The Growth of the City State*, p. 47).

and were eventually bought off for one hundred talents.[1]

One feature of this Samian history is the attempt made by the exiles to occupy the island of Hydrea, off the Argolid, and their settlement of Cydonia in Crete, which brought them into collision with the Aeginetans, whose commercial interests were threatened.[2] As we shall see more particularly when we come to examine conditions in the western Mediterranean, commercial rivalries constantly prevented peaceful intercourse by sea, and gave rise to a form of buccaneering in the truest sense of the term. Commercial rivalry and jealousies form a large part of our knowledge of the history of the Greeks during the seventh and sixth centuries B.C., and Greek morality at sea, in spite of Delphic disapproval, was never of the highest. On the open sea or off a deserted coast there was little to prevent the boarding of a smaller vessel.[3]

The recorded conduct of one of the chief commercial states of Greece throws much light

1. Hdt., III, 57 seqq.

2. See How and Wells' Notes to Hdt. III, 59, regarding Aeginetan connections with Crete (the Corintho-Samian alliance was, however, a thing of the past, III, 48). Buccaneering Samians at Cydonia would also be a serious danger to Aeginetan communications with Egypt (II, 178). For the antiquity of the feud between the Aeginetans and their trade-rivals the Samians, who also were one of the states chiefly interested in the Egyptian trade, see Hdt., III, 59.

3. Beaufort, *op. cit.*, p. 114, has an illuminating passage regarding the fear felt by the crew of Cockerell's caique on seeing the frigate approach. " Had she been a Turkish man of war, they were certain of being pillaged, under the pretext of exacting a present ; if a Barbary cruizer, the youngest men would have been forcibly seized for recruits ; and even if she had been a Greek merchant-ship, their security would have been still precarious ; for when one of these large Greek polacres meets even her own countrymen in such vessels and in unfrequented places, she often compels them to assist in loading her, or arbitrarily takes their cargoes at her own prices."

on the unscrupulous character of many of the
Greek commercial ventures. Samians were concerned in most of the great enterprises and bore
a part in all the chief commercial struggles. The
position of the island gave to its inhabitants
exceptional facilities for plundering the traffic
coming through the Cyclades, and we have
already seen that these waters were the favourite
haunt of corsairs both in antiquity and in more
recent times.[1] Plutarch has a curious story that
the Samians, driven from their island, spent ten
years at Mycale, during which they lived by
piracy. Their exile and achievements were
commemorated by a festival in honour of Hermes
Charidotes, at which theft and robbery were
authorised.[2] There is little in the story, except
perhaps a reminiscence of Samian activities in the
" boak of Samos," but we have other evidence of
their piratical behaviour. They themselves have
left us an eloquent testimony to their malpractices
in a seated statue of Hera found in the island,
which had been dedicated by a certain Aeaces the
son of Bryson[3], who is probably to be regarded as
the father of Polycrates and Syloson,[4] or at any
rate as a member of the same family. The
dedication may be assigned approximately to the
year 540 B.C.,[5] and is recorded by an inscription

1. See above, p. 19.

2. Plutarch, *Qu. Graec.*, 55.

3. L. Curtius, *Ath. Mitt.*, XXXI, pp. 151 *seqq.*; Dittenberger, *Syll.*3, 10.
The statue is reproduced by Ure, *Origin of Tyranny*, fig. 10, but by a slip it
is described as representing Aeaces himself.

4. Hdt., II, 182; III, 39, 139. Syloson's son was also called Aeaces
(VI, 13).

5. So Curtius, *l.c.*; Pomtow, in Dittenberger, *l.c.*, thinks that the letters
of the inscription were re-engraved by the younger Aeaces at the beginning
of the fifth century.

engraved on the throne on which the Goddess is seated. The statue is said to have been dedicated by Aeaces from the proceeds of σύλη collected by him in the exercise of his office. Comparing the tithes dedicated by Colaeus, the editor of the inscription concludes that the tithes of all ventures were thus dedicated to the patroness of Samos, whether they were acquired by lawful trade or piracy, and that it was the duty of Aeaces to secure and dedicate them.[1] The official piracies practised by the Samians under Polycrates were therefore no new departure, and it is probable that Plutarch is in error, when he says that it was Polycrates who first designed the *samaina*, a vessel specially constructed in Samos to combine capacity with speed.[2]

Such being the character of the Samian shippers, it is not difficult to understand the reasons for the long-standing feud between the island-state and the town of Miletos,[3] whose merchant vessels

1. Ure, *op. cit.*, pp. 81-82, misrepresents Curtius as saying that the profits of the Tartessos voyage were known as σύλη, and thinks that the term had grown to include all gains made by ventures on the sea (cf. also p. 292). As I suggested above, it is likely enough that a part of Colaeus' wealth was acquired by methods which would not bear too close scrutiny, but σύλη can mean only one thing, " Kapergut," as Curtius rightly explains it. The possibility, however, remains that σύλη may mean goods obtained by reprisal (see above, p. 65), and we should be on firmer ground if there were more evidence for Boeckh's statement (*Public Economy*, p. 757) that at Athens a tenth part of goods taken by reprisal belonged to the state. But the evidence which he cites (p. 438) scarcely warrants the assumption. (In Demosthenes' speech against Timocrates, there are obviously special circumstances, and the fact that the capture was made by a warship is probably the ground for the State's claim to the prize.) Curtius has an attractive explanation of the name of Aeaces' son, Syloson, ὃς τὸν σῦλον (τὴν σύλην) ἔσωσε. (There was an earlier Syloson, son of Calliteles, Polyaen., VI, 45.)

2. Plutarch, *Pericles*, 26. On the *samaina*, see Torr, *op. cit.*, p. 65. The two acts of piracy against Sparta recorded by Hdt., III, 47, belong to the years before Polycrates' reign.

3. Hdt., V, 99; III, 39; Thuc., I, 115. The story of the branding

putting out from home must run the risk of
meeting Samian corsairs lurking among the islands
of the Icarian sea. Similar considerations explain
the feud between Erythrae and Chios,[1] and also
the reluctance of the Chians to permit the
Phocaeans, after the capture of their city by
Harpagus, to settle in the Oenussae islands in the
sound between Chios and the mainland.[2]

It would be incorrect, however, to regard the
Samians as indiscriminate pirates. It is probable
that their depredations were limited for the most
part to their commercial rivals. During the
seventh century there are indications in Herodotus
of two great competing groups in the trade of the
Mediterranean, whose rivalries frequently resulted
in open warfare, and, we may be sure, encouraged
the activities in which the Samians excelled. So
far as the grouping of the chief commercial states
of Greece can be made out, we find Miletos,
Chios, Aegina and Eretria combined in exploiting
the trade with the Western Mediterranean through
Sybaris ; the rival group Chalcis, Samos, Corinth
and possibly Phocaea trading directly with
Syracuse and with the Chalcidian colonies in the
West.[3] This grouping was, of course, liable to
change for political reasons, but the existence of
such leagues goes a long way to explain why it was
that Samian piracy was so long tolerated. Piracy

of the Samian captives with the *samaina*, recorded by Plutarch, *l.c.*, after the
Athenian reduction of the revolt in 440 B.C., suggests that there had been
a recrudescence of the Σαμιακὸς τρόπος.

1. Hdt., I, 18.

2. *Ib.*, I, 165. On the Oenussae (Spalmadori) see above p. 19.

3. As will be recognised by many *Reginenses*, the above account is based
on Mr. E. M. Walker's notes.

was now, as on other occasions in the Mediterranean, a method of dealing with the competition
of a foreign state or league.[1] With the support
of powerful allies, Samos had little fear of direct
punishment for her depredations, so long as they
were limited to the shipping of the rival league.
At the beginning of the sixth century a rapproche-
ment had been brought about between the tyrants
of Corinth and of Miletos,[2] with a consequent
change in the grouping of the trading states.
One of the recorded acts of Samian pirates about
this time was aimed at Periander's interests, and
hostility between the two states lasted until the

---

[1]. As late as the eighteenth century, it was held that the depredations
of the Barbary corsairs constituted a useful check on the weaker competitors
in the carrying trade of the Mediterranean. The following passage from
Hakluyt (Maclehose & Sons, 1904), Vol. V, p. 275, illustrates the difficulties
of the English merchants endeavouring to secure the Levant trade during
the sixteenth century, when their rivals were using all means to exclude them.
It is from the instructions issued by the Sultan (at the instance of the British
ambassador) " to our Beglerbeg of Algier " :

" We certifie thee by this our commandement, that the right honorable
Will. Hareborne ambassador to the Queenes majestie of England hath
signified unto us, that the ships of that countrey in their comming and
returning to and from our Empire, on the one part of the Seas have the
Spaniards, Florentines, Sicilians and Malteses, on the other part our
countreis committed to your charge : which abovesaid Christians
will not quietly suffer their egresse and regresse, into, and out of our
dominions, but doe take and make the men captives, and forfeit the
shippes and goods, as the last yeere the Malteses did one, which they
tooke at Gerbi, and to that end do continually lie in wait for them
to their destruction, whereupon they are constrained to stand to their
defence at any such time as they might meet with them. Wherefore
considering by this means they must stand upon their guard, when they
shall see any gallie afarre off, whereby if meeting with any of your
gallies and not knowing them, in their defence they do shoot at them,
and yet after when they doe certainly know them, do not shoote any
more, but require to passe peaceably on their voiage, which you
would deny, saying, the peace is broken because you have shot at us,
and so make prize of them contrary to our privileges, and against
reason ; for the preventing of which inconvenience the said ambassador
hath required this our commandement." (1584).

[2]. Hdt., I, 20 ; V, 92.

time of Polycrates, when an attempt was made by
Corinth and Sparta, another victim, to put an
end to Samian aggression.[1]

In the confusion caused by the advance of the
Persians, the activities of the Samians under
Polycrates are said by Herodotus to have been
practised indiscriminately " without distinction
of friend or foe. For he argued that a friend was
better pleased if you gave him back what you had
taken from him, than if you spared him at the
first."[2] The policy ascribed to Polycrates is
difficult to understand. Samos at the time was at
the height of her power, and its ruler was not
likely to have jeopardised his schemes of empire
in the Aegean[3] by a policy which in the end must
prove fatal to his ambitions. It is difficult to
accept Ure's view that in Herodotus' account we
should see an " elaborate blockade of Persia."[4]
Possibly as the thalassocrat of his day and the
master of the islands, Polycrates was undertaking
the police of the Aegean on the principles followed
by the pasha of Rhodes, who built ships for the
Turkish government and had a frigate for his own
use, which he used for piratical purposes of his
own, while he cleared the seas of all other
malefactors.[5] In spite, however, of Herodotus, the
activities of the Samians under Polycrates pro-

1. *Ib.*, III, 47-48 ; 54-56.

2. Hdt., III, 39 (Tr. Rawlinson).

3. *Ib.*, III, 122 ; Thuc., I, 13.

4. Ure, *op. cit.*, p. 292. In the earlier part of his reign Polycrates, perhaps,
was in alliance with the anti-Persian group ; cf. his alliance with Amasis
(III, 40) and his hostility to the Persian Miletos and Lesbos (III, 39 ; on
Miletos, see I, 141 ; Lesbos, III, 13). But he had already joined the Persian
side by the time of Cambyses' expedition to Egypt (III, 44).

5. Cockerell, *op. cit.*, p. 163.

bably proceeded on the same lines as before his reign, his policy being merely a continuation of the normal Samian method of damaging enemies. We cannot at any rate point to any particular act of piracy committed under his auspices.

The thalassocracy of Polycrates belongs to an age when the whole of the Eastern Mediterranean was disturbed by the Persian advance, and the Samians, no doubt, made full use of the opportunities afforded. Greek history at this time partially reflects the conditions of the great migrations. The population of Teos had migrated from the coast of Asia Minor[1] ; the fortunes of the Phocaeans, who were similarly driven out by Harpagus, will be noticed in a later chapter. According to the counsel which Herodotus puts into the mouth of Bias, a complete migration of the Ionians to the western seas had been contemplated,[2] and the confusion in the Aegean would probably have been greater, unless the west had provided an outlet to the more explosive elements. It was to the west that the Samians and a few Milesians escaped after the battle of Lade, where they seized the town of Zancle on the Straits.[3]

Conditions in the Aegean at the beginning of the fifth century may be judged from various episodes narrated by Herodotus. When his position in Miletos was becoming impossible, Aristagoras was advised by Hecataeus the historian to establish himself in the island of Leros as a base

1. Hdt., I, 168.
2. Ib., I, 170.
3. Hdt., VI, 22-23 ; Thuc., VI, 4.

from which he might hope to regain his native town.[1] Fortunately for the peace of the Icarian sea, Aristagoras preferred to retire to Myrcinos on the coast of Thrace, a district already granted to his kinsman Histiaeus by Darius,[2] where his attacks on the natives soon brought retribution.[3] The adventures of Histiaeus himself throw a still clearer light on the conditions of the time. On the failure of his plans to establish himself as the leader of the movement in Ionia, he took station on the Hellespont at the head of eight Lesbian warships, and proceeded to attack all the vessels coming from the Black Sea which refused to obey his orders.[4] His tactics were aimed in the first instance against Miletos and consisted in an attempt to coerce the Milesians by this piratical threat to their interests in the Black Sea. After the battle of Lade, when all hopes of recovering Miletos were at an end, Histiaeus set himself to create a principality in the North-eastern Aegean and pursued the only methods available in those troubled times. We hear of a successful descent on Chios, and of an attempt on the island of Thasos, before he was finally captured by the Persians in the Atarneus district, while foraging for supplies with which to support the motley company that he had gathered.[5]

That independent bodies of pirates were active at this time might be inferred even without clear

1. Hdt., V, 125.
2. *Ib.*, V, 11.
3. *Ib.*, 126.
4. *Ib.*, VI, 5.
5. Hdt., VI, 26-30.

statement in our authorities. But there is
evidence of their existence in the mistake made
by the Ephesians, when a body of Chian refugees
after the battle of Lade came to their territory.[1]
The prevalence of piracy during all these years is
best attested by an inscription of Teos which
dates from the early years of its re-settlement after
the Greek victories of Salamis and Mycale, before
the Athenian navy had begun its work of clearing
the seas. Solemn imprecations are pronounced
against magistrates practising brigandage and
piracy, or intentionally harbouring robbers by
land or sea.[2]

1. *Ib.*, VI, 16; see above, p. 36.

2. Hicks and Hill, 23, lines 18-23; Dittenberger, *Syll.*³, 37, 38. (In the
text as restored by Hiller von Gaertringen it is interesting to find mention
of a περιπ[όλιον] in the clause which immediately precedes that dealing
with piracy. See above, p. 48.)

CHAPTER IV

THE EASTERN MEDITERRANEAN FROM 480 TO 200 B.C.

ἔτι δὲ πολέμου γενομένου καὶ τριηρῶν ἄει κατὰ
θάλατταν οὐσῶν καὶ λῃστῶν. (Andocides.)

IT was not until the naval supremacy of Athens
had been firmly established that any attempt could
be made to alleviate the conditions produced by
the confusion of the Persian wars.   A late writer
credits Themistocles with anticipating the later
Athenian policy, and with making an attempt to
destroy piracy in Greek waters.[1]   But it was only
after the establishment of the Delian confederacy
that the Athenians could seriously undertake the
task of restoring order in the Aegean.   Expeditions
are recorded against two of the principal centres
of piracy, Scyros[2] and the Thracian Chersonese,[3]
both of them districts where it was essential to
maintain an effective police.   In a period for
which our authorities are notoriously defective,
there is little direct evidence as to the measures
adopted by Athens.   Athenian settlers were
planted in both the districts mentioned, and it is
probable that one of the duties of *cleruchists*
throughout the empire was to provide protection

1. Nepos, *Themistocles*, II, 3.   See, however, Nipperdey's note *ad loc.*
as to the reliability of the statement.
2. Plutarch, *Cimon*, 8. The Dolopes of Scyros, λῃζόμενοι τὴν θάλασσαν
ἐκ παλαίου (cf. Thuc:, I, 98).
3. Plutarch, *Pericles*, 19, λῃστηρίων γέμουσα.

against piracy and brigandage. Athens also sought the co-operation of the rest of the Greek world. We hear that Pericles invited delegates from the Greek states to discuss, amongst other matters, the safety of the seas, but the proposal proved ineffective owing to opposition from Sparta.[1] The success of Athenian action is nevertheless indisputable. We have only to contrast the conditions prevailing in the Aegean both before the establishment of the Athenian hegemony and after the fall of Athens with the absolute silence in our authorities as to the practice of piracy on any considerable scale during the years preceding the Peloponnesian war, to realise the services which Athens conferred on the Greek world. There is, moreover, certain indirect evidence to be taken into account. When the Spartan commander Alcidas made his expedition to Asia Minor in 427 B.C., he found the cities of Ionia unfortified.[2] It is possible that the Athenians may have regarded such a condition as necessary to the maintenance of their empire among the Asiatic towns, but the rule, nevertheless, implies that they were able to guarantee protection not only against the Persian satraps, but also against marauders from the sea. Further evidence as to the efficacy of the Athenian police in the Aegean is afforded by the statement of Thucydides that the only parts of Greece where it was still customary to carry arms, were the districts to the north of the Corinthian gulf.[3]

1. Plutarch, *op. cit.*, 17.
2. Thuc., III, 33.
3. *Ib.*, I, 5.

It was precisely in this neighbourhood that the Athenian authority was weakest. Even if the Athenians at times abused their power, as the writer of the oligarchic tract that has come down with the works of Xenophon alleges,[1] the protection which the Athenian empire guaranteed to Greek traders and to the weaker inhabitants of the Aegean coasts was one which had never been enjoyed since the mythical days of King Minos. Yet this very real benefit is passed over almost in silence by our authorities.

Among the evils which the Peloponnesian war brought to Greece, not the smallest was the fresh impulse given to piracy by the long duration of the war and by the consequent destruction of the Athenian navy. Even before the fall of Athens it is obvious that the police of the seas had been considerably relaxed. Much of the war, as described by Thucydides, consisted of formal raids conducted by both sides on land and sea, with the additional employment of privateering on a small scale as opportunity offered. The operations of the privateers differ little in their execution from the tactics of the genuine pirate. On the Athenian side we find the Messenians of Naupactos cruising in small craft round the Peloponnese, and occupying as a base the deserted headland of Coryphasium, which the arrival of the Athenian fleet made famous as Pylos.[2] But the Athenians, having the greatest interests at sea, were naturally the chief sufferers. At an

1. (Xen.) *Respubl. Athen.*, II, 11-12.
2. Thuc., IV, 9. It is likely that Demosthenes had heard of the advantages of Pylos during the preceding year from his Messenian friends in Naupactos.

early stage of the war they were compelled to
send a squadron to check the privateering
which threatened the Athenian merchantmen
coming from Phaselis and Phoenicia.[1] At a later
date we find an enemy squadron, on the advice
of the Milesians, taking station off the Triopian
promontory to catch the merchantmen coming
from Egypt.[2] The last case belongs to a later
period of the war, when Peloponnesian warships
could operate openly in the Aegean. The earlier
work off Lycia and Caria was no doubt carried on
in small boats manned by cut-throats from the
hills, who surprised merchantmen lying-to for
the night.[3] Much of the Peloponnesian privateering in the early stages of the war was of this
character. The Megarian traitors contrived to
get the town-gates opened at night by posing as
privateers ; a sculling boat was placed on a wagon,
taken by night to the sea and brought back before
daylight. By these means the suspicions of the
Athenian post at Minoa would not be aroused by
the appearance of any vessel in the harbour during
daylight.[4] In the execution of such operations
little distinction was made between enemy and
neutral. At the beginning of the war all traders
using the sea were treated as enemies by the

1. *Ib.*, II, 69.

2. *Ib.*, VIII, 35.

3. Davis, *Anatolica*, p. 252, describes an illuminating incident on this
coast : " Just about the time we should have reached the neighbourhood
of Makri (May 18th) a band of about a hundred men had come down from
the mountains and completely blockaded Makri and Leveesi. They had
boarded some Greek ships in the port of Leveesi, and carried off their captains
into the mountains in order to extract ransom from them."

4. Thuc., IV, 67.

Peloponnesians and executed if caught,[1] and Alcidas began his raid into Ionia by slaughtering all prisoners indiscriminately.[2]

In order to cope with these inshore tactics, we find the Athenians compelled to occupy posts on the enemy coast. Usually small islands were occupied, such as Atalante,[3] an uninhabited island fortified in 431 B.C. to intercept enemy craft which put out from Opus and the rest of Locris to ravage Euboea ; Minoa,[4] off the Megarid, was similarly occupied in 427 B.C., in order to prevent the recurrence of such raids as that organised by Brasidas in 429 B.C.,[5] and to intercept the smaller privateering craft from Megara ; the post established earlier at Budorum, in Salamis, had proved insufficient for the purpose. It has been suggested that the increasing attention paid by the Athenians to the island of Melos, which culminated in the slaughter of its inhabitants in 416 B.C., was due to the use of the Dorian island by the enemy as a base for privateering.[6] Conversely the Athenians made use of the occupied stations for their own descents on the enemy coasts.[7]

Technically, the conduct of both sides could be regarded as operations of war. But a prolonged

1. *Ib.*, II, 67.
2. *Ib.*, III, 31.
3. *Ib.*, II, 32.
4. *Ib.*, III, 51.
5. *Ib.*, II, 93.
6. See Weil, *Zeitschr. für Numismatik*, XXXVIII, p. 360. The first expedition against Melos was in 426 B.C. (Thuc. III, 91). But though Melos had a bad reputation in the next century (see below, p. 115), there is no charge of this kind brought by our authorities in the fifth century.
7. e.g., Methana (IV, 45) and Cythera (IV, 53).

war of this character could produce only one result. The Athenian sea-police was fully taxed even during the first period of the Peloponnesian war.[1] If the principal combatants were careless of the rights of neutrals, it is not to be supposed that minor peoples showed any greater scruples. The seditions in the Greek cities, which were a consequence of the war, once more set bands of lawless men on the move, who sought to damage their opponents by plundering their property,[2] enlisting on occasion the assistance of the barbarian.[3] After the disaster in Sicily, when the naval forces of the Athenians barely sufficed to guard places of strategical importance and to protect the trade routes, regular piracy again began to raise its head. It is scarcely a matter for surprise to find pirates serving on the side of the Lacedaemonians. The news of Aegospotami was brought to Sparta by Theopompus, a Milesian pirate, sent by Lysander.[4]

Athens was a trading state, which Sparta was not, and during the years that followed the battle of Aegospotami there was little inducement to the Spartan government to maintain the safety of the seas for the sake of commerce, which was still concentrated for the most part in the Peiraeus. Whether Sparta continued to make active use of the pirates is uncertain. The exiled Chians of

1. Cf. Aristophanes, *Birds*, 1427.

2. e.g., the Corcyraean exiles (Thuc., III, 85 ; IV, 2).

3. As was done by the exiles from Epidamnos (I, 24). Assistance would be given readily enough in this district. For the piracy business set up by Chian exiles in Atarneus after the war, see Xen., *Hell.*, III, 2, 11.

4. Xen., *Hell.*, II, 2, 30.

Atarneus were suppressed by Dercyllidas[1] ; on the
other hand, Agesilaus is said to have exposed for
sale the Persian captives taken by pirates.[2]   But
our authorities are quite definite as to Spartan
negligence.   Isocrates, writing in the year 380 B.C.
says that the seas were infested by free-booters.[3]
A few years earlier he writes that it had been
unsafe to send valuables to the Hellespont, while
the Spartans commanded the sea.[4]   Sparta, it is
true, was carrying on a vigorous privateering war
against Athens during these years, and in 389 B.C.
occupied Aegina as a base for the purpose,[5] but
the general insecurity in home waters is shown by
the fate of Lycon of Heraclea.   Immediately
after leaving Athens he was caught by pirate
vessels in the Argolic gulf, robbed and murdered.[6]

This event took place soon after the year
378-377 B.C., when there are already signs of an
improvement in the Aegean.   There is com-
parative silence as to the existence of piracy on
a large scale during the early years of the second
Athenian confederacy.[7]   The mere fact that we
do not hear of pirates proves little in itself, but the

1. Xen., *Hell.*, III, 2, 11.

2. Xenophon, *Hell.*, III, 14, 9. It is doubtful, however, whether the
λῃσταί of whom Xenophon speaks are to be regarded as more than
Lacedaemonian raiding parties operating in Asia Minor.

3. Isocr., *Panegyricus*, 115.

4. Isocr., *Trapez.*, 35-36.

5. Xen., *Hell.*, V, 1, 2.

6. Demosthenes, LII, 5. The event took place some years before the
death of the banker Pasion in 370 B.C.   The capture of Nicostratus (Demosth.
LIII, 6) which took place in 369-8 (see Blass, *Attische Beredtsamkeit*[3], III, 1
p. 519, for the date of Apollodorus' first trierarchy), was made by a τριήρης,
a warship.

7. The early exploits of Charidemus (see below, p. 120) belong, however,
to the years preceding 368 B.C.

Athenians in the fourth century still appear to
have made claims to be the guardians of the sea.
It is difficult otherwise to explain the attitude
which was adopted towards Philip's proposal for
common action in this matter, it being distinctly
asserted by the author of the speech *On the
Halonnesos* that any such claim on the part of
Philip was an infringement of an Athenian
prerogative, and its acceptance by Athens tanta-
mount to a confession that she was no longer able
to do the work herself; while an opportunity
would be given to Philip to seduce the remnant of
Athenian allies from their allegiance.[1]   Certainly
at this time the Athenians were still endeavouring
to cope with the evil.   Another speech, which has
also come down with those of Demosthenes, informs
us that an agreement was made with the allies for
the protection of traders against pirates, and that
the Melians were fined ten talents for harbouring
pirates.[2]   The agreement in question, for which
we are told that Moerocles[3] was responsible, is
almost certainly to be regarded as later than the
secession of the principal islands from the confederacy, the weakening of Athenian sea-power
caused by their withdrawal necessitating new
provisions of this kind.   Even as late as the
year 335-334 we find an Athenian squadron being
sent out for police duty against pirates,[4] and
in 315-314 we have the record of the achievement

1. (Demosthenes) VII, 14-15.

2. (Demosth.), LVIII, 53, 56.

3. He was a contemporary of Demosthenes and Hypereides. See
Timocles, *fr.* 4 (Kock) *ap.* Athenaeus, VIII, 341e.

4. *I. G.*, II, 804.

of Thymochares, who had reduced the corsair Glaucetas of Cythnos and rendered the sea safe for navigators.[1] This was the last achievement of Athens as guardian of the seas. Her fleet had already perished in the battle of Amorgos (322 B.C.) some years previously, and the commerce of the Eastern Mediterranean was no longer centred in the Peiraeus.

But, in fact, after the Social War of 357-355 B.C. it was only too clear that Athens was unequal to the task. Already in the years 362 and 361 B.C. she had herself suffered severely from the privateers of Alexander of Pherae, who ravaged the Cyclades, occupied Peparethos in the Sporades and succeeded even in penetrating into the Peiraeus, where his crews gladly looted the tables of the money-changers.[2] A fresh impulse was given by these achievements to piracy, which came rapidly to a head in the years following the Social War. The smaller islands once more became nests of pirates. Halonnesos, which had been an Athenian possession, was occupied by a pirate named Sostratus, and when the island was cleared by Philip, there arose the famous controversy " over syllables," as to whether the Athenians were to receive it from Philip or receive it back.[3] Myonnesos too, at the entrance to the Malian gulf, gained a reputation which was proverbial.[4] In the Thracian Chersonese the promontory of

---

1. *I.G.*, II, 331. On Glaucetas, see below, p. 124.

2. Xen., *Hell.*, VI, 4, 35; Diod. Sic., XV, 95; Demosth., L, 4; Polyaenus, VI, 2, 2.

3. (Demosth.), VII, 2; *Epist. Philippi* (XII), 12-14.

4. Aesch., II, 72 (v. above, p. 23).

Alopeconnesos was full of pirates and free-booters.[1] When Athens made an attempt to eject them, they received timely assistance from the *condottiere* Charidemus. We may suspect that the λῃσταί of whom Philip complains in Thasos were no mere privateersmen.[2] Full use was made by the pirates of the confusion created by the Social War and by the prolonged war between Athens and Macedonia. The official custodian of the seas had issued general letters of marque during the Social War, with a view to destroying enemy commerce, and it is clear that in practice little distinction was made between enemy and neutral.[3] The conduct of the Athenian *trierarchs* at the same time tended to promote the evil ; Athenian warships were placed at the disposal of the highest bidder for the carrying out of private seizures and reprisals.[4] In the Macedonian war both sides resorted to energetic forms of privateering. Philip's ships raided the islands and operated off the coasts of Attica, on one occasion carrying off the state-vessel from the bay of Marathon.[5] No less energy was displayed by the Athenians,[6] whose offences were aggravated, from the Macedonian point of view, by the fact that privateering continued, while

1. Demosth., XXIII, 166.

2. See below, p. 118.

3. Demosth., XXI, 173, with *Schol. ad loc. (Or. Att.* (Didot), II, p. 689.

4. Demosth., LI, 13. The arbitrary behaviour of Athenian officers is well illustrated by the incident out of which the case against Timocrates arose (see above, p. 62).

5. Aeschines, II, 12 ; Demosth., IV, 34 (Raids on Lemnos and Imbros, capture of the corn-fleet off Geraestos, the Marathon episode).

6. See Demosth., XVIII, 145, on the damage inflicted by the Athenians.

the two states were officially at peace.   A long list
of piracies committed by the Athenians after
the peace of Philocrates could be recited.
A Macedonian herald had been kidnapped ;
pirates were allowed to use the island of Thasos,
in spite of an express stipulation in the treaty that
this was not to be permitted ; Diopeithes, the
Athenian commander in the Chersonese, had
enslaved the inhabitants of districts subject to
Philip, and had crowned his offence by arresting
and holding to ransom the Macedonian ambassador
sent to procure the captives' release.   Another
Athenian general had attacked the Macedonian
possessions on the Pagasean gulf, and had condemned all merchants sailing to Macedonia as
enemies, and sold them into slavery.[1]   To these
actions Philip replied by seizing the Athenian
corn-ships waiting at the entrance to the
Bosporus.[2]   Such was the state of affairs in the
Aegean during the years which preceded the
battle of Chaeronea.   Piratical communities
flourished unchecked, the two powers which could
have suppressed the evil refusing through jealousy
to co-operate.   Athens encouraged it so far as it
crippled her adversary, while she herself was
compelled to convoy the grain-ships on which her
existence depended.[3]   Her own citizens were

1. *Epist. Philippi*, 2-5.   On the historical value of this document,
see Pickard-Cambridge, *Demosthenes*, p. 356, note 6.

2. Didymi, *de Demosth. Commenta*, col. X, XI (Teubner, edd. Diels and
Schubart).   It is fairly certain that this is the incident to which Demosthenes
refers in *De Cor.*, 72, rather than the episode recorded by the psephism
of §§ 73-74 and the letter of §§ 77-78.

3. Demosthenes, XVIII, 73, 77.   The σίτου παραπομπή would, however,
be normal in wartime (cf. Xen., *Hell.*, I, 1, 35).   With regard to escorting
in general Professor Halliday reminds me of Democedes' vessel escorted by

guilty of the crime when it suited their interests ;
her alien generals practised it as a matter of course.
Piracy in fact during the course of the fourth
century had begun to assume a new form,
foreshadowing the conditions which the further
development of the mercenary system promoted
after Alexander. Already, in the year 380 B.C.,
Isocrates could set the conduct of the mercenaries[1]
on land beside the activities of pirates at sea.
Greece became more and more troubled with
broken men, whose sole chance of a livelihood lay
in service as mercenaries or in robbery.[2] The
financial difficulties, with which Athens was beset,
compelled her generals to resort to a variety of
shady expedients to provide the wherewithal to
pay their troops. We hear of " benevolences "
exacted by generals, the amount of which varied
in proportion to the size of the armaments under
their command, while in return the merchants of
foreign states were exempted from seizure or had
their ships escorted by the Athenian forces.
From what other sources, says Demosthenes,
could Diopeithes raise funds to pay his men[3] ?

two Phoenician triremes (Hdt., III, 136). A *strategema*, in Polyaenus, V, 13, 1,
throws some light on the tactics of escorting (παραπέμπειν): Three
merchantmen, accompanied by a trireme, were becalmed, when an
enemy trireme appeared. The captain of the escorting ship ordered the
merchantmen to close up, while he lay alongside. If the enemy ship attacked
him first, it would come under fire from the merchantmen. If it attacked
the merchantmen from the other flank, he himself would sail round the convoy
and take the enemy ship on the beam, or cut her off between his own vessel
and the convoy. Cicero, *Ad Att.*, XVI, 1, preserves the phrase ἐν ὁμοπλοίᾳ
which has every appearance of being the technical term for sailing in convoy.

1. πελτασταί (Isocr., *Paneg.*, 115).

2. Aeschines, I, 191 ; Isocrates, *Philippus*, 96. On the growth of the
mercenary system in the fourth century, see Meyer, *G. D. A.*, V, § 854 ;
Kaerst, *Gesch. des Hellenismus*, I², p. 115.

3. Demosth., VIII, 25-26.

Some of the more important *condottieri* of the age present a more than superficial resemblance to the *archipiratae* of the next century. They were always ready to sell their services to the highest bidder, and when out of regular employment, were not above practising a little piracy on their own account. Charidemus began his adventurous career, according to Demosthenes, as the captain of a pirate boat, and preyed upon the Athenian allies. Forsaking this calling, he raised a company of mercenaries, and took service under the Athenian Iphicrates. But, as we have seen, he was not averse to helping his old friends in Alopeconnesos when they were threatened by the Athenians.[1] The conduct of the Athenian Chares, according to his political opponents, was scarcely more reputable.[2] The powerlessness of Athens to protect even her own citizens towards the end of the struggle with Philip is aptly illustrated by a resolution of the *Boule* proposing a vote of thanks to Cleomis of Lesbos for ransoming Athenians captured by the pirates.[3]

The confusion of the times was increased by the naval war of Alexander on the coasts of Asia Minor, where conditions approximating to those of the earlier Persian wars were produced by his advance across the Aegean. The petty tyrants who were maintained in the Greek cities by the Persian government seized the opportunity to plunder and maltreat their subjects and joined

1. Demosth., XXIII, 148-149, 162, 166.

2. Aeschines, II, 71-73; Theopompus, *fr.* 205; Diod. Sic., XV, 95; XVI, 22, 34.

3. Dittenberger, *Syll.*[3], 263 (= Hicks and Hill, 143), *c.* 340 B.C.

with the pirates to prey upon the Greeks. One of them, Aristonicus of Methymna, was neatly caught in a trap laid for him at Chios. Unaware that the island had changed hands, he arrived with five pirate galleys[1] and was granted admission to the harbour, to find all egress barred and his forces in the power of Alexander's admirals. The judgement passed on the tyrants of Eresos gives us a vivid picture of their enormities.[2] After the battle of the Granicus the tyrants who had previously ruled in the town were expelled, but when Memnon in the following year regained possession of all Lesbos except Mytilene,[3] it seems that two new tyrants, Agonippus and Eurysilaus, were installed by the Persians, whose crimes included the levying of war on Alexander and plundering the Greeks. Having disarmed the citizens of Eresos and shut them out of the town, they imprisoned their wives and daughters in the citadel, in order to extort large sums of money. With the help of pirates they plundered and set fire to the town[4] and temples, a number of the citizens perishing in the flames.

Together with the expulsion of the tyrants a serious effort was made by Alexander to reduce

1. Arrian, *Anab.*, III, 2, σὺν ἡμιολίαις λῃστρικαῖς πέντε. Qu. Curtius, IV, 5, 19, says ten (lembi piratici).

2. *I. G.*, XII, 2, 526 (= Hicks and Hill, 157 ; Dittenberger, *O. G. I.*, 8).

3. Arrian, *Anab.*, II, 1, 1. I have followed Dittenberger's reconstruction of this episode against Droysen (II, 2, 363), whom Hicks and Hill follow.
I see no reason to regard the λαισταί mentioned in the inscription merely as mercenaries. The case of Aristonicus with his five *hemioliai* makes it clear that the Persians and the tyrants whom they supported were utilising all available means to oppose Alexander.

4. Or " citadel " according to Dittenberger, where the women were imprisoned.

piracy, his admiral Amphoterus in 331 B.C. receiving express commands to clear the seas.[1] We may suppose also that the famous rescript of 324 B.C. to the Greek cities, ordering the restoration of the exiles,[2] was occasioned not least by the necessity of ridding the Greek world of the homeless outlaws who formed a large element in the pirate bands. Although our records of Alexander's achievements have little else to tell us concerning this matter, there is enough to show that before his death he had set himself to rectify an evil which had long scourged the Eastern Mediterranean, and had correctly diagnosed one of its chief causes.

But, like other tasks to which Alexander had set his hand, the work of clearing the seas was discontinued at his death, and the Aegean became once more the scene of indescribable confusion. In an age when armies were largely composed of mercenaries, it was all the same to outlaws and adventurers whether they adopted the life of a pirate or a mercenary. Either career could be followed according to the opportunities of the moment. When a call for troops went round, pirates would not infrequently offer their services as mercenaries; in the year 302 B.C., we hear of pirates from all quarters joining the army of Demetrius against Cassander, to the number of 8,000.[3] The naval supremacy of Antigonus I and Demetrius rested in no small degree on the support which the pirates rendered. They formed

1. Qu. Curtius, IV, 8, 15.
2. Diod. Sic., XVIII, 8 (cf. *O. G. I.*, 2 = H. H. 164).
3. Diod. Sic., XX, 110.

a part of the crews in the fleet with which
Demetrius attacked Rhodes in 305-304 B.C., and
pirate vessels were used to ravage the coasts of the
island. We hear also of an arch-pirate in his
service, by name Timocles, who was captured off
the Peraea by the Rhodians. The crews of his
three undecked vessels were considered the best in
the service of Demetrius.[1] Men of this type were
particularly useful in plundering expeditions and
in operations where heavy loss of life was anticipated. Ameinias, an arch-pirate, as he is called,
was used by Antigonus Gonatas in a desperate ruse
to capture Cassandreia.[2] Not that they could
always be considered trustworthy. Demetrius'
garrison in Ephesos contained a large number of
pirates, whose chief, Andron, was corrupted by
Lycus, the general of Lysimachus. The arch-
pirate was bringing vessels loaded with plunder
into the harbour of Ephesos and was induced to
take Macedonian troops on board. They were
brought into the town with their hands tied as
captives, but were furnished with arms and
delivered the town to Lycus. It is perhaps
needless to add that after gaining possession of
the town, Lycus put no further confidence in
the pirates and dismissed them.[3]

That the pirates of this period were for the
most part bands of lawless mercenaries is clear
from the contradictory descriptions of them which
we find in our authorities. Ameinias, the arch-
pirate in the service of Antigonus Gonatas, is

1. Diod. Sic., XX, 82, 83, 97.
2. Polyaenus, IV, 6, 18.
3. *Ib.*, V, 19.

elsewhere called one of his generals,[1] and that the troops concerned in the capture of Cassandreia were mercenaries as much as pirates may be inferred from the fact that among them were certain Aetolians, who are much more likely to have been mercenaries than ordinary pirates, as Polyaenus calls them.[2] Ameinias may then be regarded as a mercenary-leader who, as opportunity offered, was not averse to plundering on his own account and hence acquired the title of arch-pirate. This was probably the case with Glaucetas, who, as we saw, was expelled from Cythnos by Thymochares.[3]

It is not difficult to realise the dangers to which the more peaceful inhabitants of the coasts of the Aegean were exposed by the presence of these large bodies of mercenary troops. The general insecurity is illustrated by an attack on the island and temple of Samothrace, which was made by lawless men who had joined with members of the troop of a certain Pythagoras, perhaps a mercenary leader stationed in the neighbourhood.[4] The excesses of which the overgrown mercenary bands were guilty, may be illustrated by examples from the western Greek world. Already in the year 339-338, Timoleon had been compelled to expel a band of disloyal mercenaries from Syracuse. They crossed to the Italian mainland and succeeded in seizing and plundering a town in

1. Plutarch, *Pyrrhus*, 29.

2. Polyaenus, *l.c.*

3. See above, p. 116. It is probable that Glaucetas was acting in the interests of Antigonus I (see Droysen, II, 2, 18; Tarn, *Antigonos Gonatas*, p. 86, compares the relations between Demetrius and Timocles).

4. *I. C.*, XII, 8, 150. See the notes in Dittenberger, *Syll.*³, 372.

Bruttium before they were finally exterminated by the natives.[1] A Campanian force serving under Agathocles treacherously seized and occupied the city of Messene, where they expelled or massacred the inhabitants, and established themselves under the name of the Mamertini. The protection which was accorded them by the Romans provides a sharp contrast to the fate of another body of Campanians who, while in the Roman service, had endeavoured to treat the city of Rhegium in the same way.[2] A striking parallel to exploits of this character is afforded by the history of the famous Catalan Company at the beginning of the fourteenth century after Christ. A force of some 2,500 knights and 5,000 men-at-arms was transported from Sicily, where their masters were anxious to be rid of them, to serve under the Byzantine emperor. On their way to the East they plundered the island of Corfu, but when they arrived at Constantinople, rendered valuable services in the Turkish wars. Quarrels, however, broke out with the Byzantine court, which ended in the murder of their leader. The Company then established itself in the Gallipoli peninsula, from which, joined by a body of 1,800 Turkish horse, they conducted raids and forays on all sides. Finally, after an adventurous march through Macedonia and Thessaly, they arrived in Greece, where they were taken into the service of the Duke of Athens. But as usual, when they had served their purpose, their employer endeavoured to rid himself of his dangerous

1. Diod. Sic., XVI, 82.
2. Polyb., I, 7.

allies. His defeat at their hands and death on the Cephissos left the Company in possession of the duchy.[1]

After the Gallic invasions we hear less of the mercenary-pirates and *archipiratae*, who are a feature of the generation after Alexander. The only case on record is that of Nicander, the *archipirata* in the service of Antiochus the Great, who took part in the trick played by the Seleucid admiral Polyxenidas on the Rhodians.[2] It is true that Aratus is said to have hired men from the ἀρχίκλωπες for his attack on Sicyon in 251 B.C.[3]; but these were probably only brigands, whose bands at this time infested the Peloponnese, as is clear from the numbers who joined Dorimachus the Aetolian in 222 B.C., and took part in his plundering expeditions from Phigaleia.[4] The reason for the disappearance of the pirates from the forces of the kings is perhaps to be sought in a change which had taken place in the mercenary system. After the Gallic invasions the kings were beginning to draw their mercenary forces more from the barbarians. It is significant that a later Ptolemaic garrison of Ephesos, in contrast to the pirate garrison placed there by Demetrius, consisted (temp. Antiochus II) of men from Thrace.[5] Bodies of this kind were ready enough to plunder if allowed to get out

1. See *The Chronicle of Ramon Muntaner* (English translation, Hakluyt Society, Series II, nos. 47 and 50), and Miller, *op. cit.*, ch. VII.

2. Livy, XXXVII, 11; Appian, *Syr.*, 24 (190 B.C.).

3. Plutarch, *Aratus*, 6.

4. Polyb., IV, 3.

5. Athenaeus, XIII, 593a.

of hand—we hear of a force of 800 Gauls in the
service of the Epirotes making common cause
with the Illyrians and destroying the city of
Phoenice.[1] But for the most part we hear no
more of pirate bands flocking to the standards of
the kings when they went to war. From the time
of Demetrius II the Macedonian kings, when in
need of auxiliaries at sea, called in the help of the
Illyrians, and henceforward every Macedonian
king in turn sought to win the alliance of the
leading Illyrian chieftain of the day.

To return to the days of the so-called thalassocracy of Demetrius I; in addition to the
excesses of native marauders, whether genuine
pirates or mercenaries, we find the Aegean being
harassed at this time by foreign visitants in
search of plunder. These are the so-called
Tyrrhenians, of whose activities in the Eastern
Mediterranean there is considerable evidence
during the later part of the fourth and in the
early third centuries B.C. There is a curious
statement in Strabo that the chief marauders in
the Mediterranean were in turn Tyrrhenians,
Cretans and Cilicians.[2] It is possible that he may
be referring to the early piracies of the
Tyrrhenians, to the days when, as we shall see,
Tyrrhenian was almost synonymous with pirate,[3]
and it is not easy to assign any specific date to
Cretan activities in this direction. Nevertheless,
it is probable that Strabo's remark was

1. Polyb., II, 5, where there is an interesting account of their previous
exploits. Serious trouble was experienced from the Gallic mercenaries of
Attalus, who were eventually destroyed by Prusias (Polyb., V, 111).

2. Strabo, X, 477.

3. See below, p. 154.

intended to apply to the three centuries before the establishment of the Roman empire. There undoubtedly was a period of Italian aggression into the Aegean about the year 300 B.C., and when it came to an end, before the rise of the great Cilician corsairs the principal disturbers of the peace were freebooters from Crete. Thanks to the vigilance of the Rhodians, the Illyrians, who scourged the western coasts of Greece in the second and third centuries B.C., seldom succeeded in penetrating into the Aegean.

Tyrrhenian activities in the Aegean begin during the last quarter of the fourth century. The Adriatic had always been full of dangers to navigators, but during the early years of the century the empire of Dionysius served to check the ravages of pirates in both the Adriatic and Tuscan seas. When his firm hand was removed, first the Italian and later the Illyrian pirates began once more to disturb the peace. Conditions, moreover, were not improved by the covenant made between Agathocles and the Iapygians and Peucetii, by which the ruler of Syracuse provided vessels for piracy and took a share of the proceeds.[1] In the year 325-324 we hear of an Athenian colony being sent to Adria (the site is unknown), to guard Athenian corn-ships and provide security against the Tyrrhenians, who are mentioned by name. A squadron was to be permanently stationed there in order to give protection to traders.[2] Other indications of Tyrrhenian activity at this time are to be found in the title of one of

1. Diod. Sic., XXI, 4.
2. Dittenberger, *Syll*.³, 305.

the speeches of the orator Deinarchus, Τυρρηνικός.[1] There was also a speech of Hypereides Περὶ τῆς φυλακῆς τῶν Τυρρηνῶν,[2] in which occurred the phrase κομιστικὰ πλοῖα,[3] which is explained as the boats used by the Tyrrhenian pirates to carry off their spoils. It is probable that the speech of Hypereides, at any rate, had reference to the more distant cruises in Greek waters which the Tyrrhenians were now making. The story that the men of Antium came into collision with Alexander may be apocryphal, but there is no valid reason for rejecting the statement of Strabo, that when some of them were caught by Demetrius, he sent them back to the Romans with a message that it was unseemly that the masters of Italy should send out pirates, and that having established a shrine in honour of the Dioscuri, they should send out plundering expeditions against the fatherland of those Gods.[4] The frequency of the visits is attested by the fact that in the year 298 B.C. it was necessary for the Delians to borrow a sum of money to put their island into a state of defence against Tyrrhenian marauders.[5] It is obvious that the " Tyrrhenians " of this time included not only the Etruscans but all corsairs from Italy. This is clear from the

1. *Oratores Attici* (Didot), II, p. 450.

2. No. LVI in Blass (Teubner), no. LIX in Kenyon (Oxford). Τυρρηνῶν s Boeckh's correction of the MSS. τριηρῶν.

3. Hypereides, *fr.* 166 (Kenyon). The MSS. have τύραννοι emended by Boeckh to Τύρρηνοι (Harpocration, *s.v.*).

4. Strabo, V, p. 232. Strabo's statement is doubted by Tarn (*Antigonos,* p. 48) on the ground that when Antium had been captured by the Romans in 337 B.C. her ships had been burnt, also that the Romans could hardly be said at this time στρατηγεῖν τῆς 'Ιταλίας. See, however, below, p. 161.

5. *I. G.*, XI, 2, 148.

account in Diodorus of the capture by Timoleon of a Tyrrhenian with his twelve piratical galleys, who infested the coasts of Sicily. The Tyrrhenian bore the good Italian name of Postumius.[1] The Romans were strong enough to prevent the native Italian pirates from mis-behaving themselves in home waters, even officially forbidding the Volscians of Antium to use the sea.[2] But the introduction of such police measures on their coasts only forced the Italian corsairs to make longer cruises, which Rome was powerless to prevent. This surely was the point of Demetrius' criticism, that if Rome claimed to be a civilised power she should exercise greater restraint over her subjects.

After the early years of the third century B.C. there is silence regarding Tyrrhenian raiders.[3] We hear nothing of them, at any rate, during the period of Ptolemaic ascendancy in the Cyclades, which followed the fall of Demetrius Poliorcetes. The Ptolemies, no doubt, were as ready as the other kings to employ privateers or even pirates against their enemies. In the second Syrian war we hear of marauders in their service over-running the domains of the Syrian king.[4] In

1. Diod. Sic., XVI, 82. See Helbig, *op. cit.*, p. 401.

2. Livy, VIII, 14.

3. The Rhodian inscription published in *Ath. Mitt.*, XX, p. 223, which records fighting with Tyrrhenians, is assigned by the editor to the end of the century on the ground of the letter forms, but in Dittenberger, *Syll.*[3], 1225, an earlier date is regarded as probable. The engagement, in any case, took place off Sicily or Italy.

4. Paus., I, 7, 3. διέπεμψεν ἐς ἅπαντας ὧν ἦρχεν Ἀντίοχος τοῖς μὲν ἀσθενεστέροις λῃστὰς κατατρέχειν τὴν γῆν, οἱ δὲ ἦσαν δυνατώτεροι στρατιᾷ κατεῖργεν. The λῃσταί are here probably irregular troops, drawn rom the usual sources, operating on land.

251-250 B.C. the Macedonian garrisons in Attica were compelled to fortify Salamis against the pirates and privateers let loose by Alexander the son of Craterus, who had revolted from Antigonus and was supported by the Egyptian government.[1] But when pirates entered the Ptolemaic sphere they were promptly dealt with by the Egyptian officers. An inscription of Thera records the assistance rendered by the Egyptian *nauarchos* on the occasion of a descent by pirates, who may perhaps have come from Allaria in Crete.[2] During the night a force was sent by sea under Hephaestius of Calynda, who landed and joined with the natives to drive the marauders back to their ships. The raid may possibly have taken place when the Egyptian ascendancy in the Aegean had already declined,[3] and the Ptolemaic possessions were limited to the southern islands.[4] A second inscription, of the years 228-225 B.C.,[5] tells us something of Egyptian

1. Dittenberger, *Syll.*³, 454, πειρατικῶν ἐκπλεόντων ἐκ τοῦ ᾽Επιλιμνίου (? on the isthmus of Corinth, see *B. C. H.*, VI, 525). Tarn, *op. cit.*, p. 356, suggests that they may have been Cretan pirates subsidised from Egypt, but offers no evidence.

2. *I. G.*, XII, 3, 1291. If Hiller von Gaertringen (*Thera*, III, p. 88) is right in connecting *I. G.*, XII, 3, 328, with this incident, the raiders were Allariotes and succeeded in getting away with a number of Theran captives. After three years' captivity they had been set free and were being employed by the Allariotes in what seem to be piratical raids, but received no share of the plunder. The Allariotes are willing to let them go in exchange for Allariote prisoners detained at Thera.

3. The *nauarchos* (? Hermaphilus) is not earlier than the Chremonidean war (see Tarn, *J. H. S.*, XXXI, 258), and may perhaps be later than the reign of Philadelphus.

4. The later possessions of Egypt in the Aegean are well described by Tarn, *J. H. S.*, XXIX, 284 : " Egypt continued to hold the southern limit of the Aegean, following the volcanic deep-water line, with a ring of posts at Methana, Thera, Astypalaea, Samos, and she remained free to expand northward at pleasure along the coasts of Asia Minor and Thrace." (The epigraphical evidence for these posts is collected *ad loc.*)

5. Dittenberger, *Syll.*³, 502.

methods in Samothrace, where the *strategos* of the
Hellespont and Thrace is thanked for the precau-
tions taken to safeguard the island of Samothrace
against the marauders who always threatened the
temple treasures,[1] a detachment of horse, foot and
catapult-men having been despatched to the
island.

If our records concerning the Egyptian control
of the League of Islanders were fuller, it is
probable that we should have heard more
regarding the police measures adopted in the
Cyclades during the Ptolemaic suzerainty.[2]   But
it is possible, perhaps, to discover something of
the Egyptian methods from the later practice
of the Rhodians, who may reasonably be held,
when the League was re-constituted, to have
adopted the methods of their predecessors.

1. See above, p. 124, and below, p. 212. The inscription contains
a further request for protection in the agricultural districts of the island.

2. For a general account of the League, see W. Koenig, *Der Bund der
Nesioten* (Halle, 1910), with the additional evidence in *B. C. H.*, XXXV,
401 *seqq.* (Roussel).   To one who is not a specialist, the note in Dittenberger,
Sylloge[3], I, p. 624, will convey the necessary information : Commune
insulanorum secundum Dürrbachium iam c.a. 314 Antigoni et Demetrii
auspiciis conditum, a. 308 Ptolemaei curis instauratum in fide regum Aegypti
mansit ;   quorum principatus, quamquam interdum Macedonum (et
Rhodiorum Ephesia pugna) victoriis navalibus interruptus, Euergetae quoque
annis quodammodo manebat, Philopatris negligentia ad Rhodios transiisse
putatur ;   sed inde demum ab alterius saeculi initio de vero Rhodiorum
dominio quodam dici potest.

A convenient summary of the evidence is given by Tarn (*Antigonos*,
Appendix, V), who shows that the league was founded originally by Antigonus
Monophthalmus and Demetrius Poliorcetes (see also Dürrbach, *B. C. H.*,
XXVI, p. 208 ; Koenig, *op. cit.*, p. 13), and points out that there can have
been no question of any serious Ptolemaic control until the overthrow of
Demetrius' sea-power.   The period of Egyptian control is roughly commensurate with the reign of Ptolemy Philadelphus (285-247), after which,
as the result of Macedonian victories, the official suzerainty of the League
appears to have passed to the Macedonians (see, however, below).   The
Rhodians are found in full control *c.* 200 B.C., and their suzerainty may be
held to have lasted till 168 B.C.   (On Rhodes and the League, see Koenig,
p. 40.)

There are indications that Rhodes had already challenged the Egyptian suzerainty before the death of Philadelphus,[1] but we do not find her as undisputed mistress of the League until the beginning of the next century.

In an inscription of the years 200-197 B.C., there is mention of a Rhodian officer, ἄρχων ἐπί τε [τῶν νή]σων καὶ τῶν πλοίων τῶν νησιωτικ[ῶν²] ; in another of the same date we find an officer in command of a Rhodian squadron, accompanied by the triremes of the islanders and by the Athenian *aphracti*.[3] He is honoured by the Delians for the care which he had shown for the safety of navigators, his protection of the island, and regard for the sanctity of the temple of Delos, as he had issued an edict forbidding privateers to make use of the anchorage at Delos. Although the immediate reference is to the war with Philip V, it is well-known that Rhodes at this time was the only naval power which endeavoured to secure the

1. This is clear from the notice in Polyaenus, V, 18, of the victory of the Rhodian admiral Agathostratus over the Ptolemaic admiral at Ephesos. The erection of a statue by the Κοινὸν τῶν νησιωτῶν to Agathostratus at Delos (Dittenberger, *Syll.*³, 455) implies a temporary relaxation of Egyptian control in the Cyclades. (It should be noted that dedications and the receipt of honours at Delos do not necessarily imply that the dedicator or recipient controlled the island, but on the other hand it may be taken as certain that in such cases as *Syll.*³, 518 (Antigonus Doson), 500 (Bucris the Aetolian), 584 (Nabis), that there was no other power in the Aegean capable *at the time* of exercising complete control.) The citation from the Lindian temple-chronicle (ed. Blinkenberg, Bonn, 1915, p. 30, XXXVII) in Dittenberger, note to no. 455, makes it clear that the Rhodian war with Egypt was concluded before the death of Philadelphus, but *Syll.*³, 455, does not prove what Hiller von Gaertringen asserts that it does in his note to *Syll.*³, 583, that there was any Rhodian *control* before the death of Philadelphus.

2. Dittenberger, *Syll.*³, 583.

3. *Ib.*, 582, ἀποσταλεὶς ὑπὸ τοῦ δήμο[υ] ἐπὶ καταφράκτων πλοίων κατὰ πόλεμον, συστρατευομένων αὐ[τ]ῶι τῶν τε νησιωτικῶν τριηρῶν κα[ὶ] τῶν Ἀθηναίων ἀφράκτων,

safety of navigators,[1] and it is a fair conjecture
that as suzerain of the reorganised League she
utilised the contingents of the islanders for policing
the Cyclades. Was Rhodes in this respect
continuing the practice of the Egyptian government ? The ἄρχων ἐπὶ τῶν νήσων καὶ τῶν πλοίων
τῶν νησιωτικῶν is usually regarded as performing
the same functions under the Rhodians as the
nesiarch under the Egyptian government.[2] In
both periods *archon* and *nesiarch* are appointed
not by the League but by its suzerain.[3] Two
inscriptions of the Ptolemaic age give us information regarding a squadron of *aphracti* maintained
in the Aegean. The first[4] tells of a certain
Zenon appointed to the command of the *aphracti*,
which in the year 290-289[5] acted as escort to the
Attic grain-ships.   In the second inscription,[6] we
find that Zenon, who had been left by Bacchon
the *nesiarch* at Ios, received a deputation from the
inhabitants regarding some slaves who had made
their way on to the *aphracti*, and whom Zenon
now caused to be handed over by his trierarchs.
The language of the second inscription makes it
plain that Zenon, the commander of the *aphracti*,
was subordinate to Bacchon, and although the
former would naturally exercise command for
tactical purposes at sea, he was clearly subject to
the authority of the *nesiarch*, whose duties were

1. See below, p. 137.
2. See notes in Dittenberger, *ad loc.*
3. See Delamarre, *Rev. Phil.*, XX, p. 112.
4. Dittenberger, *Syll.*³, 367.
5. ἐπὶ Διοκλέους [ἄρχοντος]—290-89 or 287-6. The inscription belongs
to the earliest days of Egyptian control.
6. Dittenberger, *O. G. I.*, 773.

not purely naval. If it is permissible to argue from the later Rhodian practice, the squadron of *aphracti*, under the general direction of the *nesiarch*, consisted in part of contingents sent by the islanders, by means of which the Egyptian government maintained the sea-police of the Cyclades.[1]

After the withdrawal of Egypt from the Cyclades, which is probably to be dated to the early years of the second half of the third century B.C., it is doubtful whether there was any organised police of the Aegean area other than that provided by the Rhodians. Moreover, in contrast to the preceding years, there is consider-

---

1. Contrast, however, Tarn, *J. H. S.*, XXXI, 253 : " The ships were Egyptian (it was the squadron which provisioned Athens for Ptolemy in 288, and there is no trace of any ships of the Islanders till the time of the Rhodian protectorate) ; and once on board, the slaves *were on Egyptian territory*. Bacchon had no power over Egyptian territory ; Zeno, the commander of the squadron, had : Bacchon, therefore, naturally referred the complainants to Zeno, *and went his way*, leaving [my italics] Zeno to settle the matter, which he did, after assembling and questioning his trierarchs. There is nothing, whatever, to show that Bacchon was Zeno's superior officer. He gives Zeno no *orders*."

Tarn rightly rejects the view that καταλείπειν = *déléguer* (see Dittenberger's note *ad loc.*), but the use of the word καταλειφθείς undoubtedly implies what he is at pains to deny. When an official document states that one officer is left behind by another and carries out a particular piece of work, it is difficult to believe that he is not acting on the orders of his superior. Koenig's argument (p. 74) that the slaves would not have made their way on board the *aphracti* had they consisted of contingents from the islands, is applicable only to the contingent sent from Ios.

The probabilities are that Zeno's squadron was a composite one, with a nucleus of Egyptian vessels (in 290/289 the squadron may have been entirely Egyptian), to which the islands also sent their contingents under their own officers (cf. the later τριήραρχοι τῶν νησιωτῶν attested by *I. G.*, XII, 5, 918). The whole fleet was under the command of the Egyptian officer Zenon, καθεστηκὼς ἐπὶ τῶν ἀφράκτων, (cf. the later Rhodian ἄρχων τῶν ἀφράκτων in *I. G.*, XII, 5, 913, two of whose vessels seem to have been manned and officered by Rhodians), while it is clear from *O. G. I.*, 773, that the admiral of the squadron was himself subordinate for administrative purposes to the *nesiarch*, the prototype of the Rhodian ἄρχων τῶν νησιωτικῶν.

able evidence that the islanders were suffering
severely at this time from marauders. It is
perhaps the case that the nominal suzerainty of
the League of Islanders passed to the Macedonians,[1]
but their Aegean possessions were few and it is
unlikely that kings who themselves formed
alliances with the Illyrian pirates, as did
Demetrius II with Agron,[2] and Antigonus Doson
with Demetrius of Pharos[3] (whose Cycladic raid
can only have been undertaken with the approval
of the Macedonian court[4]), were much concerned
at the depredations of smaller bands of

---

1. We find, at any rate, that Antigonus Doson commemorated his
victory at Sellasia (222 B.C.) by an offering at Delos (*Syll.*³, 518 ; cf. Holleaux,
B. C. H., XXXI, p. 95), but the Macedonian suzerainty, if it existed, can hardly
have been more than nominal. Their navy was practically non-existent.
Philip V, at his accession, was without a war-fleet and Polybius (V, 2) gives
us a lively picture of the shifts to which he was driven in order to raise a fleet
during the Social War. It is therefore difficult to believe with Beloch
(III, 2, 430) and Holleaux (*op. cit.*, p. 104) that the battle of Andros was a victory
gained by Antigonus Doson in 228, which opened the way for the expedition
to Caria (Polyb., XX, 5 ; Trogus, *Prol.*, 28). The rapidity with which in
that case the Macedonian fleet fell into decay would be extraordinary.
On the contrary, it is obvious from Polybius that the fleet with which
Antigonus was operating on the coast of Boeotia on his way to Caria was
only a small one. The epigraphical evidence cited by Delamarre (*Rev. Phil.*,
XXVI, 301 *seqq.* ; see also Beloch, p. 462 ; Holleaux, p. 106) for the Macedonian occupation of Amorgos, Naxos and Syros is not strong, though the
inscriptions point to some amount of Macedonian influence at the time, if
the king in question is Antigonus Doson (see Koenig, p. 31).
    All the evidence tends to show that during the " interregnum " (Holleaux,
p. 114), which followed the Egyptian withdrawal from the Cyclades, Rhodes
was improving her position. But it is not until the years 200-197 that we
find her as undisputed suzerain of the League, and it is probable that she
formally reconstituted the League after Philip's attempt to establish
Macedonian supremacy in 202-201. Prior to that date and to Dicaearchus'
cruise in 205-204 (Diod. Sic., XXVIII, 1 ; Polyb., XVIII, 54), Rhodes had
been on terms of friendship with Philip and would have avoided giving a direct
challenge to Macedonian pretensions. (On the doubts as to the existence of
the League, *c.* 250-200, see Roussel, *B. C. H.*, XXXV, 448-9.)

2. Polyb., II, 2.

3. *Ib.*, II, 65 ; cf. IV, 55.

4. *Ib.*, IV, 16. See Holleaux, *op. cit.*, p. 108.

marauders in the Cyclades, even if they possessed
the necessary force to stop them. The Egyptian
government, as we have seen, still offered protection to its subjects in the districts which it
controlled, but the only general police work that
can be discovered was done by the Rhodians.

As the successor of Athens as the chief trading
state of the Aegean, Rhodes from the first had set
her face against piracy, and throughout her history
her reputation stood high as the guardian of the
seas[1] and general protector of commerce. When
the Byzantines in 219 B.C. began to levy tolls on
all exports from the Black Sea, it was to Rhodes
that the trading world appealed,[2] and her high
standing is sufficiently attested by the assistance
which she received from the whole Greek world
at the time of the devastating earthquake of 224.[3]
In international politics her doctrine was that of
no interference with her trade, a course which had
already brought her into collision with Antigonus
and Demetrius at the time of the famous siege.
On that occasion the alacrity with which the
pirates hastened to join the fleet of Demetrius[4]
may be largely explained by their eagerness to
dispose of their chief enemy.

As to the methods followed by the Rhodians,
we hear of their merchandise being carried in
armed merchantmen, which were strong enough
to beat off an unprovoked attack made on them

1. Strabo, XIV, 652, ἐθαλασσοκράτησε πολὺν χρόνον καὶ τὰ λῃστήρια
καθεῖλε καὶ Ῥωμαίοις ἐγένετο φίλη.

2. Polyb., IV, 47.

3. *Ib.*, V, 88-90.

4. See above, p. 123.

by a squadron sent by Demetrius Poliorcetes.[1]
Even before the days when Rhodes was the
suzerain of the League of Islanders, there were
Rhodian guardships cruising among the islands.[2]
The strain which the maintenance of such patrols
threw on the Republic is illustrated by the
inscription already quoted, which records the
death of the three sons of Timacretes at sea, two
fighting against " Tyrrhenians," one against
pirates.[3] But the protection which these patrols
offered to the islanders was invaluable. At a time
when the coasts of Elis and Messenia were being
scourged by the Illyrians we only once hear of an
Illyrian fleet, under Demetrius of Pharos,
appearing in the Aegean, and then it was chased
away by the Rhodians.[4] It was not until the
time of Perseus that the Rhodians were overawed
by the *lembi* of Genthius.[5]

Another method adopted by the Rhodians was
the making of agreements with other states for
mutual assistance in the repression of piracy.
One of these agreements has been preserved, made
with one of the more reputable of the Cretan
cities, Hierapytna, about the years 200-197 B.C.,[6]
and it is possible that the alliance with Cnossos
of 220 B.C.,[7] and that of a still earlier date at the
time of the siege of Rhodes,[8] contained similar

1. Diod. Sic., XX, 82.
2. *Ib.*, XX, 93, ἔχων ναῦς τὰς καλουμένας παρὰ ‘Ροδίοις φυλακίδας.
3. Dittenberger, *Syll.*³, 1225.
4. Polyb., III, 16; IV, 16 and 19.
5. Polyb., XXIX, 11.
6. Dittenberger, *Syll.*³, 581.
7. Polyb., IV, 53.
8. Diod. Sic., XX, 88.

provisions. In her wars with the Cretan towns
which were habitually guilty of piracy, Rhodes
seems always to have endeavoured to secure the
active assistance of the better-behaved. The
agreement with Hierapytna provides that in the
event of an outbreak of piracy in Crete, which
necessitates action on the part of the Rhodians
against the pirates and their supporters, the people
of Hierapytna are to assist the Rhodians by land
and sea. The captured pirates and their boats
are to be handed over to the Rhodians, other
spoils to be divided among the allies.[1] If any of
the pirates' supporters retaliate on the
Hierapytnians, proper assistance is to be sent by
the Rhodians.[2] Such a clause, perhaps, was a
necessary insertion on the part of a town in Crete.

But however great the effort made by the
Rhodians, it is clear that, single-handed, the
republic was unable entirely to suppress piracy
during the second half of the third century, and
that, when the Rhodian guardships were absent,
the islands were at the mercy of casual bands of
pirates, whether from Crete or elsewhere, and
in still greater danger from the organised pillaging
of the Aetolians. An inscription of this period
from Aegiale in Amorgos[3] tells of a descent of
pirates by night on the island, when more than
thirty persons, men, women, and slaves, were
kidnapped, and the boat of a certain Dorieus,

1. Dittenberger, *l.c.*, § X.

2. *Ib.*, § XVII.

3. Dittenberger, *Syll.*[3], 521. It is possible that *I. G.*, XII, 7, 387,
records a more serious descent (see Delamarre, *Rev. Phil.*, XXVII, 112)
but the reading is uncertain. *I. G.*, XII, 8, 53 (Imbros) belongs probably
to the next century.

lying in the harbour, was taken to carry off the captives. Two of the prisoners prevailed on Socleidas, the captain of the gang, to hold the party to ransom and themselves remained as hostages. An inscription of Naxos of about the same date[1] records the capture of 280 of the inhabitants by Aetolians, who held their captives to ransom. There can be little doubt that it was by exploits of this type that the Aetolians acquired many of their overseas possessions, terrorism driving the maritime towns to join their league. (It must be remembered that the Aetolians themselves possessed nothing in the form of a war-fleet, but were dependent on the ships of the Cephallenians and privately-owned vessels, available for plundering expeditions).[2] The case is clear with regard to the island of Ceos, which was received into the league and thereby granted immunity from Aetolian raids and exercise of reprisals.[3] It would be interesting to know if the Aetolian dependencies in Thrace had been acquired by inducements of this character.[4] If Lysimacheia had joined the Aetolians in order to obtain immunity by sea, there is additional point in Philip's remarks that by so doing she had exposed herself to the incursions of the Thracians on land.[5]

1. Dittenberger, *Syll.*³, 520.

2. See Polyb., IV, 6; V, 3. For the propensities of the Cephallenians, see Livy, XXXVII, 13.

3. Dittenberger, *Syll.*³, 522. Perhaps also Chios, *Syll.*³, 443. (The grant of ἀσυλία to the *temenos* of Athene Nikephoros at Pergamon in 182 B.C. (Dittenberger, *Syll.*³, 629) belongs, of course, to a different category, as do also the Teos inscriptions (Michel, 52-66).)

4. Lysimacheia, Cius, Chalcedon (Polyb., XV, 23; XVIII, 3; Livy, XXXII, 33).

5. Polyb., XVIII, 4.

It is not easy to arrive at a just view of Aetolian operations at this time. There was much outcry at their predatory habits,[1] and Polybius, who says that they had long been accustomed to live on their neighbours,[2] exclaims against their innate wickedness and greed.[3] But Polybius cannot be regarded as an altogether unprejudiced witness against the Aetolians, and the doctrine which he ascribes to them of regarding nothing as disgraceful if profitable, is ascribed by him, in language almost identical, to his other *bêtes noirs*, the Cretans and Carthaginians.[4] It is nevertheless true that by land and sea the Aetolians were ready enough to make use of any ruffians who could serve their purpose. The following of both Dorimachus and Euripidas consisted largely of the brigands who infested the Peloponnese[5]; at sea, Scerdilaïdas the Illyrian was in their service, until he thought that he had been cheated by his employers and joined the Macedonians.[6] Aetolian depredations, according to Polybius, were so normal that they were easily overlooked.[7] Their law allowed great latitude in the interpretation of " wartime." If hostilities arose between states in alliance with the Aetolians, it was permissible for any individual to join with either of the

1. See the list of their enormities recited at the Congress of Corinth in 220 B.C. (Polyb., IV, 25).

2. *Ib.*, IV, 3. Cf. the *ithyphallos* in Athenaeus, VI, 253 f (quoted by Tarn, *Antigonos*, p. 61): Αἰτωλικὸν γὰρ ἁρπάσαι τὰ τῶν πέλας.

3. Polyb., II, 45.

4. *Ib.*, IX, 28 ; cf. VI, 46 (Cretans), 56 (Carthaginians).

5. *Ib.*, IV, 3 ; IV, 68 ; cf. 79.

6. *Ib.*, IV, 16 ; IV, 29.

7. *Ib.*, IV, 16.

combatants for purposes of plunder.[1] But the
most generous interpretation of the law could
hardly justify the conduct of Dorimachus in
Messenia,[2] or the action of the crews who seized
a Macedonian ship off Cythera and sold the master
and crew in Aetolia.[3] As these events took place
without the official approval of the league, the
government could protest, while Dorimachus was
marching through Achaia, that there was no war.[4]
Even if due allowance is made for the fact that our
knowledge of these events, which led up to the
so-called " Social War " of 219-217 B.C., is derived
from a historian who belonged to the other side,
we must nevertheless admit that on land and sea
alike the behaviour of the Aetolians was as illegal
and damaging to the Greek world as the conduct
of the Cretans and Illyrians, who are generally
recognised as pirates.[5]

After the days of King Minos, the reputation
of the Cretans was at all times bad. Already in
Homer the typical pirate boasts that he is of
Cretan race.[6] Herodotus assigns to Cretans the
chief part in the kidnapping of women from Asia.[7]
It will be remembered that the officers sent by
Alexander to suppress piracy in the Aegean began
their task by settling affairs in Crete.[8] The

1. So Philip in Polyb., XVIII, 5, ἄγειν λάφυρον ἀπὸ λαφύρου.

2. *Ib.*, IV, 3 *seqq.*

3. *Ib.*, IV, 6.

4. *Ib.*, IV, 17 (cf IV, 26, Philip's letter).

5. A closer study of the evidence has led me to change the view expressed
in *Liverpool Annals*, VIII, p. 108, that the Aetolian operations did not
transgress the ancient laws concerning privateering.

6. *Od.*, XIV, 199.

7. Hdt., I, 2.

8. Qu. Curt., IV, 8, 15.

dishonesty of Cretans was proverbial,[1] as was also their greed and love of money.[2] There is no doubt that geographical conditions were largely responsible for making the Cretan what he was, a mercenary or pirate, or both, as occasion offered. A large part of the island is barren and unable to support a large population. Whereas to-day the Cretan emigrates to the mainland or to America, in ancient times he took service abroad as a mercenary. The mountainous character of the island bred a hardy race of warriors, adepts in all kinds of guerilla warfare ; as Polybius says, they were irresistible on land and sea in ambuscades, raids, night attacks and surprises.[3] At the same time, the mountainous character of their island caused a sharp severance between communities and gave rise to endless intestinal wars, which harassed the island but served to train not only the Cretans in arms but also the more warlike spirits among the Greeks whom they summoned to their aid.[4] Strabo, whose sources of information regarding the island were exceptionally good, emphasises the close relation between the mercenaries and pirates from Crete. " It contained a large number of mercenaries and soldiers, from whom as a result the pirate

1. Polyb., VIII, 21, πρὸς Κρῆτα κρητίζειν (cf. Suidas and Hesychius s.v.) ; it was the Cretan Bolis who betrayed Achaeus, and delivered him to Antiochus. (I need not quote Callimachus and St. Paul.)

2. Polyb., VI, 46.

3. Ib., IV, 8.

4. For the savagery of these wars and their endless character, see Polyb., IV, 54 (the sack of Lyttos) and XXIV, 4. The oath of the people of Dreros is of interest : μὴ μὰν ἐγώ ποκα τοῖς Λυττίοις καλῶς φρονήσειν . . . . καὶ σπείσω ὅτι κα δύναμαι κακὸν τᾶι πόλει τᾶι τῶν Λυττίων (Dittenberger, Syll.³, 527).

boats were filled."[1] Moreover, the position of the island and nature of its coasts offered the greatest facilities both for cruises abroad and for minor operations in shore. " The island seems to be intended by nature for dominion in Hellas, and to be well situated ; it extends right across the sea, around which nearly all the Hellenes are settled ; and while one end is not far from the Peloponnese, the other almost reaches to the region of Asia about Triopium and Rhodes. Hence Minos acquired the empire of the sea, subduing some of the islands and colonizing others."[2] The less imperialistic successors of Minos found the position of Crete equally advantageous for cruises in the Cyclades[3] and southern Sporades, or to the west in the Cythera channel, the time-honoured haunt of Aegean pirates. The coast of Crete itself offers equal facilities. Admiral Spratt, whose pilot and guide was the ex-pirate Captain Manias, notes a number of places off the coast where piracy could be practised with success, to which the " patient and gentle " Manias had drawn his attention.[4]

1. Strabo, X, p. 477.   For the depredations of the Cretan mercenaries and reign of terror in Antioch after the restoration of Demetrius II (148-147), see Bevan, *House of Seleucus*, II, pp. 218, 222 *seqq.* It is noticeable that Demetrius employed Cretans against the Cilicians of his rival.

2. Aristotle, *Politics*, 1271b (Tr. Jowett).

3. For a raid on Thera see above, p. 131.   Cf. *Anth. Pal.*, VII, 654.

   Αἰεὶ ληϊσταὶ καὶ ἀλίφθοροι οὐδὲ δίκαιοι
   Κρῆτες· τίς Κρητῶν οἶδε δικαιοσύνην ;
   ὡς καὶ ἐμὲ πλώοντα σὺν οὐκ εὐπλόνι φόρτῳ
   Κρηταιεῖς ὦσαν Τιμόλυτον καθ' ἁλὸς
   δείλαιον· Κἠγὼ μὲν ἁλιζώοις λαρίδεσσι
   κέκλαυμαι, τύμβῳ δ' οὐχ ὑπὸ Τιμόλυτος.

4. *e.g.*, the Kouphonisi islands, where Spratt notes a small natural harbour between two of the smaller islets, suitable for coasting craft, or where a corsair could lie hidden and pounce on any trader drifted in by the currents

In particular he comments on the extraordinary local knowledge which his guide possessed of the Cretan coast-line, together with that of the islands of Caso, Carpatho and Casteloryzo. This, no doubt, was characteristic of all the Cretan navigators.

But owing to the excellence of its mercenaries and their numbers, Crete was an important factor in the foreign policy of the powers during the third and early second century B.C., and to obtain the troops required it was necessary to have a footing in the island. In the treaty between Rhodes and Hierapytna, it is stipulated that the Hierapytnians shall give the Rhodians facilities for raising mercenaries, but shall not countenance the raising of mercenaries to be employed against Rhodes.[1] We find the Ptolemies, in whose armies a large proportion of the mercenary troops were Cretans,[2] at all times careful to maintain their position in the island.[3] Of the Macedonian kings, Demetrius II formed an alliance with Gortyn,[4] and Antigonus Doson with Eleutherna and Hierapytna.[5] At the conclusion of the

at night (op. cit., I, p. 241). A similar snare off Cape Sidero (ib., p. 244). See also p. 279 on Gavdo, Pashley on Sudha rock (Crete, I, p. 29).

1. Dittenberger, Syll.³, 581, § VIII.

2. In Polyb., V, 65, out of a force of 8,000 mercenaries, 3,000 were Cretans.

3. See Beloch, III, 2, 283. The principal references are : O. G. I., 45 ; in the Chremonidean war certain of the Cretan states are found in alliance with the Egyptian party (Syll.³, 434/5). Egyptian relations with Itanos, attested for the reigns of Ptolemy II and III (Syll.³, 463), lasted apparently until the reign of Ptolemy VI (Syll.³, 685, O. G. I., 119). For the Egyptian position in Crete generally during this reign, see O. G. I., 102, 116. Strabo, X, p. 478, says that Ptolemy IV began to rebuild the walls of Gortyn, but his relations with the town are otherwise unknown.

4. A. J. A., ser. II, Vol. I, 1897, p. 188, no. 17.

5. B. C. H., XIII, pp. 47, 52, nos. 1 and 2. (See Tarn, op. cit., p. 471. The editor, however, refers no. 1 to Antigonus Gonatas.)

Social War, Philip V was able to establish his influence in the island[1] and thereby contrived endless trouble for the Rhodians.

We find the Cretans then taking part as mercenaries in all the wars of this period, and utilising the confusion of the times to plunder as widely as possible on the sea. An Athenian inscription of the year 217-216 B.C. sets forth the methods taken to secure the ransoming of a number of citizens and others carried off to Crete in a raid by a certain Bucris during the Social War, a war in which Athens herself was not engaged. Ambassadors were sent to recover the captives, and were successful owing to the good offices of Eumaridas of Cydonia and the payment of a lump sum of twenty talents.[2]

Fortunately for the Greek world, while a number of the Cretans found occupation abroad, much of the energies of the individual states was consumed in internal struggles, which gave Rhodes, as the guardian of the seas, an opportunity to keep Cretan piracies within bounds. The Rhodian policy with regard to Crete has already been outlined ; when that policy broke down, as it did during the closing years of the third century, the consequences were

1. Polyb., VII, 11 (see below, p. 147).

2. Dittenberger, Syll.[3], 535. Their captor is usually identified with the Aetolian Bucris, son of Daitas of Naupactos (Syll.[3], 500), hieromnemon of the Aetolians in 230 B.C. (Syll.[3], 494), and it is therefore assumed that the capture was made by an Aetolian squadron, the plunder being taken to Cnossos, which had called in the Aetolians against Lyttos in 219 B.C. (Polyb., IV, 53). The Cretans, anyhow, got the ransom-money and as Bucris, in the present inscription, is mentioned without ethnic or patronymic, it is by no means certain that he is identical with Bucris, son of Daitas. Beloch (III, 1, 657) assigns the event to the war between the Aetolians and Demetrius II (cf. Ferguson, Hellenistic Athens, pp. 204, 209).

disastrous. As Polybius describes the situation in Crete,[1] shortly before the outbreak of the Social War an alliance between Cnossos and Gortyn[2] had temporarily brought the whole island, with the exception of Lyttos, under the sway of the two towns. As Cnossos was in alliance with Rhodes, it is probable that the piratical element in Crete was kept in check. But the citizens of Gortyn, falling into civil strife,[3] gave the signal for a widespread revolt, which was increased by what was regarded as a high-handed action on the part of the commander of a Rhodian squadron, sent to aid the Cnossians. During the Social War itself we find the Cnossian group supported by the Aetolians, and their adversaries by Philip, whose succours for the most part consisted of Illyrians. The intervention of Philip in Crete had important results, enabling him to establish Macedonian influence firmly in the island. The differences of the warring Cretan states were composed, and the island united in a single confederacy under Macedonian presidency.[4] But the establishment of Macedonian influence in Crete proved a serious blow to Rhodes. In his wider schemes of conquest, begun in 205 B.C., it was essential for Philip that the Rhodians should be preoccupied, and such preoccupation could be best attained by stirring up the piratical elements in the

1. Polyb., IV, 53-55. See Head, *H. N.*², p. 451.

2. Cf. Strabo, X, 478. When the two towns were acting together, they could keep the rest in subjection. When they were at variance, the whole island was divided. The town of Cydonia formed a make-weight between the two.

3. Cf. Dittenberger, *Syll.*³, 528.

4. Polyb., VII, 11 and 14. On Cnossos, see below, p. 149.

Aegean. For this purpose the cities of Crete lay
ready to the hand of the Macedonian. A serious
outbreak of piracy took place among the Cretans,
which caused the trading world to appeal to
Rhodes, and led to a declaration of war against the
Cretans by the Rhodians.[1] There can be no
doubt that Philip was responsible. Polybius tells
us that in 204 B.C., he had instructed Heracleides
to destroy the Rhodian fleet (the two states were
at peace), and at the same time sent ambassadors
to Crete to stir up a war against Rhodes.[2]
Heracleides was so far successful that he gained the
confidence of the Rhodians by pretending to reveal
Philip's designs in Crete, and contrived to set the
arsenal at Rhodes on fire.[3] About the same time[4]
Philip gave Dicaearchus the Aetolian twenty ships,
with instructions to go pirating in the Cyclades
and help the Cretans in the Rhodian war.[5]
We have already seen how serious this war was
to the Rhodians. Cretan ships from Hierapytna
were raiding the southern Sporades, and in some
cases effecting a landing in the islands.[6] At the
same time we find Cretans in the Aegean
co-operating at sea with Nabis, the tyrant of
Sparta,[7] who, in addition to his depredations on

1. Diod. Sic., XXVII, 3.

2. Polyb., XIII, 4 and 5.

3. Polyaenus, V, 17.

4. For the date 205-204 B.C. see v. Gelder, *Gesch. der alten Rhodier*,
p. 121 ; Holleaux, *B. C. H.*, XXXI, p. 108.

5. Polyb., XVIII, 54 ; Diod. Sic., XXVIII, 1. On the altars erected
by this Dicaearchus to *Lawlessness* and *Impiety*, see Polyb., *l.c.*

6. See the inscriptions relating to this war (*Syll.*³, 567-570) discussed
above, p. 45.

7. Polyb., XIII, 8. Nabis appears from Livy, XXXIV, 25, to have
got possession of some of the smaller towns in Crete. For the citizens of

land, conducted a profitable business in piracy off Malea. The whole Aegean was ablaze, and Philip's plan was so far accomplished that for two years the Rhodians were able to do little to interfere with his wider designs.[1]

It was not until the entry of the Romans into the war with Macedonia that Rhodes was able to establish her supremacy among the Greek islands. As we have already seen, inscriptions of the years 200-197 B.C., show that she succeeded in reconstituting the league of the islanders under her own suzerainty.[2] To the same years is dated the treaty of alliance with Hierapytna,[3] which may be regarded as marking the termination of her war with Crete. We have already seen the importance of that treaty as illustrating the relations which Rhodes endeavoured to maintain with the leading states of Crete, with a view to the prevention of piracy. It is clear from the text that an alliance already existed between Rhodes and Cnossos,[4] which may possibly have been in existence since the time of the Social War. Rhodes was thus once more enabled to establish good relations with both of the principal groups of Cretan states, and it seems that many of the

Troezen carried off to Crete, see *I. G.*, IV, 756, which Herzog (*Klio*, II, p. 330) assigns to this war. (The editor of *I. G.*, IV, however, connects the inscription with Nabis' occupation of the Argolid.)

1. See Herzog, *op. cit.*, p. 327.

2. See above, p. 133.

3. Dittenberger, *Syll.*³, 581, discussed above, p. 138.

4. See § XV, where it is especially stated that Rhodes is not to send assistance to Hierapytna in the war which was then in progress between the two towns.

Cretan towns now came into the Macedonian war on the side of the allies.[1]

With her entry into the war against Philip we have reached a stage when the influence of Rome became paramount in the Eastern Mediterranean, as for many years it had been in the West, to which we must now turn our attention.

---

1. See Pausanias, I, 36. His statement, however, is somewhat vague, the Cretan alliance being ascribed to the diplomacy of Cephisodorus the Athenian.

CHAPTER V

THE WESTERN SEAS, THE ADRIATIC AND ROME

ALTHOUGH our information is defective, it can hardly be supposed that the Western Mediterranean was more free from pirates at an early age than the eastern basin.[1] The pirates and brigands of Corsica, Sardinia, the Balearic Islands and Liguria do not appear until late in history, but it is likely that their favourite pursuits at sea were followed from the earliest time. The first inhabitants of Sicily are said to have dwelt, "village-fashion," on hill-tops through fear of pirates.[2] At the time when the later books of the *Odyssey* were composed, the Sicels were known both as the purveyors of slaves and as the victims of slavers.[3] This twofold character perhaps represents the relations between the earliest Greek settlers and the native populations, now peaceful, when exchange and barter could be carried on, now hostile, when kidnapping was practised on both sides. But the traditions which have survived regarding the Greek settlements in Italy and Sicily are few and late. There is nothing, for example, to show why it was that the

---

1. In spite of Cicero's statement (*de Rep.*, II, 9): E barbaris quidem ipsis nulli erant antea maritimi praeter Etruscos et Poenos, alteri mercandi causa, alteri latrocinandi.

2. Diod. Sic., V, 6.

3. *Od.*, XX, 383, slave-merchants; XXIV, 210, 366, the Sicel slave of Laertes.

first settlers of Zancle merited the name of pirates more than their brethren who colonised other sites.[1] Perhaps the advantageous position of the town on the Straits was the reason why the reputation of the early Zanclaeans as pirates surpassed that of their neighbours.

But Greek settlers were not the only pirates in the western seas. If the Phoenicians, whom they found in occupation of Sicily, withdrew at first to the west of the island, an increasing opposition was offered on the coast of Italy. It is not without significance that " Tyrrhenian " at one time became almost equivalent in meaning to " pirate." In the Homeric *Hymn to Dionysus*, the god is carried off by " Tyrrhenian " pirates.[2] It is an ordinary case of kidnapping, a boy on shore being sighted by the crew of a pirate boat, who land and carry him off.[3] A somewhat similar story was told about an Attic youth carried off by Tyrrhenians; in this case, the captain's daughter fell in love with him and helped him to escape.[4] Another story, preserved by Suidas, points to " Tyrrhenian " operations off the coast of Caria.[5] Although, as we have seen, in the fourth and third centuries, the cruises of the Italian corsairs were extended into the Aegean, it is not necessary to believe this of an earlier date.

1. Thuc., VI, 6.

2. *Hom. Hymn.*, VII, 8, λῃσταὶ Τυρσηνοί.

3. υἱὸν γάρ μιν ἔφαντο διοτρεφέων βασιλήων.

4. Suidas, *s.v.* Κωλίας; Schol. Aristoph., *Nubes* 52. The story, however, has every appearance of a late origin; see below, p. 265. Tyrrhenians appear again in an aetiological myth of Samos, which explained the origin of the festival called Tonea (Athenaeus, XV, 672).

5. Suidas, *s.v.* Τερμέρια κακά. (A different explanation of the phrase is given by Plutarch, *Theseus*, 11.)

There may have been some confusion between the Tyrrhenians of Italy and the Tyrseni, a barbarian people of the Northern Aegean, of whom both Herodotus and Thucydides make mention.[1]   But, leaving aside the possible connection of this tribe with the Tyrrhenians of Italy, we shall probably be right in deriving the Greek use of " Tyrrhenian " as an equivalent of " pirate "[2] from the opposition experienced at the hands of the native population to the Greek advance up the western coast of Italy.[3]

According to Strabo, Greek expansion in the West was for long limited through fear of the Tyrrhenians.[4]   As he is speaking of the earliest settlements, the statement is probably little more than an inference on the part of Ephorus, whom Strabo is quoting.   As to the Etruscans themselves, as Strabo points out,[5] there is nothing in the character of their country which would naturally draw them to piracy.   Their cities for the most part were planted inland,[6] and at the date of the first arrival of the Greeks in the West there is little evidence for regarding them as a maritime people. Their only city of any consequence on the coast was Populonia, without doubt a later foundation.[7]

1. Hdt., I, 57 ; Thuc., IV, 109.

2. A good example is found in the phrase δεσμοὶ Τυρρηνοί. See Suidas, *s.v.* Hesychius has the gloss Τυρρηνοὶ δεσμοί · οἱ λῃστρικοὶ καὶ χαλεποί.

3. The date assigned to the Homeric hymn, *c.* 600 B.C. (see Allen and Sikes, p. 230) accords well enough with the view expressed above.

4. Strabo, VI, 267.

5. *Ib.*, V, 222.

6. *Ib.*, V, 223.

7. See Servius, *ad Aen.*, X, 172. It was first founded by Corsicans, from whom it was taken by the people of Volaterrae. (For Sardinian raids on the Pisatan country see Strabo, V, 225)

But aggression from the sea, whether on the part of the barbarians of Elba, Corsica and Sardinia, or of the Greeks, compelled them to look to the defence of their coasts, and with the wealth which the Etruscan cities possessed and the ample supplies of timber that were available, it is not surprising that from motives of self-defence they should build a fleet, with which to occupy the adjacent islands and close their own seas against Greek marauders. This then is probably the meaning of Tyrrhenian piracies, and the explanation of the contradictory accounts which we find concerning the participation of certain Tyrrhenian cities in the piracy of the time. Strabo, for example, tells us that the people of Agylla (Caere) held a high reputation among the Greeks and refrained from piracy, in spite of their opportunities.[1] Nevertheless, we find them guilty of the murder of the Phocaeans, whose settlement in Corsica constituted a grave menace to Etruscan and Carthaginian interests in this area.[2] It is true that the Caeretans, like other Etruscan peoples, entertained close commercial relations with the Greeks, but they would not tolerate Greek penetration into seas which they had now come to regard as their own. As Mommsen puts it, the Etruscan piracies on foreign ships, " constituted, as it were, a rude navigation act," for the protection of their own commerce.[3] The cruelty with which the captured Greek shippers were treated— apart from the stoning of the Phocaeans, we are

1. Strabo, V, 220.
2. Hdt., I, 166. See also Servius, *ad Aen.*, X, 184.
3. *History of Rome*, I, 151.

told that a favourite torture was to bind the living face to face with the dead[1]—may well have given rise to the appearance of the Tyrrhenian in legend as the proverbial pirate. Similar relations existed between the Greeks and the Carthaginians. The rise of Carthage towards the end of the seventh century set a limit to Greek expansion both in Africa and Sicily, while the Carthaginian occupation of Sardinia, not long after the Greek foundation of Massalia, proved a further barrier to the Greek advance in the Western Mediterranean. Once their power had been established, the Carthaginians jealously guarded the trade of the western seas against competitors. In the second of the two early treaties with Rome which Polybius quotes,[2] trade with Libya and Sardinia is expressly refused to the Romans. This was the traditional policy of the Carthaginians, while the savagery of the Etruscans is matched by their practice of sinking any foreign ship entering waters which they claimed as their own.[3] With the growth of Carthaginian power, the maintenance of their communications with Massalia necessitated hard fighting for the Phocaeans. It is not surprising to hear that Phocaean voyages to the West were made in

1. Val. Max., IX, 2, 10; Augustine, *Contra Julian. Pelag.*, 78, quoting Cicero, who cites Aristotle.

2. Polyb., II, 24.

3. Strabo, XVII, 802, quoting Eratosthenes, καταποντοῦν εἴ τις τῶν ξένων εἰς Σαρδὼ παραπλεύσειεν ἢ ἐπὶ Στήλας, διὰ δὲ ταῦτ' ἀπιστεῖσθαι τὰ πολλὰ τῶν ἑσπερίων. The last sentence testifies to the success of the policy. Carthaginian exclusiveness is illustrated by the well-known story of the skipper who ran his ship on to a shoal in order to destroy the Romans who were following him in an endeavour to discover the route to the Cassiterides.

warships,[1] while their enterprises assumed more and more the form of buccaneering. Their settlers at Alalia in Corsica, in face of opposition from the Carthaginians and Etruscans, maintained themselves by plundering their neighbours, until they were driven out by the combined navies of the two powers.[2] Their defeat entailed the severance of Greek communications with the West. Their compatriot Dionysius was a true buccaneer. When driven from his native town after the battle of Lade in 495 B.C., he first executed a successful raid on the shipping off the Phoenician coast. Thence he sailed for Sicily, where he abstained from pillaging any of the Greeks, but devoted his attention entirely to Carthaginians and Etruscans.[3] Buccaneering enterprises of this character were the natural outcome of the exclusive commercial policy pursued by these states, as the Spaniards also found to their cost in the seventeenth century.

One of the most interesting settlements of which we hear was that of the Cnidians and Rhodians in the Lipari Islands.[4] A band of men, led by Pentathlus, had endeavoured about the year 580 B.C. to settle in the neighbourhood of Lilybaeum[5]. When they were driven out, the

1. Hdt., I, 163; cf. Thuc., I, 13.

2. Hdt., I, 166.

3. *Ib.*, VI, 17.

4. Diod. Sic., V, 9; Paus., X, 11, 3; X, 16, 7. Thucydides (III, 88), Strabo (VI, 275) and Pausanias speak only of Cnidians.

5. Pausanias, who quotes Antiochus, says the Pachynus promontory, but this is improbable if, as he says, they reached Lipari on the return voyage. Moreover, in Pachynus they would be less exposed to the attacks of Phoenicians and Elymi, who drove them from Sicily.

survivors, on their voyage homewards, landed at the Lipari Islands, where they conciliated or exterminated the natives, and occupied the islands. Harassed by Tyrrhenian corsairs, they constructed a fleet and frequently defeated their opponents, sending tithes of the booty to Delphi. During the Peloponnesian war at any rate, only the largest of the islands was inhabited, the Liparaeans crossing in boats to cultivate the rest. As a station for corsairs the island possessed a great advantage in that lack of water made an expedition against them possible only in the winter.[1] Their resistance to the Tyrrhenians was not merely passive, but it is clear that they carried on a vigorous buccaneering on their own account. In the year 393 B.C. a Roman embassy, conveying to Delphi a thankoffering for the capture of Veii, was attacked and carried off to the islands; but, owing to the intervention of the chief magistrate, Timasitheus, " Romanis vir similior quam suis," the ambassadors were set free and their offering restored.[2]

What is of greater interest regarding this settlement is its communistic organisation, eminently suited to a piratical community of this type,[3] and imitated to some extent after many years in the colony of pirates in Madagascar, which was founded by the Frenchman Mission and our own Captain Tew.[4] The inhabitants were assigned

1. Thuc., l.c.

2. Diod. Sic., XIV, 97 ; Livy, V, 28. Plutarch's version (*Camillus*, 8) is that the Romans were mistaken for pirates.

3. See Guiraud, *La propriété foncière en Grèce*, p. 12 ; Th. Reinach, *Rev. des Et. Gr.*, 1890, pp. 86 *seqq.*

4. A short account will be found in Verrill, *The Real History of the Pirate*, p. 218.

partly to the navy, partly to agriculture, all land
being held in common, and, as would appear, the
proceeds of the raids being divided among the
population.[1] At a later stage it was decided to
divide the land in Lipara itself, and still later, that
in the other islands; but in the last case a fresh
distribution was made after twenty years.[2]

To the Greeks of Sicily this outpost of
buccaneers must have been of great value during
the early years of its existence. Tyrrhenian
aggression was steadily increasing during the sixth
century, and at the beginning of the fifth we find
that the tyrant of Rhegium was compelled to
fortify the Straits to prevent the passage of their
piratical craft.[3] It was not until the great
victory of Hiero and the Syracusans off Cumae in
474 B.C. that the menace was broken.[4] Even after
that date, in spite of a Greek attempt to re-occupy
the Pithecusae Islands opposite Cumae,
Tyrrhenian corsairs contrived to give trouble
off the Sicilian coast. A new expedition was
therefore sent against them in 453-452 B.C. under
the Syracusan Phayllus, who ravaged the island of

" A council or house of representatives was chosen, without distinction or discrimination as regarded color or wealth ; an equal division
of all cattle and treasure was made and those who had no land or were
unfamiliar with agriculture were given work they could do at wages
regulated by the state. Laws were then made and registered in a state
book and it was provided that the council was to meet annually, or
oftener if required, and that nothing of importance could be done
without the state's approbation."

The fullest account of both men is that given by Chas. Johnson, *History of the
Pirates*, Vol. II (1725).

1. So Livy, *l.c.*

2. Diod. Sic., *l.c.*

3. Strabo, VI, 257.

4. Diod. Sic., XI, 51.

Elba. His successor, Apelles, with a force of sixty triremes, overran the Tyrrhenian coast, made a descent on Corsica and reoccupied Elba.[1] But we cannot suppose that Tyrrhenian piracies were entirely stopped by these expeditions. The presence of three of their vessels with the Athenian forces at Syracuse shows that they were still ready to plunder their old enemies if opportunity occurred,[2] and it was not until the next century that the tyrants of Syracuse were able to control the Tyrrhenian Sea effectively. The continuance of piracy[3] caused Dionysius I to lead an important expedition into the northern sea, in the course of which he occupied Pyrgi, the port of Caere, and penetrated as far as Corsica.[4] It is probable that a permanent occupation of the island was attempted, and that the " Syracusan harbour " dates from this expedition.[5]

Syracusan control of the Tuscan Sea cannot long have survived the death of Dionysius in 367 B.C., and what information we possess shows that the pirates once more became active. Etruria, indeed, could no longer be reckoned as a naval power, but certain of the Etruscan cities still possessed ships, eighteen of which were serving with Agathocles in 307 B.C.[6] Besides the

1. Diod. Sic., XI, 88.

2. Thuc., VI, 103; cf. VI, 88. The Tyrrhenian sailors proved their value in one of the engagements in the Great Harbour (VII, 53).

3. Diod. Sic. (XV, 14) alleges that this was merely a πρόφασις, his real purpose being the acquisition of the temple-treasures at Pyrgi. There is a similar misrepresentation with regard to his action in the Adriatic (v. below).

4. Diod. Sic., l.c.; Strabo, V, 226; Servius ad Aen., X, 184. (A brief mention in (Arist.) Oec., II, 1349b; Polyaenus, V, 2, 21.)

5. Diod. Sic., V, 13. See Meyer, G. D. A., V, § 825.

6. Diod. Sic., XX, 61.

Etruscans themselves, we find other native Italian states taking to the sea. We have already seen that the " Tyrrhenian " Postumius, executed by Timoleon, was no Etruscan.[1] He may perhaps, as Mommsen suggests,[2] have been a native of Antium, whose fleet about this time was confiscated by the Romans, and the population forbidden the sea.[3] The fact that Postumius expected a friendly reception in Syracuse suggests that piracy was being practised on a large scale on the western coasts of Italy, Greek and Italian pirates making common cause to raid the more peaceful inhabitants. Greek pirates undoubtedly were active about the year 350 B.C. We hear that the coast of Latium was infested by them, and that on one occasion they made common cause with a band of Gauls, who had settled in the Alban hills.[4] In addition to the depredations of Greek and native marauders, there are indications that towards the end of the century the coasts of Italy were suffering also from the raids of the Carthaginians. The treaty of 306 B.C., the second which Polybius quotes,[5] contained a clause by which protection is guaranteed to the subjects of Rome, and to some extent to her allies, against Carthaginian activities.

1. See above, p. 130.
2. *History*, I, p. 425.
3. Livy, VIII, 14.
4. *Ib.*, VII, 25. Perhaps the story in Aelian (*N. A.*, VIII, 19) belongs to this date : The pig knows his master's voice. Some pirates made a descent on the Tyrrhenian coast, and carried off a number of pigs. When they put to sea, the swineherds shouted to the pigs, who all ran to one side of the vessel and overturned it. The pigs swam ashore, but the pirates were drowned. (One hopes that this is an historical incident, but see below, p. 266).
5. Polyb., III, 24.

With her growing responsibilities, it became increasingly more necessary for Rome to provide an effective defence of the Italian coasts. The piratical states in Italy were reduced, or at any rate prevented from carrying out their malpractices in Italian waters. Special protection was given to the coasts by the foundation of additional burgess colonies, the *coloniae maritimae*, whose settlers were exempted from service in the legions.[1] Rome was not the first state in the Mediterranean to be driven by pressure from marauders to organise a navy. In addition to fixed garrisons on the coast, increased attention was devoted to the organisation of the fleet. *Duoviri navales* appear for the first time in 311 B.C. and in the following year we hear of a squadron, in which the *socii navales* were serving, operating under the command of a Roman officer, who had been placed in charge of the *ora maritima*. Whether the expedition to Corsica, of which we hear about this date,[2] was connected in any way with the suppression of raiders from the island is unknown. As the suzerainty of Rome was extended over the Greek towns of Italy, the number of ships at her disposal was increased, and made the policing of Italian waters more easy. During the next half-century, except for the Carthaginian raids of the first Punic war, there is little word of piracy in the Tuscan Sea. The

1. See Mommsen, I, p. 427. The colonies of Antium (Livy, VIII, 14), Tarracina (VIII, 21), Pontiae (IX, 28) all date from the second half of the fourth century B.C. The last, which was apparently a *Latin* colony (Livy, XXVIII, 10), had originally been a Volscian settlement off the Circeian promontory, and the reason for the Roman occupation may have been similar to that which led to the occupation of Antium.

2. Theophrastus, *Hist. Plant.*, V, 8, 1-2.

fact that the more incorrigible of the Italian pirates were compelled to extend their cruises far afield into the eastern seas, testifies to the efficacy of the measures adopted by Rome in home waters.

Rome emerged from the first Punic war as the principal naval power in the Mediterranean, from the second as the mistress of the whole of the western basin. It is interesting to see how far she carried out the duties which were now imposed upon her, and to compare the methods by which she attempted to solve the problems that faced her in the different areas which she was called upon to police. The duty of policing the western seas fell to her at a time when that area had been thoroughly upset by the long Punic wars, but at the same time she had certain initial advantages. It is improbable that Carthage had tolerated piracy in the islands which she controlled. The lawlessness in the case of Corsica, which Strabo mentions,[1] seems under the Roman government to have been limited to brigandage on land. The same writer speaks of Sardinian raids on Pisa, but without any precise indication of their date.[2] Such raids may occasionally have taken place under the Roman government, but we scarcely hear of them, and in view of the necessity of keeping open the route to Spain, which was already threatened from the north, the Romans would see to it that no threat of piracy from Corsica and Sardinia would trouble their communications. The most serious threats

1. Strabo, IV, 224.
2. *Ib.*, IV, 225.

to the peace of the coasts of the Western Mediterranean came from the northern shores of the Tyrrhenian Sea, from the wild tribes of the Apennines and Maritime Alps, known generally as Ligures. For some eighty years after the conclusion of the second Punic war, the Romans were engaged in constant frontier wars and *razzias*, Liguria, as Livy puts it, forming a perpetual training-ground for the Roman armies.[1] The country was rugged, poor, and difficult to penetrate, and the inhabitants had for long been accustomed to live by pillaging their neighbours or by taking service as mercenaries abroad.[2] They were active hunters and brave mariners, and in their light barks did not shrink from distant voyages by sea, their seamanship enabling them to face all weathers.[3] The Ligurians of the Apennines had long been a source of trouble to the Etruscans of Pisa, exposed as they were to raids by land and sea.[4] But both sides of the Apennines suffered from their attacks, and after their first contact with the Romans[5] we find them making common cause with the Gauls of the Po Valley in resisting the Roman advance. In the Hannibalic war they had eagerly supported the Carthaginian generals, and in the year 200 some of their tribes were concerned with the Gauls and Hamilcar the Carthaginian in the sack

1. Livy, XXXIX, 1.

2. Ligurian mercenaries served with the Carthaginians as early as 480 B.C. (Hdt., VII, 165). We find them also with Agathocles (Diod. Sic., XXI, 3). See also Polyb., I, 17 ; I, 67.

3. Diod. Sic., V, 39.

4. Strabo, V, 223. For a great land-raid on Pisa see Livy, XXXV, 3.

5. Livy, *Ep.*, XX.

of Cremona and Placentia.[1] The pacification of
these Eastern Ligurians, which belongs rather to
the history of the Roman conquest of Italy, lies
outside our present subject. Large numbers
were exterminated by the Roman victories, or
deported from their mountain strongholds to
Central Italy.[2] To hold the remnant in check,
colonies were planted at Pisa and Luna[3] and a
military road drawn along the coast to Genoa
and Vada Sabata, the interior being opened by
roads crossing the Apennines from Vada Sabata
and Genoa to Dertona.[4]

In Western Liguria the duty of policing the
coastline was left for the most part to the
Massaliotes, whose naval stations could control
the coast as far east as Nicaea.[5] Nevertheless
about the year 181 we find the Massaliotes
complaining that the piracies of the Ingauni, who
occupied the coast opposite Genoa, were inter-
fering with sea-borne commerce as far as the
Pillars of Hercules.[6] For the first time, a Roman
squadron was detailed to act against them,
but as it at first consisted only of ten ships and
was ordered to cover the coast from Massalia to
Campania, it is unlikely that it proved particularly
effective. A vigorous offensive, however, was

1. Livy, XXII, 35; XXVIII, 39; XXIX, 5.

2. *Ib.*, XL, 38.

3. *Ib.*, XLI, 13. The MSS. vary between Luna and Luca (Luca in
Velleius, I, 15).

4. On the *Via Aemilia Scauri* of 109 B.C., see Strabo, V, 217, τὴν διὰ
Πισῶν καὶ Λούνης μέχρι Σαβάτων κἀντεῦθεν διὰ Δερθώνης. The section
of the *Via Postumia* from Dertona to Genoa had been constructed in
148 B.C.

5. See Strabo, IV, 180, 184.

6. Plutarch, *Aemilius*, 6; Livy, XL, 25-29.

begun by land under the consul Aemilius, and after what had almost proved a disaster, he succeeded in completely defeating the Ingauni, while the reinforced fleet received the surrender of thirty-two of their pirate-boats. The Romans in this district were faced with a difficult problem. It was essential for them to maintain communications with Spain both by land and sea. Already in 189 B.C. a force under the praetor Baebius had been cut up on its way to the province ; but at the same time it was clearly realised in Rome that the Ligurians of the Maritime Alps constituted a useful barrier against Gallic aggression from the North.[1] On the whole, during the first half of the second century B.C., it seems that the Massaliotes were able to cope with the situation, with occasional assistance from Rome. But in 155 B.C. they themselves, as well as their garrisons at Nicaea and Antipolis, were being severely pressed by raiders from the tribes of the Oxybii and Deciatae. An attack on a Roman deputation, sent to restore order, necessitated an expedition on a large scale under the consul Opimius. He succeeded in defeating and disarming both tribes, and ordered that hostages should be deposited with the Massaliotes, as the immediate guardians of the coast.[2] Wars with the tribes along this coast continued, however, for some years. We hear of triumphs over the Ligurians as late as the years 123, 122 and 117. After eighty years of fighting, according to Strabo,[3] the Romans

1. See Plutarch, l.c.
2. Livy, Ep., XLVII ; Polyb., XXXIII, 7-11.
3. Strabo IV, 203. On the sea-route to Spain, see Livy, XXXIV, 8.

had secured only a strip of the coast some twelve furlongs wide, to allow the passage of their armies.

The security of the sea-route to Spain was also the cause of the expedition sent in 123 B.C. to occupy the Balearic Islands. The inhabitants, if uncivilised, had the reputation of being peaceful[1]; but if they were not themselves responsible for an outbreak of piracy which occurred in these waters, it is stated that they were ready to make common cause with the pirates who had begun to infest the sea. The outbreak was perhaps due to the decline of the power of Massalia, but it was promptly dealt with by the Romans, *plurima incolarum caede*. To secure the islands, Metellus founded the towns of Palma and Pollentia, introducing three thousand Roman colonists from Spain.

A still more serious problem faced the Romans in the Adriatic, the eastern shores of which have throughout history been inhabited by wild, uncivilised tribes, who were active marauders by land and sea, and were constantly reinforced from the interior. When once she had taken the problem in hand, Rome acted with vigour. The methods which she adopted for controlling the Illyrian coast were for a long time successful; but she was eventually to find that only by a complete occupation of the interior as well as of the coasts could the fierce inhabitants of the Albanian and Dalmatian coasts be held down. Sheltered by a network of islands, the tribes known to the

1. Strabo, III, 167; Diod. Sic., V, 17, 18. A very different account, of the Balearic islanders is given, however, by Florus, III, 8; see also Orosius V, 13.

Romans as the Istrians, Iapydes, Liburnians, Dalmatians and Illyrians[1] were hard fighters, bold seamen and skilful builders of ships. From one of them was derived the name and design of the later Roman war-vessel.[2]

It is not without significance that the shores of the Adriatic had for long resisted the Greek attempts at occupation. As late as the beginning of the fourth century, the dangers of its coasts were proverbial.[3] It is true that at an early date the Greeks had been accustomed to trade with the Po-land,[4] but in spite of its harbourless character it seems that their vessels hugged the Italian coast and gave as wide a berth as possible to the pirate nests on the eastern shore,[5] where the Greeks until a late period were unable to found any settlement further north than Epidamnos and Apollonia. It was not until the beginning of the fourth century that the Greeks were able to establish any control over the Adriatic coasts, when the task was attempted by the tyrants of Syracuse.

1. I have used " Illyrian " throughout this chapter to mean the peoples south of the river Naro (proprie dicti Illyri, Pliny, *N. H.*, III, 144). For its wider sense, including the peoples between the Adriatic and the Danube, see Appian, *Illyr.*, 6.

2. Appian, *Illyr.*, 3, on the piracies of the Liburni, and the Λιβύρνιδες. (Full references in Torr, *op. cit.*, p. 16.) The *lembus* and *pristis*, which formed a considerable element in the fleets of Philip V, were similarly derived from Illyrian models (Polyb., V, 109 ; Torr, p. 115). Domaszewski, *Rhein. Museum*, 1903, p. 388, notes that the reappearance of piracy in the reign of Severus Alexander necessitated a return to the *pristis* on the part of the Roman government.

3. Lysias, *ap.* Athenaeus, XIII, 612, where the dangers of the Adriatic are vigorously expressed.

4. See Hdt., I, 163 ; IV, 33 ; V, 9 ; Strabo, V, 214 ; IX, 421 (Spina is called a Greek city possessing a treasury at Delphi). See Meyer, *G. D. A.*, II, §424.

5. Livy's description of the voyage of Cleonymus in 303 B.C. (X, 2) perhaps illustrates the Greek route up the Adriatic.

We have already examined the policy of Dionysius I in the western sea. A similar attempt was made by him to establish his supremacy in the Adriatic. In addition to Syracusan settlements on the Italian coast, at Ancona and in the Po Valley,[1] we find Dionysius forming an alliance with the so-called Illyrians, and utilising them to establish his influence in Epiros by means of the restoration of the Molossian king Alcetas. His settlement of Lissos on the mainland, where a large dockyard was built, lay not far to the south of the later Illyrian capital of Scodra, and was an important factor in his schemes for controlling this coast. Syracusan influence reached as far north as the Dalmatian Islands, where the Greek settlements of Pharos, and probably also Issa and Corcyra Nigra, were established about this time under Dionysius' protection.[2] It is impossible to say how far Dionysius was successful in reducing the piracy of the Adriatic, but it is clear that after his death it was again rampant. The younger Dionysius was compelled to occupy two cities on the Apulian coast to serve as a base against marauders, who were extending their raids into the Ionian Sea.[3] We have already noted a similar attempt on the part of the Athenians to protect their commerce in the Adriatic by the establishment of a naval base. The inscription which

1. Strabo, V, 241 ; *ib.*, 212. See Meyer, *G. D. A.*, V, § 822. (Plutarch, *Dio*, 11 ; Pliny, *N. H.*, III, 121.)

2. Diod. Sic., XV, 13-14 ; Strabo, VII, 315. (Pliny, *N. H.*, III, 140 ; Scylax, 23 ; Scymnus, 413-4, 426-7 ; *C. I. G.*, 1837 *b* ; Dittenberger, *Syll.*³, 141.)

3. Diod. Sic., XVI, 5.

records the attempt makes it clear that after the
fall of the Syracusan power in the Adriatic,
Italian as well as Illyrian pirates were active in
that sea.[1]

As is well known, the first appearance of the
Roman legions in the East was occasioned by the
piracies of the Illyrians under Queen Teuta.
The decline of the Epirote kingdom after the
death of Alexander, son of Pyrrhus, had given an
opportunity to the Illyrian prince Agron to
build up a formidable power, which extended
from the neighbourhood of Epirus as far as the
Dalmatian Islands, where the Greek settlements,
with the possible exception of Issa, all acknow-
ledged his suzerainty. It is probable that their
population had by this time become very mixed,
under the rule of petty princes of half-Greek
origin, amongst whom is to be reckoned the
famous Demetrius of Pharos.[2]

1. See above, p. 128.

2. On the πολιδυνάσται of Polyb. V, 4, see Niese, II, p. 278. Issa was
the scene of Teuta's reception of the Coruncanii; she was besieging it at
the time, but it is by no means certain that it had not obtained freedom by
a revolt. See Polyb., II, 8, ἐπολιόρκει τὴν ῎Ισσαν διὰ τὸ ταύτην ἔτι μόνον
ἀπειθεῖν αὐτῇ. This follows a statement that a wide-spread revolt in Illyria
had elsewhere been put down. The later authorities do not help. From
Appian, Illyr., 7, and Dio Cass., fr. 151, it would seem that Issa was independent during Agron's reign, but Zonaras, VIII, 19, implies that a revolt
had taken place : ἐθελοντal τοῖς ῾Ρωμαίοις παραδεδώκασιν ἑαυτοὺς τῷ σφῶν
κρατοῦντι ἀχθόμενοι ᾿Αγρῶνι τῷ τῶν Σαρδιαίων βασιλεῖ.

It is not easy to determine the extent of Agron's kingdom. Polybius
(II, 2) merely says that he controlled larger forces by land and sea than any
previous Illyrian prince. Appian's account (Illyr., 7) is demonstrably
incorrect. The capital in the reign of Genthius was Scodra (Livy, XLV, 26 ;
cf. Polyb., XXVIII, 8), but this is nowhere stated to have been the case in
Agron's reign. We should perhaps look for it at Rhizon, on the Bocche di
Cattaro, to which Teuta fled for refuge. (Cf. Zippel, Die Römische Herrschaft
in Illyrien, p. 44.) Of the tribes mentioned by Polybius as surrendering
to the Romans, the Atintanes were probably not subject to Agron at the
time of his death (see Polyb., II, 5, § 8 ; contrast, however, Zippel, p. 43) ;
the Parthini, whom Strabo (VII, 326) places with other tribes above

The raids of the Illyrians at this time were extended along the whole of the western shores of Greece. They had long been in the habit of plundering the coasts of Elis and Messenia[1]; Pausanias has a story of their dealings with Mothone, which illustrates both their cunning and effrontery. A party of Illyrians anchored near the town and opened a trade with the inhabitants, very much to the profit of the latter. When all suspicion had been allayed and a brisk trade was proceeding on the shore, the Illyrians swept a number of men and women on board their ships and put to sea.[2] A very similar trick was attempted at Epidamnos. The Illyrians landed from their ships, professedly to get water. But concealing their short swords in the water-jars, they cut down the guard at the city gate and were only kept from seizing the town by the bravery of the inhabitants.[3] At sea their tactics resembled those of the Moorish pirates of a later date. Enemy ships were overwhelmed by the swift rush of a boarding party. In the fight with the

Epidamnos and Apollonia, appear from the account of Scerdilaidas' march (Polyb., II, 6) to have been dependent, but the alacrity with which they joined the Romans shows that Agron and Teuta's sovereignty was not very secure. The hostility of Epidamnos and Apollonia shows also that the coast to the south of Lissos was not completely in Agron's hands. (The peace-terms show that Lissos itself was Illyrian.) The centre of Agron's kingdom was formed by the Ardiaei (cf. Dio Cass., fr. 49; Zonaras, VIII, 19, 20), whom Polybius mentions as alone offering a serious resistance to the Romans. Appian (Illyr., 3) speaks of them as the leading seamen of the coast, and their importance at an earlier date is attested by Theopompus (fr. 39, a and b, ed. Hunt). The Dalmatians, according to Polybius, XXXII, 9, were later subject to Pleuratus, and it is probable that Agron's kingdom reached as far as Delminium.

1. Polyb., II, 5.

2. Pausanias, IV, 35.

3. Polyb., II, 9.

heavy Achaean warship off Paxos they lashed together four of their vessels, presenting them broadside to the enemy ship, which rammed. While her prow was encumbered with the wreckage, the Illyrians leapt on board, and overcame the crew by their numbers.[1]

An impetus was given to Agron's ambition by an alliance with Demetrius II of Macedon.[2] Probably the Macedonian sought to paralyse the dangerous attacks of the Dardani by embroiling them with the Illyrians of the coast ; the Illyrian fleet would in any case be useful in his war with the Aetolians.[3] On the suggestion of Demetrius, Agron sent a force to oppose the Aetolians, which was successful in relieving the town of Medion and inflicted a heavy defeat on the Aetolians. Agron himself is said to have met his end in celebrating his first victory over regular Greek troops, but his widow Teuta, in addition to sending out plundering expeditions to attack all whom they might meet, embarked on a career of conquest in the South, capturing Phoenice, the chief city of Epiros, and establishing Illyrian suzerainty over the country.[4] Thanks to the support which had been rendered in the affair at Medion, Illyrian influence was also supreme in Acarnania.

Hitherto the Romans had abstained from all interference, in spite of long-continued attacks

1. *Ib.*, II, 10. At Medion we hear of 5,000 Illyrian troops embarked in 100 *lembi* (II, 3), but perhaps the number of fighting men was greater on this occasion, since land operations were in prospect.

2. Polyb., II, 2.

3. See Polyb., II, 6, § 5, and Niese, *l.c.*

4. Polyb., II, 7.

on vessels sailing from Italy.[1]   But at the time of the capture of Phoenice Illyrian detachments from the main body had attacked Italian traders, killing and capturing a large number.[2] A predatory state, whose influence now extended as far as the entrance to the Corinthian Gulf, was bound to be a matter of concern to the Senate, and now (230 B.C.) in response to representations from many quarters, an embassy was sent to Queen Teuta to expostulate.[3] The Queen had recently succeeded in putting down a serious revolt among her subjects, and was fired by the amount of booty obtained from Phoenice to undertake further exploits. To the expostulations of the Roman ambassadors, the brothers Gaius and Lucius Coruncanius, she replied that it was not customary for the Illyrian kings to interfere with the pursuits of their subjects by sea, but that she would see to it that the Romans suffered no public wrong. When the younger of the two brothers replied that Rome would make it her business to teach the Illyrians a better custom, the Queen, in return for a freedom of speech that was " salutary but scarcely opportune," caused him to be murdered on his return journey.

Thus for the first time a Roman force crossed the sea to Greece. But before its arrival the Queen had sent out a new fleet, which defeated an armament fitted out by the Achaean and

1.   This point is strongly emphasised by Holleaux, *Rome, La Grèce et les Monarchies Hellénistiques*, pp. 25 *seqq.*

2.   Polyb., II, 8 ; cf. Dio Cass., *fr.* 49.

3.   Appian (*Illyr.*, 7) states that the Roman embassy was sent in answer to an appeal from Issa, whose envoy Cleemporus was murdered at the same time as Coruncanius.

Aetolian leagues, captured the town of Corcyra, and laid siege to Epidamnos. Unfortunately for Teuta, the Illyrian garrison of Corcyra had been placed under the command of Demetrius of Pharos. Having already incurred the Queen's suspicions and fearful of her displeasure, he opened treacherous communication with the commander of the Roman fleet now on its way, and delivered the Illyrian garrison of the town into his hands. Under the guidance of Demetrius of Pharos the Roman forces, which, according to Polybius, consisted of 200 ships, 20,000 foot and 200 horse, had little difficulty in overcoming the Illyrian Queen. Epidamnos and Issa were relieved, a number of Illyrian towns on the coast captured, the resistance of the Ardiaei broken, and a display of Roman power made in the interior. In the spring of the following year (228), Teuta capitulated.[1]

It is not easy to discover the terms of the settlement which the Romans now imposed on Illyria. According to Polybius, Teuta was compelled to surrender the greater part of her kingdom, to pay tribute, and to give an undertaking not to sail beyond Lissos with more than two *lembi*, both unarmed. The greater part of the kingdom was placed under Demetrius of Pharos, who thus acquired a large dominion.[2] The account given by Appian, however, says that Demetrius of Pharos, whom the Romans already had come to distrust, was given only a few

1. Polyb., II, 8-11. Zippel, *op. cit.*, p. 51, interprets the words προῆγον εἰς τοὺς εἴσω τόπους τῆς Ἰλλυρίδος (Polyb., II, 11, § 10) as referring only to an advance up the Adriatic.
2. Polyb., II, 12.

places as a reward for his treachery, but that the bulk of Teuta's kingdom was left to Pinnes, the infant son of Agron by a former wife.[1] But although Polybius makes no mention of the infant Pinnes, there can be little doubt that his version of the settlement is otherwise the correct one. The policy adopted by the Romans was one of their first attempts to control a dangerous district through a client prince. Demetrius of Pharos seemed at the time the obvious man for the post, but lest he should prove intractable, the old royal house was not entirely dispossessed, and apart from the infant Pinnes it had another representative in Scerdilaidas.[2]

We first hear of Scerdilaidas as the commander of the troops which were sent by land to reinforce Teuta's armament besieging Phoenice.[3] He next appears in company with Demetrius of Pharos at the head of a pirating expedition, which, in defiance of the treaty with Rome, set out to plunder the western shores of Greece in 220 B.C. To this expedition Demetrius contributed 50 *lembi*, Scerdilaidas 40.[4] Demetrius himself, as we have seen, had already formed a connection with the Macedonian court by the year 222.[5] It is impossible that a Roman protectorate of Illyria could have been viewed with favour by the Macedonians ; during the three wars with Rome the question of

1. Appian, *Illyr.*, 7-8. According to Dio Cassius, *fr.* 46, Demetrius of Pharos became guardian of Agron's infant son Pinnes (see below, p. 179).

2. Possibly a brother of Agron, see Niese, II, p. 279.

3. Polyb., II, 5.

4. *Ib.*, IV, 16.

5. See above, p. 136.

the control of the Illyrian coast assumes an ever-increasing importance. Relying on Macedonian support and encouraged by the preoccupation of the Romans with Gallic wars and threats from Carthage,[1] Demetrius seized the opportunity to attack the Illyrian cities subject to Rome, and further defied the Romans by leading a plundering expedition south of Lissos, to the Peloponnese and Cyclades.[2]

The Romans were fully alive to the situation. A hostile Illyria, in alliance with Macedonia, would constitute a risk that might well prove fatal during the coming struggle with Carthage.[3] Vigorous action was taken, and a second armament was sent to the Illyrian coast in 219 B.C.[4] The storming of the fortress of Dimale, believed to be impregnable, struck terror into Demetrius' supporters ; next, sailing to Pharos, the Romans captured and destroyed it after a short defence. Demetrius fled for protection to Philip of Macedon, whose evil genius he was now to become.[5]

We have no direct statement as to the territorial arrangements made by the Romans after either expedition. There is no doubt that in 228 B.C., the Greek cities of Corcyra, Epidamnos, Apollonia

1. See Polyb., III, 16.

2. Polyb., IV, 16. According to Appian *Illyr.*, 8, he also induced the Istrians to begin hostilities with Rome.

3. See Polyb., III, 16, εἰς ἃ βλέποντες Ῥωμαῖοι καὶ θεωροῦντες ἀνθοῦσαν τὴν Μακεδονίαν ἀρχήν.

4. For the date see Polyb., IV, 37.

5. Polyb., III, 18-19. Our authorities again differ as to Demetrius' end. Appian, *Illyr.*, 8, asserts that he returned to the Adriatic and was killed by the Romans. This is absolutely at variance with Polybius' account of his death at Messene (III, 19).

and Issa were declared free and placed under Roman protection. Polybius states, as we have seen, that during the operations against Teuta the Ardiaei were reduced, the Parthini and Atintanes surrendering voluntarily. During the winter of 228-227 a legion was enrolled locally to watch the Ardiaei and other tribes which had surrendered.[1] The subsequent fate of the Ardiaei is uncertain. If it is the case that they had formed the principal part of Agron's kingdom, it is probable that they were restored to Teuta and Pinnes.[2] The position with regard to the Parthini is also uncertain; we find Demetrius in possession of Dimale, one of their principal towns,[3] but this may well have been one of the Illyrian towns subject to Rome which he is said by Polybius to have captured.[4] The Atintanes were now, as in 219 B.C., placed on the footing of subject allies of Rome.[5]

The settlement in 219 B.C. is fortunately clearer. In the treaty between Hannibal and Philip it is stipulated that the Romans shall no longer remain in possession of Corcyra, Apollonia and Epidamnos, Pharos, Dimale and the Parthini, or of Atintania.[6] The list enumerates the states

1. Polyb., II, 12.

2. They certainly formed part of the kingdom of Scerdilaidas and Pleuratus. In the negotiations of 208 B.C. (Livy, XXVII, 30) a demand is made for their restoration to Scerdilaidas and Pleuratus; they had apparently been conquered by Philip in his Illyrian campaigns of 211/210 (Livy, XXVI, 25; Polyb., VIII, 13-15).

3. Livy, XXIX, 12.

4. Polyb., III, 18 (cf. III, 16).

5. See Appian, *Illyr.*, 8, where Demetrius is said to have detached them from the Romans.

6. Polyb., VII, 9.

of Southern Illyria and Northern Epiros over
which Rome in 215 B.C. claimed to exercise a direct
suzerainty. The Greek cities were nominally
free, but the character of their freedom, as it
appeared to the Greek mind, may be judged from
the unprintable jest about Corcyra preserved by
Strabo.[1] It is clear that in 219 B.C., Rome
established a protectorate in Southern Illyria and
Northern Epiros as a makeweight both to
Macedonian and Illyrian ambitions, the kings of
Illyria being still to some extent her dependents.
It is likely enough that a similar arrangement was
attempted after the first pacification, the greater
part of Illyria being handed over to Demetrius,
but with a possible rival to him remaining in the
old royal house, which was not entirely dispossessed.

Roman calculation had been upset in the first
experiment by the faithlessness of Demetrius.
In the second, fortune was more favourable.
Scerdilaidas, who had at first joined with
Demetrius in his plundering raid, parted company
with him after their failure at Pylos. He then
for a time put his forces at the disposal of the
Aetolians (220 B.C.), but soon quarrelled with
them and joined Philip,[2] who promised him

1. Strabo, VII, *frag.* 8.

2. The chronological sequence of events in Philip's dealings with
Scerdilaidas is important and can be made out with fair accuracy from
Polybius :

220-219 Winter: Agreement between the two, Polyb., IV, 29. (Zippel,
        op. cit., p. 60, is guilty of a serious blunder in dating it to 217 B.C.)
219.   Roman expedition against Demetrius of Pharos.
218.   Scerdilaidas sends only fifteen ships to Philip at Cephallenia owing
        to disturbances among the πολιδυνάσται of Illyria (Polyb., V, 4).
217.   Scerdilaidas' vessels attack Taurion's squadron at Leucas, and
        proceed to their plundering raid off Malea (V, 95). Philip
        attempts to catch them (V, 101).
        (Peace of Naupactos (V, 105).)

assistance in reducing Illyria. In his agreement with Scerdilaidas, Philip counted on the active assistance of the Illyrian fleet, but, when demanded, the assistance sent was small, and fortunately for the Romans a quarrel soon broke out between the two. Scerdilaidas felt himself cheated by his ally. His ships made a treacherous attack on a squadron belonging to Philip's allies in the harbour of Leucas, and sailing to Malea started new piracies in that ancient haunt. Scerdilaidas himself, in the same year, invaded the Macedonian frontier.

There is no mention in Polybius of the Roman embassy which, as Livy says, was sent at this time (217 B.C.) to Pinnes, but the statement in Livy is so definite that it is difficult to reject it.[1] The ambassadors demanded the payment of the tribute or, if a postponement was necessary, that hostages should be furnished. (At the same time an embassy was sent to Philip demanding the surrender of Demetrius of Pharos.) It was vital to the Romans at this time (the year of Trasimene) to maintain their influence in Illyria, and it is

> After the conclusion of the peace, Philip returns to Macedonia and finds that Scerdilaidas has invaded his frontiers. He retaliates before the winter (V, 108).
> The Roman embassy to Pinnes (Livy, XXII, 33) is also to be dated to this year.
> 217-216 Winter : Philip's preparations to raise a fleet (Polyb., V, 109).
> 216. Philip advances by sea to Apollonia (V, 110) where he hears that a Roman squadron is on its way to help Scerdilaidas.
> There is, unfortunately, absolute silence as to the position of Scerdilaidas in the important year 219. We hear of him in the previous winter preparing, with Philip's help, to make himself master of Illyria, and still in alliance with Philip in 218, when he is troubled by disturbances in Illyria. In 217 (the year of the Roman embassy to Pinnes) he has thrown Philip over and is engaged in direct hostilities with him, receiving help from Rome in the following year.

1. Livy, XXII, 33, Ad Pineum quoque regem in Illyrios legati missi. The year 217 is certain, but Livy gives no indication of the season.

more than probable that a part of the message to Pinnes was that the alliance with Macedon should be brought to an end. The name Pinnes, or Pineus, can hardly be an invention on the part of Livy, and he must, though a minor, have been the nominal king at the time. But all power was in the hands of Scerdilaidas, and he alone is mentioned by Polybius.[1] The Roman embassy coincides with Scerdilaidas' quarrel with Philip ; there was no further alliance with Macedon, and henceforward the conquest of Illyria becomes an important part of Philip's schemes. As both sides knew well, it was a necessary preliminary to an invasion of Italy ; it was vigorously prosecuted by Philip,[2] but Scerdilaidas stood firmly by Rome, and when hard pressed received such assistance as she could spare.[3] In later documents we find him officially recognised as the ally of Rome, and his son Pleuratus continued his father's policy.[4] The Roman experiment worked well, when they had found the right man for the position of client

1. According to Zippel, *op. cit.*, p. 59, Scerdilaidas was appointed Pinnes' guardian in 219 after the Roman expedition against Demetrius of Pharos, Demetrius having filled the position before that date. Cf. Dio. Cass., *fr.* 46, Δημήτριος ἔκ τε τῆς τοῦ Πίννου ἐπιτροπεύσεως καὶ ἐκ τοῦ τὴν μητέρα αὐτοῦ Τρίτευταν τῆς Τεύτας ἀποθανούσης γῆμαι. In *frag.* 151, Teuta is again said to be the stepmother of Pinnes (cf. Appian, *Illyr.* 7) ; but the passage of Dio is the sole authority for Triteuta and for Demetrius' guardianship. It is far more probable, to my mind, that Scerdilaidas had been the guardian of Pinnes from the first, and that the Romans had in 228 set up two independent chieftains in Illyria, Demetrius of Pharos and Scerdilaidas, the latter representing Pinnes and the royal house. In the year 222 they appear together, each at the head of an independent force.

2. Polyb., V, 101, 108 ; VIII, 13-15 ; Livy, XXIV, 40 ; XXVI, 24-25.

3. Polyb., V, 109-110 ; Livy, XXIV, 40.

4. Livy, XXVI, 24 (211 B.C.). The reading is uncertain ; possibly Scerdilaidas alone is meant. In XXVII, 30 (208 B.C.), Scerdilaidas and Pleuratus are spoken of as reigning together, but in XXIX, 12 (205 B.C.) Pleuratus is reigning alone, Scerdilaidas, presumably, being dead.

king of Illyria. During the second Macedonian war, Illyria constituted a serious menace to Philip's flank. We hear of no further disturbances of a piratical character in the reign of Scerdilaidas himself or of his successor. Pleuratus continued to assist the Romans in the war with Antiochus and the Aetolians,[1] and he was mentioned by the Scipios, with Massinissa, as the ideal client king.[2]

After some years of peace the Adriatic again fell into a disturbed state, at the close of the reign of Pleuratus. In 181 B.C. the inhabitants of Brundisium and Tarentum were complaining of descents on their coasts, and when the piracies of the Ligurians necessitated the maintenance of a special squadron to patrol the Tuscan Sea, a similar force was commissioned to protect the southern part of Italy as far as Barium.[3] In the complaints received by the Romans from Apulia there was special mention of the Istrians, and the praetor, Duronius, was empowered to act against them. In his report he stated that all the pirate vessels operating in the Adriatic came from the kingdom of Genthius, the new king of Illyria, but apart from a demand for the release of Roman citizens detained at Corcyra, no action was taken at the time against Genthius himself.[4] It is probable enough that the Istrians were being encouraged by Genthius. Their country, the Pola Peninsula, was not indeed a part of his

1. Livy, XXXVIII, 7.

2. Polyb., XXI, 11.

3. Livy, XL, 18. See above, p. 164. Probably the ten ships under Duronius (Livy, XL, 42), of which we hear on the Illyrian coast, were this squadron.

4. Livy, XL, 42. Corcyra Nigra is intended.

kingdom, but like all the inhabitants of the coast
they were reckoned as Illyrians,[1] and at an earlier
date are said to have been induced by the intrigues
of Demetrius of Pharos to engage in war with
Rome.[2] At the present time they were disturbed
by the preparations to found the colony of
Aquileia at the head of the Adriatic,[3] which,
together with its main purpose of protecting
Italy on the land side, would also serve to limit
Istrian activities by sea. After its foundation an
" Istrian " war was necessary during the years
178 and 177 to secure its safety, in which the Romans
suffered one serious disaster before the country
could be pacified.[4] During the war it is noticeable that additional protection was necessary on
the Adriatic coast. The squadron of ten ships
was doubled, ten ships covering the coast from
Tarentum to Ancona, ten, which were ordered
also to co-operate with the land forces, operating
from Ancona to Aquileia.[5]

For some years there was no open breach with
Genthius, but it was obvious that the success of
the system which had prevailed during the reign
of Pleuratus was at an end. Relying on
Pleuratus' loyalty, the Romans had for long
neglected the Illyrian coasts, but after his death[6]

1. Strabo, VIII, 315 ; on the harbour of Pola, see V, 215.

2. Appian, *Illyr.*, 8. See also Eutropius, III, 17 ; Orosius, IV, 13 ;
Zonaras, VIII, 20. Niese, II, 437, regards this war as suspicious, but the
notice in Livy, Ep. XX (cf. XXI, 16) seems conclusive. Istrian piracies are
mentioned by Livy (X, 2) as early as 301 B.C., but only in a very general way.

3. Livy, XXXIX, 55 ; XL, 26, 34.

4 ; *Ib.*, XLI, 1-5, 10-11.

5. *Ib.*, XLI, 1.

6. Genthius succeeded before 181 B.C. (Livy, XL, 42).

a widespread revolt had taken place in the northern part of the kingdom. The Dalmatians, to the north of the river Naro, had declared their independence and reduced the neighbouring territories, from which they levied tribute.[1] The report of the praetor in 180 B.C., as we have seen, indicated that all the Illyrian coast was disturbed, and before the outbreak of the third Macedonian war the people of Issa were complaining of plundering attacks on their territory and of the doubtful attitude of Genthius. It was further alleged that his ambassadors in Rome were nothing more than the agents of Perseus.[2] The Illyrian, however, was able partially to allay suspicion by the bribery of the agent sent to visit his court.[3]

Genthius himself is said to have been a weak man, addicted to wine and oppressive to his subjects. Early in his reign he had executed his brother Plator through jealousy of the influence he was likely to acquire by marriage with a princess of the Dardani.[4] It is possible that he saw in him a rival whom Roman diplomacy could easily raise against himself. During the early years of the Macedonian War the Romans secured his loyalty by an adroit manoeuvre on the part of the commander of their fleet, who requisitioned fifty-four of his *lembi* at Dyrrhachium on the assumption that they had been sent to co-operate with his own forces.

1. Polyb., XXXII, 9.
2. Livy, XLII, 26.
3. *Ib.*, XLII 37, 45.
4. Polyb., XXIX, 13; Livy, XLIV, 30.

But in the following year it was necessary to send troops and ships to Issa and Illyria to watch his wavering attitude.[1] It was not, however, until the year 168 that Genthius finally declared against Rome. In the previous year Perseus had been unwilling to pay the price at which Genthius hinted,[2] but finally an offer of 300 talents was wrung from him, and on receipt of ten, Genthius committed himself by imprisoning the Roman ambassadors at his court.[3] Though the balance of the sum promised by Perseus was never paid, the Illyrian king was now the openly declared enemy of Rome.

Perseus expected much from the new alliance. He was careful to have it proclaimed before his army,[4] and Illyrian envoys appeared with his own at Rhodes. But the Romans were fully alive to the dangers which the addition of the Illyrian fleet to the Macedonian would entail. A large armament was at once dispatched to reinforce the troops already in the country and, assisted by widespread disaffection among the subjects of Genthius, the praetor Anicius forced him to capitulate within thirty days.[5] Genthius was deprived of his kingdom, and carried to Rome for the triumph of his conqueror. The district which he had controlled was divided into three

1. Livy, XLIII, 9 (170 B.C.).

2. For the negotiations of 169 see Polyb., XXVIII, 8-9; Livy, XLVII, 19-20.

3. Polyb., XXIX, 3-4, 9; Livy, XLIV, 23, 27; Appian, *Mac.*, 18. According to Appian, *Illyr.*, 9, he accused them of being spies, perhaps in recollection of the charges brought against his own envoys by the Issaeans.

4. Polyb., XXIX, 4.

5. Livy, XLIV, 30-32.

parts, half the annual tribute which had formerly been paid to him being imposed on the majority of the tribes, while those which had voluntarily deserted him were exempted.[1] What was most important, all the Illyrian ships, to the number of 220, were confiscated and made over to the people of Corcyra, Apollonia and Epidamnos.[2]

By these measures, for a time at any rate, peace was restored in the lower Adriatic. Probably the Greek states with the help of the. confiscated Illyrian fleet were able to protect the coast, although we hear of raids from the interior on the weakened tribes which were subject to Rome.[3] But to the North, hard fighting still awaited the Romans. The Dalmatians, who had revolted from Genthius at the beginning of his reign, were still unsubdued and continued to raid the island of Issa and the friendly tribe of the Daorsei on the river Naro.[4] In 158 B.C. their complaints caused the Romans to send a deputation to inquire into the state of affairs on the Illyrian coasts. Its members were roughly handled (as a crowning insult their horses were stolen), and the Romans took the opportunity to make a display of their power on the Illyrian coast by sending an expedition in the following year, which almost destroyed the capital Delminium.[5] This was the first of

1. Livy, XLV, 26; cf. Diod. Sic., XXXI, 8. We, unfortunately, do not possess Polybius' version; Livy's account leaves much to be desired.

2. Livy, XLV, 43.

3. Appian, *Illyr.*, 10. The Ardiaei were still causing trouble in 135 B.C. (Livy, *Ep.* LVI; Appian, *Illyr.*, 10).

4. Polyb., XXXII, 9. For the Daorsei or Daorizi, see Strabo, VIII, 315, and Livy, XLV, 26.

5. Polyb., XXXII, 9, 13; Livy, *Ep.*, XLVII; Strabo, VIII, 315; Florus, IV, 12; *C.I.L.*, I, p. 176.

the series of " Dalmatian " wars. We hear of further expeditions against the Dalmatians in 119,[1] and against their northern neighbours the Iapydes in 129.[2] Unfortunately, we are very imperfectly informed as to the Adriatic for many years, but the pacification of the inhabitants of the upper Adriatic remained far from complete. The Dalmatians were active again in the year 78,[3] and it is clear that at the time of the civil wars they were thoroughly disturbed. In Strabo's day, even after the subjugation by Augustus, both Iapydes and Dalmatians still remained at a very low stage of civilisation.[4]

In spite of frequent reductions of the piratical states and confiscation of their ships, the Roman policy in the West can be said to have been only partially successful. No standing fleet was maintained under the Republic for patrolling the seas, and Rome was always inclined to leave the actual task of policing dangerous coasts to dependents, who could only be successful if properly supported. In the West Roman interests were too great for the matter to be altogether neglected ; the importance of maintaining communications with Spain necessitated that adequate support should be given to Massalia, when the Ligurian activities became too great ; similarly, the danger to the coasts of Italy was a sufficient reason for supporting the Greek states charged with the task of safe-

1. Livy, *Ep.*, LXII ; Appian, *Illyr.*, 11, who says that they had been guilty of no offence and offered no opposition ; *C.I.L.*, I, p. 177.

2. Livy, *Ep*, LIX ; Appian, *Illyr.*, 10 ; *C.I.L.*, I, p. 176.

3. Eutrop., VI, 4 ; Oros., V, 23.

4. Strabo, VIII 315.

guarding the lower Adriatic. Of the various experiments which the Romans made, the system of maintaining client kings as guardians of the peace was successful only when the loyalty of the ruler could be absolutely relied upon, and when he possessed sufficient power to keep both his subjects and his neighbours in check. The failure of the Illyrian policy in the reign of Genthius was due not only to his disloyalty but also to his weakness, which allowed the Dalmatians to become independent. The system of depopulation and extermination could have only a limited success. It could be pursued in islands like the Baleares, where Rome was able to plant settlers in the place of the original inhabitants ; but on the Illyrian and Ligurian coasts, where new tribes were pressing forward to take the place of the dispossessed, even a partial reduction of the inhabitants brought new dangers with it. This was realised by the Romans in the case of Liguria. In Illyria the defeated tribes lay at the mercy of their neighbours, and in spite of endless wars on the coast and in the interior, piracy was still liable to break out until Augustus organised the interior as far as the Danube. The fact that he was not faced with a Ligurian as well as a Dalmatian question at the beginning of his reign was due to the earlier penetration of the Hinterland and the carrying of Roman arms and civilisation beyond the Western Alps.

With their first interference in the affairs of Greece the Romans had appeared as the guardians of law and order, and their vigorous action had won for them a high reputation among the leading Greek states. But when, after the war with Philip of Macedon, Roman influence became predominant in Greece, their action against piracy lacked the vigour that had been shown in the Adriatic. We have already seen what were the special problems in the East, and to what extent the powers of the law-abiding states sufficed to solve them. In spite of the increasing importance of Italian trade, the Romans as yet had no direct political motives for maintaining large fleets in the Eastern Mediterranean, and at first the policy which had been pursued, when possible, in the West of allowing others to carry out the actual work of police, proved easy in the Aegean. The second Macedonian war had raised the Rhodians to the height of their power. Their navy was supreme, and for the purpose of suppressing piracy the forces of the reconstituted League of Islanders provided, as we have seen, a peculiarly valuable addition. In normal times, therefore, the Rhodian forces were likely to be sufficient for the task, with occasional assistance from the Romans. The activities of Nabis, for example, were curtailed by Flamininus in 195 B.C., and we hear that a force from Rhodes, as well as from Eumenes, took part in the campaign.[1] To a maritime people like the Rhodians, the importance of Nabis lay in the relations which he still maintained with certain of the Cretan cities, and in Crete lay the most difficult part of the problem which Rhodes was

1. Livy, XXXIV, 29; cf. chh. 33 and 36: fuerat autem ei magno fructui mare, omnem oram Maleae praedatoriis navibus infestam habenti.

called upon to solve. In the Syrian war, when both the Roman and the Rhodian fleets were fully occupied, bands of pirates were again active,[1] and the number of Roman and Italian prisoners who are reported to have been carried to Crete makes it probable that a large proportion of the pirate forces were drawn thence. A proclamation was issued by the Romans to the Cretans that they should compose their differences and surrender the prisoners. Their numbers must have been considerable if the statement of Livy's authority, Valerius Antias, is correct that the Gortynians, who alone obeyed the order, handed over as many as four thousand.[2] It has been suggested that the Roman intervention took place in response to the representations of the Rhodians,[3] but we are in fact ignorant of the relations which Rhodes maintained with Crete at the time.[4]

In spite of the confusion which prevailed in Crete, and the predatory character of its inhabitants, it seems that Rhodes was able, for the most part, to keep the seas clear during the interval between the second and third Macedonian wars, although the outbreak of piracy which accompanied the Syrian war showed that in abnormal times the Rhodian police was not sufficient. But with the rapid decline that followed the with-

1. Livy, XXXVII, 27 (cf. ch. 11). Pirates were also active off Cephallenia and interfered with the Roman supply-ships (ch. 13).

2. Livy, XXXVII, 60 (189 B.C.).

3. Niese, II, p. 750.

4. The only information which we possess concerns the year 168 B.C., when at the time of the Rhodian intrigues with Perseus an attempt was made by the republic to renew friendly relations with the Cretan towns (Polyb., XXIX, 10).

drawal of Roman favour after the third Macedonian war, it became obvious that the Rhodians were no longer equal to the task. A war with Crete that broke out about the year 155-154 taxed their resources to the utmost, and during its course we hear that a Cretan fleet ravaged the island of Siphnos.[1]

Roman jealousy had weakened the one power in the Aegean that was capable of dealing with the pirates, and nothing was put in its place. In another quarter of the Eastern Mediterranean a similar policy was promoting one of the most dangerous outbreaks of piracy that ever threatened the ancient world.

1. Polyb., XXXIII, 4, 13, 15-16; Diod. Sic., XXXI, 38, 43, 45; Trogus, *Prolog.*, XXXV, Bellum piraticum inter Cretas et Rhodios. See van Gelder, *Gesch. der alt. Rhodier*, pp. 160-1.

CHAPTER VI

THE PIRATES OF CILICIA

Satis mali sunt et frequenter latrunculantur.

THE last hundred years of the Republic saw one of the most remarkable developments of piracy that the Mediterranean has known. It was the more remarkable in that the sea was controlled by a single power, which, when it put forth its strength under a capable leader, had no difficulty in putting an end to the evil in the short space of a three months' campaign. The ease with which Rome finally achieved its suppression has naturally led to a severe condemnation of her negligence and apathy in permitting piracy to flourish for so long a period.

The headquarters of the pirates at this time were the southern slopes of the Taurus range, more particularly where the mountains come down to the sea in Cilicia Tracheia. The range, which forms the southern boundary of the central plateau of Asia Minor, is a long chain stretching from the Amanus on the east to the Aegean Sea, the mountains of Lycia and Caria having their natural prolongation in the islands known as the Sporades, off the western coast. The range is by no means of uniform character nor of equal altitude throughout. In its eastern part, the northern face of the Bulghur Dagh forms a steep

wall above the plains of Eregli and Nigdeh ; to
the south of the mountain wall stretches the
alluvial plain formed by the deposits of the rivers
Cydnos, Pyramos and Saros, and known to the
ancients as the level Cilicia. To the west of
the Bulghur Dagh, in the central section of the
range, to which Mr. Hogarth has given the name
of the Low Taurus,[1] altitudes are lower and
gradients on both sides of the central ridge less
severe. To the west of this section, the line of
the main ridge, which has hitherto pursued a
general direction from east to west, is broken.
Numerous spurs are thrown out to the north,
which enclose large lakes and fertile plains
capable of supporting a considerable population.
The principal mass, which comprises the hill-
country of the Pisidians, consists of an irregular
table-land, crossed by ridges and cleft by deep
river valleys. The southern rim of this plateau
is in the form of an arc, and falls sharply into the
Pamphylian plain, which lies at the head of a gulf
bounded on the east by the mountains of Cilicia
Tracheia, on the west by the lofty spur of Taurus,
known formerly as the Solyma mountains in
eastern Lycia. The whole range terminates in
the tangled mass of the Lycian and Carian
mountains, which attain to an elevation
of 8,000 to 10,000 feet, and except where the
river valleys have formed alluvial plains, fall
steeply into the sea.

The hillmen on both sides of the Taurus were

---

1. See the paper, *Modern and Ancient Roads in Asia Minor*, by D. G.
Hogarth and J. A. R. Munro (*Royal Geographical Society, Supplementary
Papers*, vol. III), to which I am much indebted in the following
description of the geographical features of Cilicia Tracheia.

noted at all times for their military qualities and predatory habits. From their mountain fast-nesses it was easy to raid their more settled neighbours of the plains without fear of reprisals,[1] while the forests with which the hills are covered provided the robbers on the coast with an abundant supply of timber for shipbuilding. With the piracy of the coasts and brigandage on land thus intimately connected, the suppression of one or the other necessitated for the Romans the penetration of the whole district. The pirate war, which may be said to have lasted from 102 to 67 B.C., is therefore to be regarded as a part of the Roman reduction of southern Asia Minor, a task which entailed hard fighting with the tribes on both sides of the Taurus, and led to a variety of political expedients, while the country was still in a state of tutelage, and unable to support the full Roman rule. At no time can the district be said to have been completely pacified. The reputation of the inhabitants as warriors and robbers was maintained until a late date. Rebellions and outbreaks of brigandage on a large scale remain a feature of the history of the Isaurians, even when they themselves provided the best troops in the Byzantine armies.

The district known during the later Roman empire by the general name of Isauria is roughly commensurate with the section of the range which we have called for convenience the Low Taurus, and which was known to the Greeks as

1. Cf. Strabo, p. 569, τοὺς ἐκ τοῦ Ταύρου κατατρέχοντας Κίλικας καὶ Πισίδας τὴν χώραν ταύτην (Phrygia Paroreios and Lycaonia) ; p. 570, οἱ δὲ Πάμφυλοι πολὺ τοῦ Κιλικίου φύλου μετέχοντες οὐ τελέως ἀφεῖνται τῶν λῃστρικῶν ἔργων οὐδὲ τοὺς ὁμόρους ἐῶσι καθ' ἡσυχίαν ζῆν.

Cilicia Tracheia. In the north it comprised the
country of the Homanadeis,[1] of the Isauri in the
narrower sense as used by Strabo,[2] and of the
inhabitants of Derbe and Laranda (Karaman),
who were active as brigands under their prince
Antipater in the middle of the first century B.C.
The natural centre of the district is Laranda,
from which radiate the principal roads to the
south, crossing the main ridge by easy tracks
towards the coast.[3] The whole district has the
form of an elevated plateau, which varies from
4,000 to 6,000 feet and falls, as Mr. Hogarth
says, in a series of steps to the sea.[4] The country
is roughly divided into two parts by the lower
valley of the Calycadnos, a deep cleft which in places
is 4,000 feet below the level of the surrounding
country, and is as much as twenty miles across.
The eastern part of the country is described by
travellers as a solid mass of calcareous rock,
covered with scrub and containing only a few
cultivable patches.[5] The mass is scored by
water-courses, which have carved deep ravines

1. Politically, the Homanadeis were not included in Isauria, but racially
were regarded by Strabo as Cilices. See Ramsay, *J. R. S.*, VII, p. 251.

2. On the Roman use of the name Isauria as contrasted with Strabo's
Isauri (*i.e.*, the inhabitants of the district immediately surrounding the two
towns of Isaura Vetus and Nova), see Ramsay, *op. cit.*, p. 277.

3. Davis, *Life in Asiatic Turkey*, p. 315; Ramsay, *Historical Geography
of Asia Minor*, p. 361; Hogarth, *op. cit.* A full bibliography of exploration
in this district (up to 1903) is given by Schaffer, *Petermann's Mitteilungen,
Enganzungs-heft no. 141* (1903), p. 98; see also Herzfeld, *Petermann's Mitt.*,
1909, pp. 25-26.

4. Hogarth, *op. cit.*, p. 645. Compare his description of this section of
the range as seen from the sea: "a vast level-crested ridge, falling to the
sea in a succession of parallel shelves" (*J. H. S.*, XI, p. 156).

5. See especially Bent, *Proc. Royal Geog. Society*, XII (1890), pp. 445 *seqq.*,
J. H. S., XII, pp. 206 *seqq.*; Heberdey und Wilhelm, *Reisen in Kilikien*,
(*Denkschr. der k. Akad. der Wiss., Wien, Philos.-Hist. Cl.*, XLIV (1896),
no. VI).

on their way to the sea. One of the most
impressive is the Lamos gorge, which is described
by Mr. Theodore Bent as reminding him of
a " sheet of forked lightning which had eaten its
way into the heart of the range." The gorge,
which is some fifty miles in length, is never more
than half-a-mile across, the walls on either side
being stupendous precipices, sometimes as high
as 2,000 feet ; frequently, for miles, there is no
possibility of descent from the heights to the
river-bed. Other ravines which open to the sea
in the neighbourhood are hardly less impressive.
The frequency of such fissures renders lateral
communication difficult, but since the plateau
falls steeply into the sea, it is only by the water-
courses that access to the interior is made possible.
All these approaches were guarded by defensive
works, many of which appear to date from the
period preceding the Roman conquest. In the
Lamos gorge at intervals of three or four miles occur
the ruins of towers, often built of vast blocks of
polygonal masonry, on steep cliffs above the
stream. One of the most remarkable is described
as being situated on a peak jutting out into the
gorge like a promontory ; two sides of it are
protected by the river, the third approached only
by a narrow ledge from the heights above. As a
means of approach from the river-bed, a stairway,
which is no longer practicable, had been cut in the
rock to a height of not less than 1,000 feet.
An interesting feature of these hill-castles is the
heraldic devices which they bear, some of which
recur on the coins of the district.[1] Not less

---

1. Illustrations are given by Bent in *Class. Rev.*, IV, p. 321 *seqq.*

interesting are the numerous rock-tombs and
reliefs of men in armour cut in the precipitous
walls of the ravines.

In spite of its apparent barrenness the district
enjoyed great prosperity, as may be judged from
the profusion of ancient remains,[1] and was at all
times famous for its religious associations. Near
the coast are situated the caves of the Corycian
Zeus, of Typhon, and another dedicated to the
Zeus of Olba, which was hardly less revered.
All this district, with much of Western Cilicia,
was dependent on the priestly dynasty of Olba,
the members of which styled themselves Teucer
and Ajax, and claimed descent from the Homeric
heroes. But the name Teucer is to be regarded
as the graecised form of a name which recurs in
various parts of Asia Minor and is especially
common in this district.[2] In an earlier chapter
I have suggested that we should perhaps seek
the ancestors of this house in one of the tribes who
raided Egypt at the end of the thirteenth century.
Whether that is the case or not, the Teucrid
house of Olba was ruling an extensive principality
at the close of the third century B.C., and retained
some of its former power even after the reduction
of Cilicia Tracheia by Pompeius.[3]

1. See Bell, *Rev. Arch.*, 1906, p. 388.

2. The religious phenomena of the district are discussed by Frazer,
Adonis, etc., p. 111 *seqq.* On the forms of the names Ταρκυ-, Τροκο-, Lycian
Trqqñta, etc., see Kretschmer, *Einleitung in die Geschichte der Gr. Sprache*,
pp. 362-364.

3. For the history of the Teucrid house, see Strabo, XIV, 672. The
Teucros inscription at Kanytelideis (*J. H. S.*, XII, p. 226, no. 1, the dating
of which is confirmed by Heberdey and Wilhelm) shows the Teucrid house
to have been reigning at Olba, *c.* 200 B.C., over a district which, at any rate,
reached to the coast. The imposing ruins of Olba are fully described by
Bent, and Heberdey and Wilhelm. Two inscriptions throw light on the

The western half of the country, with the
exception of the coast, has been less thoroughly
explored, and there are few remains that can be
said to be of pre-Roman date. The plateau is
of a more or less uniform elevation, but is broken
by ridges and contains fertile little plains surrounded by hills. The southern part is well
wooded and contains forests of oak, beech,
juniper and pines, some of which grow to a great
height.[1] Near Ermenek, Davis saw tall pines of
120 to 150 feet in height[2]; but the finest forests
are those between Anemurium and Selefke.[3]
The plateau is bounded on the west by the lofty
range of mountains which starts near the southern
end of Lake Caralitis and is continued in a direction east of south above the western shore of
Lake Trogitis, culminating in the peak known as
Ak-Dagh, some ten miles inland from Coracesium.[4]
The range may be regarded as the natural
boundary of Cilicia Tracheia on this side; its
height and difficult character would prove an
efficient barrier against incursion from the west.
On its eastern slopes rise the two arms of the river
Calycadnos which, above their junction at Mut

savagery of the inhabitants and their pursuits: the imprecation on a tomb
(*J. H. S.*, XII, p. 267, no. 59), ὃς δ' ἂν τολμήσῃ ἢ ἐπιτηδεύθῃ ἕξει πάντα
τὰ θεῖα κεχολώμενα καὶ τὰς στιγέρας 'Ερεινύας καὶ ἰδίου τέκνου ἥπατος
γεύσεται. Their predatory habits are illustrated by *J. H. S.*, XII, p. 263,
no. 49 (first century, B.C.), recording the dedication of the tithe of spoils from
a sack of Xanthus. The editor refers it to the sack by Brutus in 43 B.C.

1. Kinneir, *Journey through Asia Minor, etc.*, p. 206. For the cedars
of which Strabo speaks (XIV, 669), see p. 202, and Schaffer, *op. cit.*, p. 72.

2. Davis, *op. cit.*, p. 349.

3. *Ib.*, p. 449.

4. The range is called Akseki-Dagh in Murray's handbook. Strabo
(XIV, 670) makes the coast of Cilicia begin with Coracesium, but quotes
the view of Artemidorus that it began with Celenderis.

(Claudiopolis), divide the western part of the plateau into three more or less equal sections. The northern arm, which has excavated for itself a tremendous gorge throughout its whole length,[1] at first follows a course to the east of north to a point near Isaura Vetus, where it turns to the south-east. It is rapidly increased in volume by numerous small tributaries from the north and south, which have similarly eaten their way into the plateau and present many points of interest to the geologist.[2] The watershed between the two arms is formed by the ridge known as the Top Gedik Dagh, a chain of rounded peaks running in a north-westerly direction from above the point of junction of the two streams.[3] The gorge of the southern arm is of similar character to the northern. Except at Ermenek, it is if anything narrower and more precipitous, and presents an even greater obstacle to approach from the south. Between the southern arm of the Calycadnos and the sea a ridge, known perhaps to the ancients as Mount Imbaros,[4] rises above the general level of the plateau and attains a height of some 5,500 feet above sea-level. It is described for the most part as a dreary waste of rock, deeply scored by the short watercourses which run from its southern flanks to the sea. The penetration of this country, covered with forests in the south, and rent by the great cañons of the rivers and their

1. See Ramsay's description, *J. R. S.*, VII, p. 233.

2. Schaffer, p. 48 ; Sterrett, *Wolfe Expedition to Asia Minor*, p. 52.

3. Sterrett, p. 79 ; Schaffer, p. 70.

4 So Schaffer, *op. cit.*, p. 72 and his map 1, but the name rests only on the doubtful testimony of Pliny, *N. H.*, V, 93.

tributaries, must at all times have presented a difficult problem to the invader. The character of the inhabitants was in keeping with their surroundings. Even after the Roman conquest they remained in a backward condition, the so-called Clitae, who inhabited the district above Anemurium, on two recorded occasions in the first century after Christ breaking into open rebellion.[1]

To east and west of the mouth of the Calycadnos the plateau which forms the interior falls steeply to the sea, and forms a rocky coastline with bold, precipitous forelands, difficult of approach to an attacking squadron, but providing hidden refuges and safe anchorage to men who knew the coast.[2] On these rugged headlands and precipitous crags above the sea, whose natural strength was increased by fortification,[3] were the eyries of the pirates who in the last century of the Republic were masters of this coast. From these look-out points the presence of any vessel rash enough to

1. Tacitus, *Annals*, VI, 41 (36 A.D.): Clitarum natio . . . . quia nostrum in modum deferre census, pati tributa adigebatur, in iuga Tauri montis abscessit. (One is reminded of Kinneir's host, p. 201, who left his guest at Cylindre and retired to the hills, when word was received of the approach of a party to collect the tribute). The outbreak necessitated the presence of a force of 4,000 legionaries and auxiliary troops to suppress it. An even more serious revolt occurred sixteen years later (XII, 55).

As Ramsay has shown, the *Clitarum* of the MSS. should probably be altered to *Cietarum* (*H. G.*, pp. 364, 455 ; see also Wilhelm, *Arch. Ep. Mitt.*, XVII, p. 1).

2. Compare Strabo, XIV, 671, εὐφυοῦς γὰρ ὄντος τοῦ τόπου (the whole district of Cilicia Tracheia) πρὸς τὰ ληστήρια καὶ κατὰ γῆν καὶ κατὰ θάλατταν, κατὰ γῆν μὲν διὰ τὸ μέγεθος τῶν ὀρῶν καὶ τῶν ὑπερκειμένων ἐθνῶν, πέδια καὶ γεώργια ἐχόντων μεγάλα καὶ εὐκατατρόχαστα, κατὰ θάλατταν δὲ διὰ τὴν εὐπορίαν τῆς τε ναυπηγησίμου ὕλης καὶ τῶν λιμένων καὶ ἐρυμάτων καὶ ὑποδυτηρίων.

3. See Beaufort's account of Anemurium (*Caramanian Coast* p. 194), Karaburun (Heberdey-Wilhelm, *op. cit.*, p. 135), Cape Cavalliere (H.-W., p. 97 ; Beaufort, p. 213). On Coracesium, see below, p. 205.

approach the coast could be detected, and a wide
view be obtained across the channel between the
Cilician coast and Cyprus, by which the Levant
traffic must pass.[1] Many of the small islands
which lie off the coast are of great natural strength
and were similarly occupied.[2]

The original mistake of Roman policy, which
permitted piracy to become established on these
coasts, was committed at the time of the settlement with Antiochus the Great, when, as Strabo
puts it,[3] Rome cared little as yet for the districts
outside Taurus. The powers which had hitherto
policed the Levant and controlled the districts
where piracy threatened, had been weakened or
destroyed, and Rome had failed to create a
standing fleet to carry on the work. Such
information as we possess regarding Cilicia before
the battle of Magnesia all goes to show that the
Seleucids and Ptolemies were fully alive to the
dangers which might threaten from this coast,
and that, so long as they were able, they maintained an effective police. Even before the death
of Alexander a beginning was made towards the
reduction of the tribes of the interior, and though
the first expedition of Balacrus against Isaura and
Laranda was unsuccessful, both towns were
reduced by Perdiccas.[4] Diodorus gives us a

1. Beaufort, p. 178, and Cockerell, *Journal*, p. 179, on the view of
Cyprus from Selinty; Heberdey-Wilhelm, p. 152, from Antiocheia ad
Cragum; Langlois, *Voyage dans la Cilicie*, p. 116, from Selefke.

2. *e.g.*, Provençal Island (Beaufort, p. 206; Heberdey-Wilhelm, p. 97),
Papadoula Islands (Beaufort, p. 209); see also Heberdey-Wilhelm, p. 159,
on the island called by them Nagidussa.

3. Strabo, XIV, 667.

4. Diod. Sic., XVIII, 22.

graphic account of the capture of Isaura, the inhabitants of which, rather than surrender, preferred to perish with their families in the flames which they themselves had lighted. No doubt the establishment of the Macedonian treasures at Cyinda in Cilicia[1] made it necessary to give a lesson to all the mountaineers.

The coastline of Cilicia Tracheia was firmly held by the early Seleucids, and it seems that they were strong enough in this quarter to maintain order in the interior. The centre of their power was the town of Seleuceia, founded by Seleucus I, Nicator. The new foundation, to which the inhabitants of Holmi were transplanted, was of great natural strength, on an acropolis above the right bank of the Calycadnos, near the point where it leaves the hills. The river itself is said by Strabo to be navigable as far as this point.[2] The site thus chosen is the centre of the road system of southern Tracheia. It is the principal station on the important coast road from east to west, which provides almost the sole means of lateral communication. To the north-east runs an easy road to Olba, and to the north-west the road to Claudiopolis (Mut) and Laranda, from which branches the hill track to Ermenek (Germanicopolis).[3] The success of the foundation may be judged by the fact that of the towns of Cilicia Tracheia Seleuceia alone at a later date refrained from the " Cilician and Pamphylian mode of life," and was specially exempted by

1. Strabo, XIV, 672. See also Menander, *fr.* 24 (Kock).
2. Strabo, XIV, 670.
3. See Heberdey and Wilhelm, *op. cit.*, p. 101 ; Herzfeld, *op. cit.*, p. 30.

Augustus, when the rest of the country was placed under the police supervision of Archelaus.[1] There is reason to believe that Seleucus endeavoured to control the interior through the priest-kings of Olba, with whom a later inscription of Olba shows that he maintained friendly relations.[2] His own occupation of the coast and an alliance with or protectorate over this family, who, as we saw, governed a large part of Cilicia Tracheia, would serve to keep the country quiet.[3]

There are indications that the Seleucid control of this coast had already been challenged by the Egyptian government during the reign of Ptolemy II. But it was not until the third Syrian war that Cilicia passed into the hands of the Ptolemies. A Papyrus fragment, which preserves an account of the operations off the coast of Syria and Cilicia in 246 B.C., shows that the Syrian kings were still in the habit of keeping reserves of treasure in this district and that a Syrian governor was maintained in Cilicia. It is clear, however, that there was considerable disaffection among both the troops and the natives. A treacherous agreement seems to have been made between the people of Soli in Cilicia

1. Strabo, XIV, 670-671.

2. Heberdey and Wilhelm, p. 85, no. 166, Ἀρχιερεὺς μέ[γ]as Τεῦκρος Ζηνοφάνους [τοῦ] Τεύκρου Διὶ Ὀλ[β]ίωι τὰς [σ]τέγας ἐκαίνωσεν [τ]ὰς πρότερο[ν γεγε]ημένας ὑπὸ βασιλέω[s] Σελεύκου Νικάτορος. The inscription, which is on the *peribolos* wall of the great temple of Zeus at Olba, is dated by the editors to the end of the second or beginning of the first century B.C.

3. Other Seleucid foundations in this district are Antiocheia ad Cragum (Ptolemy, V, 7; see Droysen, II, p. 680; Wilhelm, in Pauly-Wissowa, I, 2, 2446). For the existence of another Antioch in the interior, see Sterrett, *op. cit.*, p. 85, who quotes Davis, *op. cit.*, p. 367, and *B. C. H.*, 1878, p. 16. The site is at Tchukur to the north of Ermenek.

Pedias and the Syrian troops, and when the
governor attempted to escape into the interior,
he was murdered by the hillmen.[1]

For some fifty years the Cilician coast remained
in the possession of the Ptolemies, who, like their
predecessors, endeavoured to consolidate their
power and commemorate the names of their house
by the foundation of cities.[2] There is little
evidence regarding the character of the Egyptian
government in Cilicia. After its conquest by
Ptolemy III the district apparently formed part
of the great coastal province which extended from
the Ionian coast to Cilicia.[3] Its value to Egypt
consisted in the materials, especially cedar wood,
which were exported for shipbuilding, and whatever lawlessness may have been tolerated among

---

1. An attempt made by Ptolemy I on this coast in 310 B.C. had been
defeated by Antigonus and Demetrius (Diod. Sic., XX, 19). The evidence
for an Egyptian occupation of Cilicia under Philadelphus rests on the name
of the town Arsinoe (cf. the re-naming of Patara in Lycia by Philadelphus,
Strabo, XIV, 666), and on the statement of Theocritus, XVII, 87:
Παμφύλοισί τε πᾶσι καὶ αἰχμηταῖς Κιλίκεσσι σαμαίνει. On the
other hand, in the Aduli inscription (Dittenberger, *O. G. I.*, 54)
Pamphylia and Cilicia are not mentioned in the list of possessions inherited
by Euergetes, but occur among his conquests. The evidence of the Petrie
Papyrus is in agreement. Bevan, *House of Seleucus*, I, p. 148, inclines to the
view that Philadelphus may have temporarily occupied strong points on the
Cilician coast, but lost them before his death. See also Beloch, III, 2, p. 263.
Kock, *Ein Ptolemaeer Kreig*, p. 2, cites numismatic evidence for a Ptolemaic
occupation for a few years after 271 B.C. It is, however, extremely hazardous to assume that the Egyptians lost their Cilician possessions owing to
the battle of Cos in 261 B.C.

In the Petrie papyrus I have followed Bilabel's text, *Die Kleineren
Historikenfragmente*, Bonn, 1923, pp. 23 *seqq.*, where full references to
modern literature are given.

2. Berenice (Steph. Byz., *s.v.*; Stadiasmus, § 190), Arsinoe (Strabo,
XIV, 669; Ptolemy, V, 7; Pliny, V, 92; Steph. Byz.); Ptolemais, between
the river Melas and Coracesium (Strabo, XIV, 667, and therefore strictly
in Pamphylia).

3. See Bevan, *op. cit.*, I, p. 189, following Haussoulier, *Rev. de Phil.*
1901, p. 145.

the tribes of the interior, the Ptolemies are
unlikely to have permitted the inhabitants of the
coast to interfere with this traffic.   Later, as the
Egyptian power declined, the maritime towns
were encouraged to raid the Syrian coast in order
to damage the old enemy.[1]   Even the Rhodians
who, as we have seen, did their utmost to suppress
piracy elsewhere, acquiesced.[2]

We may conclude that it was the troublesome
character of the Cilicians not less than the
weakness of Egypt that induced Antiochus III to
make the attempt in 197 B.C. to regain the
Cilician coast for Syria.   Its masters were still
nominally the Egyptians,[3] but it is significant
that the only point at which Antiochus met with
opposition was Coracesium,[4] which later was the
recognised headquarters of the pirates.   It was
while laying siege to this town that he received the
ultimatum of the Rhodians, and the news of
Philip's defeat at Cynoscephalae.   The further
conquests of Antiochus, by which the remnants
of the Ptolemaic province were finally lost to
Egypt, do not here concern us.   His ambitions
were crushed by the Romans at Magnesia ; but
the humiliating terms of peace which were

1.   Polyb., V, 73, shows that Ptolemaic influence had seriously declined
in Pamphylia by 220 B.C.

2.   The notice in Strabo (XIV, 669) to this effect must refer to a period
before the battle of Magnesia.   So far as concerns Egyptian relations with
Syria, such a policy is equally understandable in the second century, but we
can hardly understand the connivance of the Rhodians after the defeat of
Antiochus.   Strabo's chronology is vague, and the notice regarding
Coracesium and Diodotus Tryphon, to whose presence in Cilicia he ascribes
the origin of piracy, very difficult (see below, p. 205).

3.   Livy, XXXIII, 19.

4.   *Ib.*, XXXIII, 20.

imposed upon him were more than all else responsible for the trouble which not long afterwards came to a head on this coast. Although Cilicia Tracheia was left to the Syrian king, his navy was limited to ten ships of war, and no armed vessel might be sent by him to the west of the Calycadnos. The effect of such an ordinance was that Cilicia Tracheia became practically independent ; invasion by land could be attempted only by the coast-road, much of which is impracticable for a large force.[1] The country, therefore, ceased to be of interest to the Syrian kings, except in so far as it offered a base of operations to rival claimants of the throne. We hear that one of these pretenders, Alexander Balas, was established by Eumenes or Attalus of Pergamon in 159 B.C. with the Cilician prince, Zenophanes.[2] After his expulsion from Syria, Alexander retired again to Cilicia, where he organised a second expedition. Strabo ascribes the beginnings of piracy at Coracesium to another Syrian usurper, Diodotus Tryphon, who used it as a base for privateers ; though he himself was destroyed by Antiochus Sidetes, the weakness of the Syrian kingdom was such that his adherents

1. Cf. Kinneir's account of the road between Anemurium and Celenderis (*op. cit.*, p. 198), and to the east of Celenderis (p. 202), where it consists of a track about two feet wide on the face of a precipice above the sea.

2. Diod. Sic., xxxi, 32a. It is tempting to connect this Zenophanes with the Teucrid house of Olba (see also Niese, III, p. 259, n. 5). The " Great High Priest " Teucer, mentioned in the inscription quoted on p. 201, who was reigning *c.* 100 B.C., was the son of Zenophanes, the son of Teucer. Was this Zenophanes the protector of Alexander ? The name, however, is not an uncommon one in this district (see the Corycian lists in Heberdey and Wilhelm), and was also borne by the father of Aba, who, having married into the Teucrid house, contrived to seize the remains of the principality (Strabo, XIV, 672).

in Coracesium could not be touched. It is probable that the activities of Diodotus increased rather than originated the growth of piracy on this coast. Henceforward, it flourished unchecked. What remained of the principality of the Teucrids was seized by a number of petty chiefs whose sole business was robbery.[1] The most important of their strongholds was Coracesium, perched on a precipitous rock above the sea and connected with the land only by a narrow isthmus, from which it rises abruptly. Two sides of the promontory are described as perpendicular cliffs from five to six hundred feet high. The eastern side is so steep that the houses of the modern Alaya seem to rest one upon the other.[2]

During the thirty-five years which followed the death of Diodotus we have few details of the pirates' activity. In the early stages of their career the home waters provided abundant prey along the Levant routes,[3] but as their strength grew, their depredations were extended to the whole coast-line of Asia Minor. To this period may be assigned the tactics employed along the Erythraean coast, when the pirates were still working with few ships. By fraternising with and eavesdropping on the crews of merchantmen which utilised the harbours, they would find out their destination and cargo. The pirate vessels

1. Strabo, XIV, 672. We hear of Κιλίκων τύραννοι in the triumph of Pompey (Appian, Mithr., 117).

2. Beaufort, op. cit., p. 172. There is a view of the site on p. 136. Cf. Heberdey-Wilhelm, p. 136 : " Haus an Haus und Haus über Haus liegt die heutige Stadt."

3. The dedication at Delos made by a merchant of Ascalon, σωθεὶς ἀπὸ πειρατῶν (C. R. Ac., 1909, p. 308) perhaps belongs to this period. (The editor, however, regards the letter-forms as of the first century B.C.).

would then be warned to rendezvous at sea and attack the merchantmen after they had left port.[1] Under the leadership of a certain Isidorus they soon began to infest the whole of the Eastern Mediterranean, sweeping the " golden sea " from Cyrene to Crete and the Peloponnese.[2] Such depredations called for no particular show of energy on the part of the Roman government. Diplomatic representations were made to the foreign states which were held to be responsible, Scipio Aemilianus himself on one occasion making a tour of inspection in the East.[3] Special protection might be granted in certain cases,[4] but defence against the raiders was left for the most part to the initiative of the natives, either singly or in co-operation with their neighbours.[5] As is to be expected, the record of such matters is slight and is to be found only in occasional

1. Strabo, XIV, 644. cf. Alciphron, I, 8 : ὁ λέμβος οὖν οὗτος ὃν ὁρᾷς ὁ κωπήρης < ὁ > τοῖς πολλοῖς ἐρέταις κατηρτυμένος Κωρύκιόν ἐστι σκάφος, λῃσταὶ δ' Ἀτταλῆς τὸ ἐν αὐτῷ σύστημα, where, however, it is obvious that there is a confusion between the Ionian Corycos and Corycos, the former name of Attaleia. See J.R.S., XII, 44, n. 2.

2. Florus, III, 6. The author is not precise in his chronology, but implies, I think, that Isidorus, of whom there is no other record, belonged to the period before the Mithradatic wars. (An Isidorus who was in command of a squadron of thirteen quinqueremes and was defeated by Lucullus off Lemnos (Plutarch, Lucullus, 12) may, however, have been the same man taken into the service of Mithradates.)

3. Strabo, XIV, 669. Probably in 141 b.c. (P.-W., IV, 1, 1452).

4. e.g., in the case of Ilion (I. G. Rom., IV, 196 ; Dittenberger, O. G. I., 443), to which a detachment of troops was sent from Poemanenum. The event, however, is dated to the year 80-79, and we are not informed of the exact circumstances.

5. A decree of Ephesos (end of second century, b.c.) records the gratitude of the community to the people of Astypalaea, who, on receipt of news that pirates were raiding a shrine of Artemis in the Ephesian territory, successfully attacked them and rescued their captives (I. G., XII, 3, 171). An inscription of rather later date (? middle of first century b.c.) from Syros records co-operation between the people of that island and of Siphnos in face of a piratical attack.

inscriptions. The Roman crime, however, was not mere negligence and failure to provide an adequate police of the seas. The pirates had their place in the economic scheme, and the growing demand for slaves in Italy was not the least of the causes which led to their prosperity and to their toleration by the government. Posing as ordinary slavers, they frequented the port of Delos, where we are told that tens of thousands of slaves changed masters in a day,[1] the principal purveyors being the pirates and the tax-farmers. The depredations of the latter vied with those of the pirate, so that when Nicomedes of Bithynia was asked for a contingent at the time of the Cimbrian wars he replied that the majority of his subjects had been carried off by the tax-farmers and were now in slavery.[2] As a result of this competition between pirate and tax-farmer, it is little to be wondered at if the inhabitants of the provinces and the client states sought to avoid the ravages of the one by joining the ranks of the other, to the no small advantage of the pirate communities. Their numbers were increased by men from all countries, especially by their neighbours in the Levant.[3] Not only were the pirates joined by individuals, but in default of protection from the Roman government, the cities themselves formed open alliances with the pirates.[4]

1. Strabo, XIV, 668.

2. Diod. Sic., XXXVI, 3. On the depredations of the tax-farmers in Asia in the time of Lucullus, see Plutarch, *Lucullus*, 20 ; on the slave-hunts, Mommsen, III, p. 78. Similar methods were employed in Italy to fill the *ergastula* (Cic., *pro Cluentio*, 21 ; Suetonius, *Aug.*, 32 ; *Tib.*, 8).

3. Appian, *Mithr.*, 92.

4. Dio Cass., XXXVI, 20.

The neighbouring town of Side put its dockyards
at their disposal and provided a market, second in
importance only to Delos, for the disposal of their
captives.[1] Phaselis, on the Lycian coast, was
connected with them for purposes of trade, and
later by a definite alliance.[2] Other towns
followed the course of purchasing exemption from
their raids by a fixed annual tribute.[3]

The first recorded action against the Cilicians
on the part of the Romans was not taken until
the year 102 B.C., when a force was sent against
them under M. Antonius.[4] The literary evidence
regarding the expedition is small and gives no
hint of its immediate cause.[5] It seems probable

1. Strabo, XIV, 664.

2. Cic., *Verr.*, II, 4, 22 (see below, p. 217).

3. This is recorded at a slightly later date of the Lipari islands (Cic.,
Verr., II, 3, 85). The practice of buying off the corsairs must have been
common in all ages. There is an interesting case recorded by Spon and
Wheler, *op. cit.*, II, p. 220, where it is stated that an arrangement had been
made by the French consul in Athens, by which the Christian population of
Megara paid a fixed tribute (in cheeses) to Crevilliers, the principal corsair
of the time, in order to secure immunity from raids. (Crevilliers apparently
shared the tastes of Ben Gunn.)

4. In *I. G. Rom.*, IV, 1116, he is called στρατηγὸς ἀνθύπα[τος; cf.
Cicero *de Or.*, I, 18. The inscription informs us that the Rhodians provided a
contingent, and it is probable that the bulk of his fleet was composed of
contingents from the maritime states of the East. (The inscription, which
also informs us that his quaestor was an Aulus Gabinius, has been assigned
to the campaign of M. Antonius Creticus (Th. Reinach, *Rev. Et. Gr.*, XVII,
p. 210, and Hiller von Gärtringen in Dittenberger, *Syll.*3, II, p. 435, note 15
to no. 748.) We have no evidence for the fact that the operations of Antonius
Creticus ever reached the Cilician coast, as the inscription would imply, and
though Creticus may have had more than one quaestor assigned to him, we
should have heard of it had the quaestor captured by the Cretans (Dio.
Cass., *fr.* 108) been the tribune of 67 B.C. But the use of the title
στρατηγὸς ἀνθύπατος makes it impossible that the reference is to Antonius
Creticus (see Foucart, *Journal des Savants*, 1906, p. 576, and Holleaux' study
ΣΤΡΑΤΗΓΟΣ ΥΠΑΤΟΣ, pp. 31 *seqq.* and 56 *seqq.*)

5. Livy, *Ep.*, LXVIII; Obsequens, 104; Trogus, *prol.*, 39. From
Cicero, *Brutus*, 5, 168, we learn that his prefect M. Gratidius was killed in
Cilicia.

however that the complaints from the provinces and client states had become so serious that the Romans were forced to take action at this time against both the tax-farmers and the pirates. As a result of representations made by Nicomedes,[1] we hear that the Senate had decreed that all the allies of free birth who were now in slavery should be set free, and that the provincial governors should make it their business to see that the decree was carried out. Clearly the government intended that all forms of kidnapping of free provincials should cease.

Although Antonius was accorded a triumph for his victories,[2] there is little evidence as to the extent of his success in suppressing the piracy of this district. The campaign, however, produced one important result. A permanent command was created in Cilician waters, to which the name of the province of Cilicia was given, although at first it can have comprised little more than the former Attalid possessions in south-western Asia Minor.[3] But the new command remained a permanent threat to the pirates in Cilicia Tracheia, and, with the loss of the valuable market at Delos, proclaimed that the long-continued toleration by the Romans would no longer be enjoyed. The pirates therefore sought and found a new protector. Within fifteen years they reappear in history as the close friends and allies of Mithradates.

The alliance now formed between Mithradates

1. Diod. Sic., XXXVI, 3.
2. Plutarch, *Pompeius*, 24.
3. See Marquardt, II, pp. 312 *seqq*. (French translation of 1892).

and the pirates closely resembles the position held by the Barbary corsairs of the sixteenth century under the Sultan of Turkey. After its capture by the brothers Uruj and Kheyr-ed-din Barbarossa, Algiers had been formally made over to the Sultan, and Kheyr-ed-din appointed his viceroy. The corsairs were thus assured of the Sultan's protection and favour, while the Turks, never by nature a seafaring people, derived their main strength at sea from the corsairs, becoming their pupils in all matters pertaining to seamanship and naval construction. The principal officers of the Turkish fleet up to the battle of Lepanto, such men as Kheyr-ed-din, Torghut Reis and Ochiali, were all pirates who had learnt their seamanship off the Barbary coast. A similar union with the Cilicians gave Mithradates that command of the sea which in the first Mithradatic war was nearly fatal to Sulla. It is impossible to say how much of the development of their organisation was due to the direct suggestion of Mithradates in view of the coming struggle with Rome, but it is as a compact naval power that we next meet them, fully organised for regular warfare. It is probable that much of the organisation which is recorded at a slightly later date was already in existence during the first Mithradatic war. We are told at any rate that at this time their vessels were organised in squadrons, resembling fleets rather than independent hordes.[1] The value to Mithradates of such bodies of privateers, not paid by him but content with the proceeds of their raids, is obvious. The war

1. Appian, *Mithr.*, 63, στόλοις ἐοικότα μᾶλλον ἢ λῃσταῖς.

against the pirates became, in fact, identical with
the war against Mithradates.

The pirates were so closely identified with the
king's fleet that Mithradates himself on one
occasion, when in danger of shipwreck, had no
hesitation in transferring himself to a pirate vessel,
and was safely landed at Sinope.[1] The tactics
pursued by both sections of the fleet were so much
alike that it is not always easy in the records of the
war to distinguish the achievements of the pirates
from those of his regular navy. The first sack
of Delos, a feat which was imitated a few years
later by an independent pirate, is ascribed to
a certain Menophanes, who, though called an
admiral of Mithradates, was not improbably the
leader of a squadron of pirates acting under the
general direction of Archelaus.[2] It is not specified
whether the cruisers operating on the coasts of
the Peloponnese and Zacynthos, which burnt the
advance guard of Flaccus' fleet, outside
Brundisium,[3] were pirates, but it was the pirates

1. Appian, *Mithr.*, 78 ; Plutarch, *Lucullus*, 13 (who says Heraclea).
The incident occurred in the third war. Orosius, VI, 2, 24, says that the
pirate's name was Seleucus (in myoparonem Seleuci piratae). The same
Seleucus, " archipirata," was in command at the siege of Sinope (VI, 3, 2) ;
cf. Memnon, LIII, Μιθριδάτου στρατηγὸς ἰσοστάσιος τῶν εἰρημένων
(Leonippus and Cleochares). (The position held by Mithradates' favourite
pirate recalls the orders given to the Turkish generals at the siege of Malta to
undertake no action of importance until the arrival of Torghut Reis).
Seleucus was responsible for the capture of the Roman convoy off Sinope
Memnon, *l.c.*)

2. According to Poseidonius (*ap.* Athenaeus, V, 215) a first attempt on
the island was made by Apellicon of Teos, sent by Aristion, which failed with
heavy loss to the Athenians. Appian (*Mithr.*, 28) says that the second attack
was made by Archelaus, who sent the spoils to Athens, but in Pausanias (III
23, 3) the actual commander is said to have been Menophanes, Μιθριδάτου
στρατηγός, (? cf. Seleucus) and Pausanias is uncertain whether Menophanes
was carrying out an order of Mithradates or acting on his own initiative.

3. Appian, *Mithr.*, 51 ; cf. 56.

themselves who harassed Lucullus on his voyage
to the East, while the fleet of Mithradates
prevented the Rhodians from putting to sea.
Lucullus could only reach Alexandria from Crete
by way of Cyrene, and escaped his pursuers by
changing from ship to ship.[1]   To the pirates also
at this time is ascribed the capture of Iassos,
Samos, Clazomenae and Samothrace, from the
temple of which plunder to the value of 1,000
talents was carried off, though Sulla himself was in
the neighbourhood.[2]   How far Mithradates had
restrained them earlier in the war is unknown.
According to Appian, when he realised that he
could no longer retain his conquests, free license
was given to them.   The depredations just
mentioned may, in fact, have taken place after
the conclusion of peace.[3]

There can be no doubt that Sulla was fully
alive to the necessity of a rapid settlement with
the Cilicians.   He had himself held the Cilician
command in 92 B.C., and the campaign against
Mithradates had taught him the value of their
support to his enemy.   Security in southern
Asia Minor depended not only on the suppression
of piracy at sea, but on the reduction of the
kindred tribes on both sides of the Taurus range,
from whom the sea rovers drew reinforcements,
and with whom a refuge could be found in the
event of trouble on the coast.   The task to be
attempted was two-fold : the policing of the
southern coast of Asia Minor, and a vigorous

1. *Ib.*, 33 ; a variant in Plutarch, *Lucullus*, 2.

2. Appian, *Mithr.*, 63.

3. See Reinach, *Mithradate*, p. 209.

penetration of the Taurus and reduction of the Highlanders.

The area occupied by the pirates at this time was as follows : In Cilicia Tracheia it is clear that they held the whole of the coast together with the interior on both sides of the Taurus. The Pamphylian coast, if not entirely occupied by them, was deeply implicated in their malpractices. The town of Side was practically in their hands, and Servilius Isauricus found it necessary to chastise the people of Attaleia. On the western shore of the Pamphylian Gulf a robber chieftain had made himself master of the Solyma mountains and of Olympos, Corycos and Phaselis.[1] In the *Hinterland* of Lycia, in spite of Strabo's encomium of the rule of Moagetes,[2] it is probable that the Cibyratis was disturbed, perhaps as a result of the Mithradatic war. Disturbances in this district constituted a threat to the inhabitants of Lycia, whose loyalty to Rome had been demonstrated in the late war. Moreover, a disturbed population in the Cibyratis offered the same support to the brigands of Mount Solyma as did the Isaurians and Homanadeis to the Cilician pirates.

The plan of campaign for the pacification of this district comprised an attack by sea on the southern coasts of Asia Minor, together with a simultaneous advance by land along the northern face of the Taurus, so as to attack the pirate country from

1. For a fuller discussion of Servilius' operations, I may refer to my paper, *The Campaigns of Servilius Isaurians against the Pirates* (*J. R. S.*, XII, pp. 35 *seqq.*), of which the following pages are a summary.

2. Strabo, XIII, 631.

the north and south. For this purpose Murena,
the successor of Sulla, whose share in the pirate
war has been largely forgotten, gathered a fleet
from the subject states to be used against the
pirates, and by land proceeded to the occupation
of the Cibyratis.[1] An end was made of the rule
of Moagetes, a part of his kingdom being assigned
to the Lycians, while the remainder, comprising
the later *conventus* of Cibyra, was annexed by
Rome. Murena's unfortunate adventure against
Mithradates, while interrupting any concentrated
action against southern Asia Minor, led to his
own recall in 81 B.C. We know little of his
successor, Nero, except that he weakly abetted
the depredations of Verres, who was *legatus* to the
governor of Cilicia in the years 80 and 79. That
governor, Dolabella, was himself impeached, and it
is highly probable that the misconduct of him and
his *legatus* created further disturbances,[2] which
necessitated the vigorous action of the new
proconsul in Cilicia, Servilius. During the years
of Servilius' command a forward policy was once
more adopted by the Romans, and a beginning
made towards the complete reduction of the whole
district.

The information which we possess regarding the
campaigns of Servilius during the years 77 to 75 B.C.
is unfortunately very meagre. Enough, however,
remains to show that they were a part of a general
scheme now undertaken by the Romans for the
pacification of southern Asia Minor. His first
operations were directed against eastern Lycia

1. Appian, *Mithr.*, 93; Strabo, *l.c.*; Cic., *Verr.*, II, 1, 90.
2. Cic., *Verr.*, II, 1, 56; cf. 86.

and Pamphylia ; during the last year of his command he appears to have moved from a base in Pamphylia against the tribes dwelling to the north of the Taurus, and to have attacked the Orondeis, Homanadeis and Isaurians. It would seem that these operations were to be preliminary to a combined movement by land and sea against the pirates of Cilicia Tracheia, who were to be attacked simultaneously from the North and from the southern coast. In spite of the statements to be found in later writers that Servilius himself achieved the reduction of the Cilicians there is little evidence to show that he succeeded in penetrating into Tracheia itself.[1]

Apart from the reduction of Isauria and the alleged over-running of Cilicia, we have the following definite statements regarding Servilius' movements : that he captured Phaselis, Olympos and Corycos in Lycia ; that his operations were extended into Pamphylia, where he took territory from the people of Attaleia. In connexion, probably, with the campaign against Isauria, he annexed territory from the Orondeis, gaining also for the Romans the otherwise unknown Ager Aperensis and Ager Gedusanus. Cicero gives us a further detail, to the effect that a pirate chief, Nico, about whom nothing otherwise is known, was captured. It is noticeable that the information regarding the Lycian cities is common to almost all writers, the campaign on the eastern

---

1. The only district in Cilicia Tracheia which Servilius or his officers can be said to have visited was Corycos. In *J R. S.*, XII, p. 40 *seqq.*, I have endeavoured to show that the Cilician Corycos is confused with the Lycian.

coast of Lycia being obviously an important part of the whole, in any case the best recorded.[1]

The people of Lycia receive high praise from Strabo for their good behaviour at this time. Though their country offered facilities not less than those enjoyed by the Cilicians, under the good government of the Lycian league they refrained from the piracies practised by the Pamphylians and Cilicians, and were seduced by no motives of base gain.[2] In a later passage, however, he explains the situation which prevailed on the eastern coast and necessitated the interference of the Romans. In this district a chieftain, Zenicetes, whose chief stronghold was the mountain Olympos and town of the same name, had made himself master also of Phaselis and Corycos and many places of the Pamphylians. On the capture of the mountain by Servilius, Zenicetes burnt himself and his household.[3]

The district, which Zenicetes controlled, formed a compact principality, cut off from the rest of Lycia by the mass of the Solyma mountains, and ethnically perhaps distinct from it. Zenicetes himself may have been a Cilician pirate, who had invaded Lycia from the sea and established himself at Olympos, extending his sovereignty along the coast to Phaselis and into Pamphylia.

---

1. The principal authorities for Servilius' campaigns are : Ammian. Marc., XIV, 8, 4 ; Ps.-Asconius, in Verr., II, p. 171 (Orelli) ; Cic., de leg. agr., I, 5, II, 50 ; Verr., II, 1, 21 ; II, 3, 211 ; II, 4, 22 ; II, 5, 79 ; Eutropius VI, 3 ; Festus, Brev., 12, 3 ; Florus, III, 6 ; Frontinus, III, 7, 1 ; Livy, Epp., XC, XCIII ; Orosius, V, 23 ; Sallust, Fragmenta (Maurenbrecher) ; I, 127-132 ; II, 81, 87 ; Strabo, XII, 568-9 ; XIV, 671 ; Suetonius, Julius, 3 ; Velleius, II, 39.

2. Strabo, XIV, 664.

3. Strabo, XIV, 671.

The description, however, which Strabo gives of
his principal stronghold, called by him Mount
Olympos, with its wide view over Lycia,
Pamphylia, Pisidia and the Milyas, makes it clear
that the mountain in question is not the Olympos
already described by him,[1] but the modern
Tachtaly Dagh (Solyma mountains). Zenicetes
must then be regarded as a native chieftain of
the Solyma mountains, whose power had grown
during the disturbances of the first Mithradatic
war, when Lycia was invaded by Mithradates,
and, as we have seen, the *Hinterland* was disturbed.
Commanding the Solyma Mountains, he could
control the eastern coast of Lycia, and reach
Pamphylia by way of the Tchandyr valley;
while he held Mount Solyma and the passes, he
was secure from attack by land; by sea, an
alliance with the Cilicians would ensure his safety
on that side. The security of the master of
Phaselis was a matter of the first importance to the
Cilicians,[2] so that the great naval battle of which
we hear in this campaign,[3] had probably to be
fought by Servilius against the Cilician allies of
Zenicetes, before he could deliver his attack on
the Lycian coast.

When order had been restored on the Lycian
and Pamphylian coast, it was the task of Servilius

1. Strabo, XIV, 666.

2. On Phaselis and the pirates, see Cicero, *Verr.*, II, 4, 22. Its importance
to the Cilicians lay in its convenient situation as a port of call for vessels
which followed the coast instead of sailing directly across the Pamphylian gulf.
Cf. Leake, *Journal of a Tour in Asia Minor*, p. 133 : " In passing by sea from
Alaya [Coracesium] to Castel Rosso [Casteloryzo], I was compelled to follow
the coast of the gulf of Adalia, the sailors begin afraid in this season [March]
of crossing directly to Cape Khelidoni."

3. Florus III 6.

to attempt the pacification of the tribes inhabiting the northern slopes of the Taurus range. A beginning had already been made in the west by Murena's occupation of the Cibyratis. Servilius' passage of Mount Taurus was considered one of the most brilliant feats of his campaign, and his reduction of the Isaurians secured for him the title Isauricus.

There is fortunately no doubt as to the position of the two towns Isaura Vetus and Nova, both of which were now reduced. The former has long been identified with the modern Zengibar Kalesi; the latter has now been located with certainty by Sir William Ramsay at Dorla, some twenty miles to the north-east of Isaura Vetus.[1] In addition to these two towns, the territory occupied by the Isaurians comprised several other villages, all swarming with brigands.[2] The district lay on the northern slopes of Taurus, within the boundaries of Lycaonia, marching on the north-west with the territory of the turbulent Homanadeis, with whom, in common with other tribes occupying the northern face of Taurus, the Isaurians offered a strenuous resistance to the Roman advance.

I have elsewhere tried to show that Servilius advanced across the Taurus range by a route which would bring him directly into the country of the Orondeis,[3] and that the Ager Orondicus, which Cicero says that he annexed, is to be regarded as this district. With regard to the otherwise

1. *J. H. S.*, 1905, pp. 163 *seqq.*
2. Strabo, XII, 568.
3. *J. R. S.*, **XII**, p. 49.

unknown Ager Gedusanus it has been suggested
that Gedusanus is probably a corruption of
Sedasanus,[1] Sedasa, which is located on the east of
Lake Trogitis, being a town of the Homanadeis,
whose territory according to Sir William Ramsay
lay around three sides of Lake Trogitis, and
extended from the neighbourhood of Isaura to
the confines of Selge and Katenna.

If these suggestions are accepted, the operations
of Servilius on the northern side of Taurus were
directed against the three peoples of the Isauri,
Homanadeis and Orondeis, and extended over
a district reaching from Isauria in a north-
westerly direction along the eastern shore of the
lakes Trogitis and Caralitis.

By these conquests on the northern face of
Taurus, the necessary preliminaries had been
accomplished for a combined attack on Cilicia
Tracheia by land and sea. The following year,
74 B.C., therefore saw the creation of a new command, the *maius imperium infinitum*, conferred on
M. Antonius for three years, with orders to clear
the whole of the Mediterranean coast of pirates,
a command which anticipated that which was
entrusted to Pompeius in 67.[2] Land operations,
however, at first delayed by the death of Servilius'
successor, Octavius,[3] were indefinitely postponed
owing to the outbreak of the third Mithradatic
war. By sea, the Roman plans were stultified by

1. The suggestion was made by Professor Calder (See *J. R. S.*, XII,
pp. 47-48). The suggestion that the Ager Aperensis may be the Ager
Ateniensis, Atenia being a town on Lake Caralitis, is perhaps less probable.

2. See below, p. 234.

3. Plutarch, *Lucullus*, 6.

the incompetence of the admiral, before their fleets could even approach the Cilician coast.

However well-earned his triumph, the victories of Servilius, which had failed to touch the Cilician coast, produced few results so far as concerned the suppression of piracy. The preparations for the complete reduction of the tribes of the Taurus had to be abandoned owing to the outbreak of a third war with Mithradates, in the course of which the northern districts were again disturbed by a raid conducted by the king's general Eumachus.[1] Thanks to the arrangements made by Sulla for the provision of a fleet and to the genius of Lucullus, in the third war Mithradates never possessed the command of the sea that he had held in the first. He began the war, it is true, with a force of 400 triremes and a considerable number of fifty-oared ships and lighter craft,[2] which we may suppose consisted principally of pirate vessels, which had joined him as in the former war. Squadrons were despatched to create trouble in Crete and to effect a junction with Sertorius in Spain.[3] But in spite of an initial success which enabled him to destroy Cotta's fleet at Chalcedon,[4] the king's regular fleets in the Aegean were soon defeated by

1. Appian, *Mithr.*, 76.

2. Memnon, XXXVIII ; cf. Strabo, XII, 576. (See, however, Kromayer, *Philologus*, LVI, p. 475, who thinks these figures are exaggerated.)

3. Memnon, XLIII. The commanders were probably Fannius and Metrophanes (see Maurenbrecher, *ad Sallust, fr.* IV, 2), who may have been identical with the Metrophanes of Appian, *Mithr.*, 29, perhaps a pirate like Seleucus.

4. Appian, *Mithr.*, 71 ; Plutarch, *Lucullus*, 8.

Lucullus, and the bulk of the remainder destroyed in Pontus by the accident of a storm.[1]

To Lucullus, indeed, belongs most of the credit for the later successes gained by Pompeius against both the pirates and Mithradates. His victories over Mithradates at sea prepared the way for the subjugation of the pirates no less than his successes on land broke the king's power. In the meantime, however, the power of the Cilicians was untouched, and just as after the battle of Lepanto the depredations of the Barbary corsairs continued unabated until their country was occupied in the nineteenth century, so too the Cilicians, although deprived of the active assistance of Mithradates since the close of the first war, had extended their raids over the whole Mediterranean.[2] Their elaborate organisation, of which there are already traces in the first Mithradatic war, had by this time been brought to a high state of perfection. The miseries entailed by the constant wars in which Rome was engaged had added greatly to their numbers, which are given as many tens of thousands.[3] Ruined men, who " preferred to act rather than to suffer " flocked to them from all quarters, especially from the East. No doubt the refugees provided them with many of their boldest leaders, men who knew the more distant coasts and could lead profitable raids, like the Christian

---

1. Appian, *op. cit.*, 77-78 ; Plutarch, *op. cit.*, 11-13. The ships which had been sent to Crete and the West were caught by Triarius on their return and destroyed off Tenedos (Memnon, XLVIII).

2. Appian, *Mithr.*, 93 ; Plutarch, *Pompeius*, 25.

3. Appian, *l.c.*

renegades of a later date.[1] Like their successors
on the Barbary coasts, they kept their arsenals
manned with captives, who were chained to their
tasks, and vast quantities of naval stores and
munitions were captured by the Romans after
the fall of Coracesium.[2] The pirate ships are said
to have numbered more than a thousand,[3] and
were richly adorned with gold, silver and purple.[4]
They were giving up their lighter craft—hemioliae
and myoparones—and building biremes and
triremes ; they sailed in organised squadrons
commanded by admirals (στρατηγοί), disdaining
the name of pirates, and dignifying the proceeds
of their raids as pay (μισθὸς στρατιωτικός). The
closest connection was maintained between the
pirate bands all over the Mediterranean, money
and reinforcements being sent as required.[5] Their
seamanship enabled them to keep the seas even

1. Plutarch, *Pomp.*, 24, χρήμασι δυνατοὶ καὶ γένεσι λαμπροὶ καὶ τὸ
φρονεῖν ἀξιούμενοι διαφέρειν ἄνδρες ἐνέβαινον εἰς τὰ ληστρικὰ καὶ
μετεῖχον.

2. Plutarch, *l.c.*

3. Plutarch, *l.c.* The only materials that we possess for arriving at an
estimate of their strength are those given at the time of Pompeius' operations.
Appian, *Mithr.*, 96, states that 71 ships were captured, 306 surrendered ;
Plutarch (*l.c.*) that Pompeius captured 90 χαλκέμβολοι and " many others."
There must be some exaggeration in Strabo's statement that he burnt more
than 1,300 σκάφη (XIV, 668). Regarding the numbers of the pirates themselves, Appian says that about 10,000 were killed in battle, and according to
Plutarch 20,000 were captured. The towns, fortresses and bases which
they occupied in the Mediterranean are given as 120. A large quantity of
material was captured by Pompeius, ships under construction, bronze, iron,
ropes, sail-cloth, and timber. A number of captives were found awaiting
ransom, many of whom had long been given up for dead.

4. This detail, which is recorded by Plutarch, is significant, and though
in part, no doubt, due to oriental love of splendour, serves to distinguish the
disciplined Cilician corsair from the dirty Aegean pirate of the ordinary
type. See what Beaufort has to say of the " contemptible appearance " of
the Mainote vessel which he captured (*op. cit.*, p. 227).

5. Appian, *l.c.* ; Dio Cass., XXXVI, 23.

in winter, and the swiftness of their vessels to avoid capture when pursued.[1] Although Cilicia still remained their headquarters,[2] pirates by this time swarmed on all the coasts of the Mediterranean, possessing everywhere fortified bases and watch-towers, and carrying out their raids on all sides.[3] They were ready at all times to render assistance to the enemies of Rome. Already in the year 81 a squadron of Cilicians had helped Sertorius to capture the Pityussae islands in the Balearic group.[4] A Cilician fleet in the year 70 B.C. agreed with Spartacus to transport 2,000 of his men to Sicily, in order to raise a new rebellion of slaves in the island. The Cilicians, however, after receiving his gifts played him false.[5] In the Black Sea pirate vessels remained, as we have seen, with Mithradates after the defeat of his fleet in the Aegean, and Cilicians formed the main part of the garrison of Sinope. Before its surrender they burnt the town and made their escape by night ; Lucullus, however, succeeded in capturing some 8,000 of them.[6] The Cilicians who were put to death in Crete by Metellus had probably found their way there as allies of the Cretans.[7]

Allusion has already been made to the command

1. Dio Cass., XXXVI, 21.

2. Cilices became in fact the general term for all pirates at this time (Appian, *Mithr.*, 92). See above, p. 24.

3. Appian, *Mithr.*, 92 ; Plutarch, *Pomp.*, 24 ; Dio Cass., XXXVI, 20-22 ; Zonaras, X, 3.

4. Plutarch, *Sertorius*, 7.

5. Plutarch, *Crassus*, 10.

6. Plutarch, *Lucullus*, 23 ; cf. Appian, *Mithr.*, 83.

7. Dio Cass., XXXVI, 18.

which was conferred on the praetor Antonius in the year 74.[1] He was the son of Marcus Antonius the orator, who had commanded against the Cilicians in 102 B.C., and the father of the triumvir. Plutarch describes him as generous but weak[2] ; elsewhere we hear that he was worthless and his friends worse.[3] The character of his command is important, since in every respect it anticipated that which was later, in spite of opposition from the Senate, conferred upon Pompeius. By the intrigues of Cotta and Cethegus Antonius received supreme command of all the naval forces of the Romans in the Mediterranean ; but as Velleius points out, in the case of an Antonius such powers were viewed by the Romans with equanimity.[4] Since a part, at any rate, of the existing Roman fleet was employed against Mithradates, his duties included the raising and manning of ships from among the provincials, a source of extortion of which he and his officers made full use.[5] We hear, in fact, more of his extortions than of his opera-

1. The date is fixed by Velleius, II, 31, who says that Antonius was appointed seven years before Pompeius, *i.e.*, in 74 B.C. Cf. Sallust, *Hist.*, *frag.* III, 116, triennio frustra trito (Antonius died in 71). On the whole campaign, see Foucart, *Journal des Savants*, 1906, pp. 569 *seqq.*, " Les campagnes de M. Antonius Creticus contre les Pirates*, 74-71," to which I am much indebted in the present section.

2. Plutarch, *Antonius*, 1.

3. Ps. Asconius (Orelli), p. 121.

4. Velleius, II, 31. Cicero twice alludes to the *imperium infinitum*, which had been conferred on Antonius (*Verr.*, II, 2, 8 ; II, 3, 213).

5. On his behaviour in Sicily, see Cicero, *ll. cc.* His prefect carried off the choristers belonging to Agonis of Lilybaeum, on the plea that they were required for the fleet (*Div. in Caec.*, 55). A fragment of Sallust (III, 2) obviously refers to Antonius : Qui orae maritimae, qua Romanum esset imperium, curator <nocent> ior piratis. Cf. Dio Cass., XXXVI, 23, who says that the allies suffered more at the hands of the Roman generals sent against the pirates than from the pirates themselves. (Cf. Ps.-Asconius, p. 206).

tions during the first two years of his command.
Two fragments of Sallust refer to operations
undertaken by him on the Ligurian and Spanish
coasts, the success of which was, to say the least,
doubtful.[1] A third fragment, which is probably
to be referred to Antonius, records the destruction
of a transport carrying a cohort by two of the
pirates' *myoparones*.[2] His principal achievement,
however, was the invasion of Crete in the year 72
for which in mockery he was given the title of
Creticus.

It is not easy to discover the position held by
the Cretans in the world of piracy at this time.
Plutarch says that the island was its principal
source after Cilicia,[3] and in the past the Cretan
record had been of the worst. During this
century, however, there is not much evidence.
It is difficult to believe that the Cilician corsairs
of the " golden sea " had been prevented from
using Cretan harbours, or that the Cretans had
refrained from occasional acts of piracy on their
own   account.   Nevertheless   the   Cretans,
according to Strabo, had themselves suffered at
the hands of the Cilicians,[4] and in the first
Mithradatic war it is clear that Lucullus, touch-
ing at Crete on his way to Cyrene, had been
able to arrange affairs in the island in a way

1. Sallust, *fr.*, III, 5-6. According to Foucart, *op. cit.*, p. 575, the
operations in the Western Mediterranean were undertaken to ensure the
communications of the army in Spain and to reopen the land-route on the
Ligurian coast (summer of 73). Pompeius had experienced difficulties on
his march to Spain in 77 B.C. See Rice-Holmes, *Roman Republic*, I, p. 145.

2. Sallust, *fr.*, III, 8.

3. Plutarch, *Pompeius*, 29.

4. Strabo, X, 477.

satisfactory to Rome.[1] We hear, too, that the Romans were charged with having undertaken the Cretan war through lust of conquest rather than on account of any special provocation.[2] On the whole, it seems probable that the Cretan cities, though not officially countenancing piracy, at the same time did nothing to prevent its being practised on their coasts either by foreigners or by their own citizens. They were now accused of favouring the cause of Mithradates, and there is no doubt that negotiations had been going on with him,[3] and of furnishing him with mercenaries, a charge which was only too much in accord with Cretan custom. A further charge was added by Antonius that they were supporting the pirates, and were openly assisting them when pursued.[4] The accusations made by the Romans were answered with defiance, and Antonius prepared to reduce the island. There is little information regarding the expedition itself,[5] except that it

1. Plutarch, *Lucullus*, 2.

2. Florus, III, 7.

3. Memnon, XLVIII.

4. Appian, *Sic.*, VI.

5. Foucart, *op. cit.*, p. 581, argues from the Cloatius inscription (Dittenberger, *Syll.*,³ 748) that Antonius was mustering at Gytheion, and would assign to this occasion an inscription (*I. G.*, IV, 932) which records the establishment of a garrison in Epidauros by M. Antonius, ὁ ἐπὶ [πάν]των στραταγός. (Cf. Wilhelm, *Ath. Mitt.*, 1901, p. 419 [= Beitrage, p. 112] who reads in line 21 τὸ τέταρτον καὶ ἑ[βδ]ο[μή]κοστον ἔτος and regards the era as the normal one for Achaia (146 B.C.), against the editor in *I. G.*, who would identify Antonius with the triumvir and dates the era 125 B.C.) The garrison, however, was clearly not placed there to give protection against the pirates' attacks, as the Epidaurians had themselves to provide a contingent for the operations that were in progress.

The notice in Tacitus, *Ann.*, XII, 62, that the Byzantines sent a contingent, may refer to this occasion or to the war of 102 B.C. In view of its position in the order in which their services are mentioned, the former is more probable.

was a complete failure. The fetters with which Antonius had loaded his ships were used by the victorious Cretans to bind the Roman captives.[1] Amongst the prisoners was Antonius' quaestor,[2] and Antonius himself was compelled to conclude a humiliating peace before his death (71 B.C.).[3]

The further history of the Cretan war lies outside the present subject. The peace which Antonius had concluded was set aside by the Roman government, and impossible demands were made of the Cretans—the surrender of all prisoners and of the Cretan leaders, of all pirate boats, and 300 hostages, together with the payment of a sum of 4,000 talents of silver. When the Cretans refused, the Roman general Metellus was sent against the island ; he conducted the war efficiently, but with the greatest brutality.[4]

During all these years the depredations from which the coasts of the Mediterranean suffered were among the most terrible in history. Islands and towns on the coast were deserted. Four hundred cities are said to have been sacked, both fortified and unfortified. Fortified towns succumbed to storm or mining, some even to a formal siege, so great was the impunity of the pirate, who, without fear of molestation, caroused on every shore and carried his raids inland, till all the coastal districts were uncultivated, and the Romans themselves were deprived of the use of

1. Florus, III, 7.
2. Dio Cass., *fr.* 108.
3. Diod. Sic., XL, 1 ; Livy, *Ep.*, XCVII.
4. Diod. Sic., XL, 1 ; Dio Cass., *fr.* 108 ; Velleius, II, 34 Appian, *Sic.*, VI.

the Appian Way. We hear no more of quick descents and hasty re-embarkations ; the pirate stayed openly on shore to dispose of his captives ; cities as well as individuals were held to ransom. Their chief weapon was terrorism. Those who submitted were mildly treated, but any who resisted or attempted retaliation suffered the most terrible reprisals.[1]

Cicero has left us a graphic description of the operations of the pirates off Sicily during the governorship of Verres. Some allowance is, perhaps, to be made for rhetorical exaggeration, and it must be remembered that not every governor was a Verres. But the account throws light not only on the audacity of the pirates, but on the whole system of protection of the subject states which the Romans employed, a system which offered as many facilities for extortion as an unjust governor could desire.[2]

Earlier praetors had requisitioned ships and a fixed number of troops and sailors for the protection of the coasts. Verres compounded with the favoured town of the Mamertines, who were bound by treaty to furnish a bireme, that they should provide instead a merchantman to convey his stolen property to Italy, the materials for its construction being requisitioned from Rhegium. In every province it was customary for the cities to supply a fixed sum for the pay and commissariat of the crews,[3] the money being

1. Appian, *Mithr.*, 93 ; Plutarch, *Pomp.*, 24 ; Dio Cass., XXXVI, 20-22 ; Cicero, *de imp. Cn. Pomp.*, 31-33.

2. Cicero, *Verr.*, II, 5, 42 *seqq.*

3. One of the counts in the charge against Flaccus, governor of Asia, was that he had extorted money for the maintenance of a fleet, although the danger from the pirates had ceased to exist (Cicero, *pro Flacco*, § 12).

entrusted to their own *nauarchos*, who rendered an account of his expenditure. Verres, on the contrary, ordered the money to be paid to himself ; he took additional sums from the cities, which enabled them to avoid sending crews, and from individuals to purchase their discharge. All this was done in the face of imminent attacks from the pirates, and so openly that the pirates themselves were aware of it.

Two engagements took place. In the first his officers, with ten half-manned ships, "found" a pirate ship, so laden with booty that she was almost sinking, and towed her to Syracuse. The old and ugly on board were treated as enemies, the young and useful distributed to Verres' son and retinue, or sent to friends in Rome. No one heard what happened to the captain, though the people of Syracuse were waiting expectantly for the pleasure of seeing him executed. The remainder were brought out for execution from time to time ; for those whom he had himself abducted, Verres substituted Roman citizens, some of whom he accused of being Sertorians ; others, who had themselves been captured by pirates, he charged with having joined them on their own account.

The second engagement was a more serious affair. In order to enjoy the favours of the lady Nice in greater tranquillity, Verres had given the command of the Sicilian squadron, previously commanded by his *legatus*, to her husband Cleomenes of Syracuse. The squadron consisted of six undecked vessels and one quadrireme, which acted as flagship. Thanks to the governor's malversations, the vessels were undermanned and the crews half-starved, but Cleomenes put to sea and took up his position at Pachynus. While the admiral was drinking on shore, a pirate squadron was reported at the neighbouring harbour of Odyssea, whereat the admiral hastily embarks, cuts his cables, and flies in the direction of Syracuse, ordering the rest of the squadron to follow. They do so as best they may, but the two rearmost vessels are cut off by the pirates. At Helorus the admiral leaves his ship, and the other captains run their own aground. The whole squadron was captured and burnt by Heracleo, the pirate leader, at nightfall, the flames of the burning ships giving the signal to Syracuse that pirates were off the coast.

When the news was received at Syracuse, a tumult nearly broke out against the governor, which was only prevented by the self-restraint of the citizens and presence of mind of the resident Romans. Immediate measures for defence are taken by the latter against the now imminent attack. Heracleo's four galleys, having passed the night at Helorus, sail on to Syracuse. They visit first the summer pavilion of Verres on the shore, but finding it empty, enter the harbour. As they cruise about at will, they throw on shore the palm roots which the starving sailors in the captured ships had gathered, and finally retire unmolested, " overcome not by fear, but boredom."

Such is the picture which Cicero draws. It was some consolation to the Sicilians that Lucius Metellus, the successor of Verres, defeated the pirates by land and sea, and drove them from Sicilian waters.[1]

The coasts of Italy were suffering not less than the provinces. Already, in the year 75, the Consul Cotta announced that the shores of Italy were filled with enemies.[2] The people in the neighbourhood of Brundisium and on the coasts of Etruria and Campania are said to have been the chief sufferers.[3] Two Roman praetors were carried off, with their lictors and twelve axes.[4] Caieta was sacked under the eyes of the praetor, and the temple of Juno Lacinia. Noble Roman ladies were captured and held to ransom ; among them the daughter of the Antonius who had led the first expedition against Cilicia was carried off from Misenum.[5] A pirate squadron entered the harbour at Ostia, capturing and destroying a consular fleet which lay there.[6] The pirates were attracted to the Italian coast, partly by the richer booty which it offered, partly by policy, thinking that by injuring the Romans themselves they could the more easily terrorise over the provincials.[7] There is a certain humour in their treatment of Roman citizens. When a captive proclaimed his name and origin, they would feign alarm and humbly beg for pardon, and lest the

---

1. Orosius, VI, 3. The name of the pirate leader is given as Pyrganio, who is clearly regarded by Orosius as the leader of the pirates who had entered the harbour of Syracuse.

2. Sallust, *frag.* III, 47, 7.

3. Appian, *Mithr.*, 93 ; Florus, III, 6.

4. Plutarch, *Pompeius*, 24 ; Appian, *l.c.* ; Cicero, *de imp. Cn. Pomp.*, 32.

5. Cicero, *l.c.* ; Plutarch, *l.c.* It is to be noted that all three localities are promontories, which it would be easy to cut off.

6. Cicero, *l.c.* ; Dio Cass., XXXVI, 22.

7. Dio Cass., *l.c.*

error should occur again, dress him in his boots and toga, and send him home by water.[1] Much, of course, depended on the individual. There is the well-known story of Julius Caesar reading aloud his youthful compositions and threatening his captors with crucifixion for their lack of appreciation. Their treatment of him was an amused tolerance, in gratitude for which, when he had pursued and caught them after his release, he cut their throats before nailing them to the cross. The ransom they had asked was twenty talents, which Caesar thought unsuitable for such a person as himself and proposed fifty.[2]

In spite of such protection as the fleets of Lucullus could offer, the year 69 seems to have been an especially bad one in the Greek archipelago. In addition to the long list of towns and temples which were sacked at various times,[3] to that year can be assigned the overrunning of Aegina,[4] and the second sack of Delos by the pirate Athenodorus. All that Lucullus' officer, Triarius, could do was to repair the damage as best he might, and protect the island for the future with a wall.[5] The miserable

1. The ancient equivalent for "walking the plank" was for a ladder to be lowered into the sea, by which the captive went home. Compulsion was occasionally necessary (Plutarch, *l.c.*; Zonaras, X, 3).

2. Plutarch, *Julius*, 2; *Crassus*, 7; Suetonius, *Julius*, 4, 74; Velleius, II, 41.

3. Plutarch, *Pompeius*, 24, mentions the temples at Claros, Didyma, Hermione, Epidauros, the Isthmus, Taenarum, Calaureia, Actium, Leucas, Samos and Argos. Cicero (*l.c.*) adds Cnidos and Colophon. On Didyma see, however, Haussoullier, *Rev. de Philologie*, XLV, p. 57.

4. *I. G.*, IV, 2, 2. For the dating, see Fraenkel *ad loc.*

5. Phlegon, *F. H. G.*, III, p. 606, 12. See Roussel, *Delos*, p. 331. Remains of the wall have been discovered by the French excavators in the eastern part of the island. There is an allusion to the sack of Delos in Cicero.

condition of the Cyclades at this time is reflected by an inscription of Tenos, which portrays the island as ruined by the continual descents of the pirates and crushed by a load of debt.[1]

The seas were now almost closed. Roman fleets dared not venture from Brundisium except in the depths of winter.[2] Trade was at a standstill, and Rome itself threatened with a famine.[3] It is scarcely to be wondered at if the business classes and people combined to demand that the extraordinary command against the pirates should be revived and conferred on the most capable general available.[4]

No name was mentioned in the original proposal of the tribune Gabinius,[5] but it was universally understood that Pompeius was intended, and that he himself had been waiting for such an opportunity as was now offered. The senatorial party, which had acquiesced in the earlier appointment of Antonius, now offered the bitterest opposition,

de imp. Cn. Pomp., 55. An inscription found in Myconos and published in *B. C. H.*, XLVI, pp. 198 *seqq* (see also *Supplement. Epigr. Gr.*, I, 335) contains the text of a *Lex Gabinia Calpurnia de Deliis*, a consular law of 58 B.C., decreeing the restoration of temples and shrines in Delos, and the grant of *libertas* and immunity from taxation to the Delians. Qu[o]mque praedones, quei orbem ter[r]arum complureis[annos vexarint ? fan]a delubra sumu[la]cra deorum immor[t]alium loca religio[sissuma devast]arint, lege Ga[b]inia superatei ac deletei s[i]nt, et omneis rel[iqua] praeter insu[l]am Delum sedes Apollinis ac Dianae in antei[quom splendor]em sit rest[it]uta . . . . etc.

1. *I. G.*, XII, 5, 860.

2. Plutarch, *Pomp.*, 25 ; Dio Cass., XXXVI, 23 ; Cicero, *op. cit.*, 31.

3. Livy, *Ep.*, XCIX ; Plutarch, *op. cit.*, 27 ; Dio Cass., XXXVI, 31.

4. The chief authorities for Pompeius' campaign are : Appian, *Mithr.* 94-96, 115 ; Cicero, *de imp. Cn. Pomp.*, 31-35 ; Dio Cass., XXXVI, 20-37 ; Eutropius, VI, 12 ; Florus, III, 6 ; Orosius, VI, 4 ; Plutarch, *Pompeius*, 24-27 ; Velleius, II, 31 ; Zonaras, X, 3.

5. On the so-called Lex Gabinia, see Appendix E (p. 242).

maintaining that the creation of such a command was a revival of the ancient monarchy, and threatening that the holder would meet the fate of the ancient kings. As a last resort the tribune Roscius endeavoured to introduce an amendment by which the command should be made collegiate, a proposal which would not only have been fatal to Pompeius' ambitions, but as likely as not have wrecked his strategic scheme.

By the terms of his appointment, Pompeius was given proconsular power for three years over the whole Mediterranean, his authority to run concurrently with that of existing governors for a distance of fifty miles inland from the coast. Client kings and allied states were ordered to co-operate. His staff was to consist of fifteen legati of senatorial rank with the title of pro-praetor, whose number was later increased to twenty-five.[1] Troops, ships and money might be raised by him as required. He is said to have raised 120,000 men (twenty legions), and 4,000 cavalry, requisitioned 6,000 talents of money and had 270 ships in commission.[2]

It is obvious that Pompeius had already framed

1. Plutarch and Dio Cassius say 24 and 2 quaestors. The grant of praetorian rank is confirmed by Dittenberger, *Syll.*3, 750 (= *I. G. Rom.*, I, 1040), a decree of Cyrene in honour of Lentulus Marcellinus, who is styled πρεσβευτὰς ἀντιστράταγος.

2. The figures vary slightly in the authorities. Those given above are Appian's. Plutarch gives 5,000 cavalry and authority to raise 200 ships, though he says that 500 were commissioned.

The figures are discussed by Groebe, *Klio*, X, pp. 375 *seqq.* The conclusions which he reaches are that Appian's 270 νῆες σὺν ἡμιολίαις = 200 warships (cf. Plutarch) and 70 light vessels, the total 270 being that of the existing Roman fleet (cf. Appian, ναῦς ὅσας εἶχον; Dio Cass., τὰς ναῦς ἁπάσας.) The total of 500 which Plutarch states were commissioned was made up by new construction (and ? allied contingents). But any results are problematical.

his scheme of operations before the appointment
was made. The Gabinian law was passed at the
beginning of 67, probably in January, and after
a few weeks spent in the necessary preparations
he was ready to sail at the very beginning of the
Spring. There had already been a fall in prices
at Rome on his appointment, but one of his first
measures was to secure the food supplies of the
capital.

His plan of campaign was a masterpiece of
strategy and was carried out triumphantly in all
its details. The Mediterranean and Black Seas,
with the adjoining coasts, were divided into
thirteen commands, each district being placed
under the control of a group-commander, who
was responsible for coast-defence, the rounding-up
of pirate forces, and the reduction of strongholds
within his own area. The commands were
arranged so as to isolate the scattered bands of
pirates over the whole Mediterranean, co-operation between the commanders of adjoining
districts being an essential feature of the scheme.
So far as it is possible to discover it, the distribution
of forces was as follows :[1]

1. For a detailed discussion of the question I must refer to my paper,
The Distribution of Pompeius' forces in the Campaign of 67 B.C. (*Annals of
Archaeology and Anthropology*, X, pp. 46 *seqq.*) For convenience I give the
passage of Appian (*Mithr.*, 95) and of Florus (III, 6), with the readings and
punctuation that should be adopted :

Appian, *Mithr.*, 95 : ἐπέστησεν Ἰβηρίᾳ μὲν καὶ ταῖς Ἡρακλείοις
στήλαις Τιβέριον Νέρωνα καὶ Μάλλιον Τορκουᾶτον, ἀμφὶ δὲ τὴν
Λιγυστικήν τε καὶ Κελτικὴν θάλασσαν Μᾶρκον Πομπώνιον, Λιβύῃ δὲ
καὶ Σαρδόνι καὶ Κύρνῳ, καὶ ὅσαι πλησίον νῆσοι, Λέντλον τε Μαρκελλῖνον
καὶ Πόπλιον Ἀτίλιον, περὶ δὲ αὐτὴν Ἰταλίαν Λεύκιον Γέλλιον καὶ
Γναῖον Λέντλον. Σικελίαν δὲ καὶ τὸν Ἰόνιον ἐφύλασσον αὐτῷ Πλώτιός
τε Οὔαρος καὶ Τερέντιος Οὐάρρων μέχρι Ἀκαρνανίας, Πελοπόννησον δὲ
καὶ τὴν Ἀττικήν, ἔτι δ' Εὔβοιαν καὶ Θεσσαλίαν καὶ Μακεδονίαν καὶ
Βοιωτίαν Λεύκιος Σισιννᾶς, τὰς δὲ νήσους καὶ τὸ Αἰγαῖον ἅπαν καὶ τὸν
Ἑλλήσποντον ἐπ' ἐκείνῳ Λεύκιος Λόλλιος, Βιθυνίαν δὲ καὶ Θρᾴκην καὶ

In the west, the Spanish seas were entrusted to
Tiberius Nero and Manlius Torquatus, the former
patrolling the Straits and the arm of the sea
between Mauretania and southern Spain, the
latter stationed in the Balearic islands. The two
commands effectually controlled the whole of the
sea between Mauretania and Spain. The Gallic
and Ligurian gulfs were under Marcus Pomponius,
whose sphere of operations in Ligurian waters
overlapped that of Atilius, based on Corsica and
Sardinia. Sicily was held by Plotius Varus, and
the whole of the northern coast of Africa from the
point of contact with the Spanish command by
Lentulus Marcellinus. The district is a wide one,
but his duties would consist principally in
maintaining contact with other groups, to the
west with Nero and Torquatus, to the north with
Atilius in Sardinia, Plotius in Sicily, above all
with Varro in the Ionian Sea, perhaps also with
Metellus in the Levant.

Italy was guarded by two powerful fleets under

τὴν Προποντίδα καὶ τὸ τοῦ Πόντου στόμα Πούπλιος Πείσων, Λυκίαν δὲ
καὶ Παμφυλίαν καὶ Κύπρον καὶ Φοινίκην Μέτελλος Νέπως.

Florus III, 6: Gellius Tusco mari impositus, Plotius Siculo; Atilius
[Gratillius, codd.] Ligusticum sinum, Pomponius [Pompeius, codd.] Gallicum
obsedit; Torquatus Balearicum, Tiberius Nero Gaditanum fretum, qua
primum maris nostri limen aperitur; Lentulus Libycum, Marcellinus
Aegyptium, Pompeii iuvenes Hadriaticum, Varro Terentius Aegaeum et
Ionicum [Ponticum, codd.]; <et> Pamphylium Metellus, Asiaticum Caepio,
ipsas Propontidis fauces Porcius Cato sic obditis navibus quasi porta observavit.

It will be seen that for the Gnaeus Lentulus, L. Lollius, and Publius Piso
of Appian are substituted Pompeii iuvenes, Caepio, and Porcius Cato, all of
whom I believe to have been subordinates. L. Sisenna has been omitted.
It is for this reason that I believe the reading of the MSS. Lentulus Libycum,
Marcellinus Aegyptium to be original. To arrive at the total of thirteen
commanders, and assisted probably by a confusion with Gnaeus Lentulus
(Clodianus), the actual commander in the Adriatic, for whose name he has
substituted the subordinate Pompeii iuvenes, Florus has created two persons
out of the single name Gnaeus Lentulus Marcellinus. (His name is given in
Dittenberger, Syll.³, 750, as Cn. Cornelius P. f. Lentulus Marcellinus.)

the consulars Lucius Gellius (Poplicola) and
Gnaeus Lentulus (Clodianus), the one based on
the western coast and covering the Tuscan Sea,
the other, on the east, being responsible for the
Adriatic, and it is to be presumed, the dangerous
Illyrian coast.[1] One of the most important
commands was that of Terentius Varro, who
covered the coast of Epiros, from the mouth of the
Corinthian gulf as far as the straits of Otranto,
and patrolled the sea between Sicily and the
Cyclades.[2] One of his duties was to close the
straits of Otranto by means of patrols between
Hydruntum and Apollonia.[3] Further to the
south his patrols, maintaining contact with the
forces of Lentulus Marcellinus off the Cyrenaica,
would provide an effective barrier between the
eastern and western halves of the Mediterranean.
The protection of the coasts of the Peloponnese
fell to his colleague Lucius (Cornelius) Sisenna,[4]
whose district comprised also the western shores
of the Aegean and included Macedonia. The
Greek archipelago and the Aegean as far as the
Hellespont were entrusted to Lucius Lollius, and
it is to be presumed that he was also responsible

1. See Groebe, *op. cit.*, p. 385. Appian's περὶ δὲ αὐτὴν 'Ιταλίαν
Λεύκιον Γέλλιον καὶ Γναῖον Λέντλον is made quite definite by Florus : Gellius
Tusco mari impositus, and Cicero, *op. cit.*, 35 : Italiae duo maria maximis
classibus firmissimisque praesidiis adornavit. But what is to be made of
Florus' Pompeii iuvenes Hadriaticum ? The eldest was not more than
thirteen (see Groebe), but were they being given their first introduction to
warfare under the consular Lentulus, who is not mentioned by Florus ?
The Teubner reading in Florus, which is followed by Groebe, Libycum
Lentulus Marcellinus, Aegyptium Pompeii iuvenes ; Hadriaticum Varro
Terentius, is of course impossible.

2. See his own statement, *De re rust*, II, *proem.*

3. See Pliny, *N. H.*, III, 16, 3, with my note in *Annals*, p. 49, n. 1.

4. Dio Cass., XXXVI, 18.

for the Aegean coastline of Thrace to the east of the Macedonian frontier, as well as the western coast of Asia Minor, which Florus assigns to the otherwise unknown Caepio.[1] The Propontis and Euxine were assigned to Piso, under whose direction, if there is any ground for Florus' statement, M. Porcius Cato commanded a squadron in the Propontis. Finally, the southern coast of Asia Minor was allotted to Metellus Nepos, whose district, as described by Appian, was Lycia, Pamphylia, Cyprus, and Phoenicia. The omission of Cilicia is not without significance. There was no question of Metellus attempting to reduce the Cilician coast until the rest of the Mediterranean had been cleared, and the commander-in-chief himself should arrive in Cilician waters. It was Metellus' business to patrol the Levant and engage the pirates as they issued from or sought to retire to their Cilician fastnesses.

Simultaneous attacks were to be opened by the *legati* on all the pirates' strong points and anchorages throughout the Mediterranean, and a cordon drawn round each group. Concerted action of this character would frustrate their known tactics of sending reinforcements to any of their brethren who were threatened. The pirates in Cilicia would be effectually blockaded by Metellus, and any that were able to evade him would fall in with Varro's patrols, if they attempted to seek the West.[2] Pompeius himself

1. "Asiaticum Caepio." The omission of the name by Appian is probably due to the fact that Caepio was acting under the orders of Lollius. This is almost certainly the relation between M. Porcius Cato and Piso.

2. Varro received the naval crown for these operations (Pliny, *N. H.* XVI, 3, 1; VII, 31, 7).

commanded a mobile force of sixty ships, which was first to sweep the western seas, driving the pirates on to the stationary forces already assembled, or if they fled eastward, into the squadrons of Varro and Metellus.

The pirates were taken by surprise owing to the rapidity of the Roman movements, operations beginning at the earliest possible season.   In alarm, they fled to their accustomed headlands and anchorages, where they were reduced according to plan by the *legati*.   Pompeius thus cleared the west in forty days.   We hear of his presence in Sicily, Africa, and Sardinia, and it is probable that he visited the coast of Gaul, where his officer Pomponius was experiencing trouble from the consul Piso, governor designate of Gallia Narbonensis.   Piso had carried his feud with Pompeius as far as a petty attempt to thwart a subordinate in the raising of troops.   At the end of forty days Pompeius returned, by way of Etruria, to Rome, where the consul's activities necessitated his presence, but having obtained through his agent Gabinius pledges for good behaviour, he sailed once more from Brundisium.

There is little information regarding his movements in the East.   We hear of him in Athens, where he was received with fulsome flattery, and at Rhodes.   It is probable that both visits were made with the purpose of collecting forces from the allied states, previously ordered to rendezvous at the Peiraeus and at Rhodes.

By this time the cause of the pirates was desperate.   Even before Pompeius arrived in the East, many of them had surrendered.   No small part of his success was due to the moderation which was shown towards captives, which induced men whom he had spared to give information about the rest, and brought about further surrenders. The most desperate, however, placed their families and treasures in the castles of the Taurus and prepared for a final resistance.

The task that remained appeared the most serious part of the campaign, and for it Pompeius made careful preparations. A siege train and a force equipped for all kinds of fighting were gathered, before the final attack was delivered on the strongholds of the Cilician coast. The pirates, however, realised that their cause was desperate. When they offered battle off Coracesium, they were heavily defeated and blockaded in the fortress. The defenders soon threw themselves on the mercy of the invader, and were followed by the remnants of the pirates throughout Cilicia.[1] Pompeius did not betray their trust. It is one of his chief merits that he diagnosed the causes of piracy in the misery of the times, and took the most effective steps possible to prevent its recurrence. Many of the survivors were settled by him in districts where the temptation to relapse into their old habits would not exist,[2] and where the ruined men who had

1. Plutarch, *op. cit.*, 28. Appian's statement (*Mithr.*, 96) that Cragos and Anticragos were the first fortresses to be reduced raises a small difficulty, since it would imply that western Lycia had gone over to the side of the pirates, of which there is no other record, and which is directly contradicted by Strabo. From his words it seems certain that Appian imagined Cragos and Anticragos to be in Cilicia—πρῶτοι μὲν οἱ Κράγον καὶ 'Αντίκραγον εἶχον, φρούρια (sic) μέγιστα, μετὰ δ' ἐκείνους οἱ ὄρειοι Κίλικες (*i.e.*, those in the interior). There is an obvious confusion between the Lycian mountains Cragos (ἔχων ἄκρας ὀκτὼ καὶ πόλιν ὁμώνυμον, Strabo, 665) and Anticragos and the Cilician Cragos, πέτρα περίκρημνος πρὸς θαλάττῃ (Strabo, 670).

2. Plutarch, ἐς γῆν μεταφέρειν ἐκ τῆς θαλάσσης.

joined the ranks of the pirates could obtain a fresh start in life. The cities of Cilicia Pedias had been depopulated by Tigranes, and Pompeius settled many of his captives there, especially in Mallos, Adana, Epiphaneia and Soli, which was re-named Pompeiopolis. Some were settled in Dyme of Achaia,[1] and it is a pleasing thought that the old man of Corycos, whom Vergil knew in Calabria, was a reformed pirate, who supported his old age by bee-keeping.[2]

The moderation displayed by Pompeius had one result that was unexpected. During the war with Crete, which was now drawing to a close, Metellus had treated the island with the utmost savagery. The towns which he was still besieging accordingly sent to Pompeius, who at the time was in Pamphylia, and made their surrender to him. Pompeius, who had hitherto refrained from encroaching on the sphere of Metellus' operations, accepted the surrender and sent Octavius, one of his officers, to the island with orders to protect the Cretans. Finding himself ignored, Octavius summoned Sisenna, Pompeius' officer in Greece, and after his colleague's death actually met Metellus with force. It was but a slight consolation to Pompeius for the rebuff which he had received, that he could induce one of the tribunes in Rome to compel Metellus to give up Lasthenes and Panares, the Cretan leaders, on the ground that they had surrendered to himself.[3]

1. Appian, *Mithr.*, 96, 115; Strabo, XIV, 665; Plutarch, *Pomp.*, 28; Dio Cass., XXXVI, 37.

2. Virgil, *Georg.*, IV, 125; see Servius, *ad loc.*

3. Plutarch, *Pomp.*, 29; Dio Cass., XXXVI, 18, 19; Livy, *Ep.*, XCIX; Florus, III, 7.

APPENDIX E (Chapter VI, p. 233).

The so-called *Lex Gabinia* from Delphi.

An attempt has been made by E. Cuq (*C. R. Ac. Inscr.*, 1923, pp. 129 *seqq.*) to prove that the law engraved on the Monument of Aemilius Paulus at Delphi, the full text of which was first published in *Klio*, XVII, p. 171, is the famous *Lex Gabinia* of 67 B.C. It is unfortunate that the editor of this inscription in *Suppl. Ep. Gr.* (I, no. 161) has also adopted this view. It must be confessed that if this law is the *Lex Gabinia*, it adds little to our knowledge regarding its most important provisions, the creation of the *imperium infinitum* and the powers to be conferred on its holder, according to Cuq's view, having been contained in the missing first section. It is surprising, however, as Levi (*Rivista di Filologia*, 1924, pp. 80 *seqq.*) has pointed out, to find that the Gabinian law was a *lex satura* of the type which the Delphic inscription would show it to be. Cuq is undoubtedly right when he points out that the consulship of C. Marius and L. Valerius (100 B.C.), mentioned in the inscription, cannot be taken as the actual date of the law, which would naturally have been given in the missing preamble. But an examination of the chronology of Pompeius' campaign against the pirates is enough to show that this is not the *Lex Gabinia*. Cuq's principal argument for dating the present law to the year 67 B.C. is based on Cap. VI, which contains instructions that the Senate shall give audience to the Rhodian ambassadors ἐκτὸς τῆς συντάξεως. This provision was necessitated, in his view, by an earlier *Lex Gabinia de Senatu Legatis dando* of the same year, which would prevent audience being given to ambassadors from foreign states after March 1 ; but since the co-operation of the Rhodians was essential to Pompeius' plans, it was necessary to make a special exception in favour of the Rhodian ambassadors, who had arrived late. The present law must, therefore, be later than March 1, 67. The effect of this is to make Pompeius' campaign fall in 66 B.C. " Pompée fit ses preparatifs à la fin de l'hiver et entra en campagne au début du printemps 66 " (*op. cit.*, p. 142. Cf. Cicero, *de imp. Cn. Pomp.*, 35 : extrema hieme apparavit, ineunte vere suscepit, media aestate confecit). This is absolutely at variance with the known chronology. On Cuq's own showing Gabinius was elected tribune in July 68 and entered office on December 10, 68. His term of office would therefore expire in December, 67. We know, however, that Pompeius' campaign took place during Gabinius' tribunate and Piso's consulship (67 B.C.). After the conclusion of the operations in the West, Pompeius was compelled to visit Rome owing to the machinations of Piso, who was still consul, ὅθεν ὁ Πείσων ἐκινδύνευσε τὴν ὑπάτειαν ἀφαιρεθῆναι, Γαβινίου νόμον ἔχοντος ἤδη συγγεγραμμένον. Ἀλλά καὶ τοῦτο διεκώλυσεν ὁ Πομπήιος. (Plutarch, *Pomp.*, 27).

The contents of the inscription all point to a date soon after 100 B.C. An essential part of the law is the provision that instructions to prevent pirates from using their ports should be sent by the consul to the king reigning in the island of

Cyprus, the king reigning in Alexandria and Egypt, the king reigning in Cyrene, and the kings reigning in Syria, οἷς πᾶσι] φιλία καὶ συμμαχία ἔ[στι. This implies a date when there was a dual monarchy in Syria, when Egypt and Cyprus were separate kingdoms, and when there was still a king of Cyrene, with whom φιλία καὶ συμμαχία could be said to exist. The only period which satisfies all these conditions after 100 B.C. (the *terminus post* for the inscription) lies between the years 100 and 96 B.C.

The crucial case is Cyrene. After the death of Ptolemy VII of Egypt in 116 B.C., it had passed to Ptolemy Apion, who reigned until 96 B.C., and at his death bequeathed Cyrene to the Romans (Sallust, *fr.* II, 43 ; Tacitus, *Ann.*, XIV, 18 ; Justin, XXXIX, 5 ; Appian, *Mithr.*, 121). We are now asked to believe that the inscription proves that Cyrene was governed by a king in 67. (Cf. *Suppl. Ep.* : Cyrenam a. 67 nondum in provinciae statum redactam esse ex hac lege apparet.) It is true that Pompeius claimed to have reduced the Cyrenaica (Diod. Sic., XL, 4), but a fragment of Sallust (II, 43, Maurenbrecher) shows that it was already regarded as a Roman province in the year 75 : P(ublius) que Lentulus Marcel⟨linus⟩ eodem auctore quaest-⟨or⟩ in novam provinci⟨am⟩ Curenas missus est, q⟨uod⟩ ea mortui regis Apio⟨nis⟩ testamento nobis d⟨ata⟩ prudentiore quam ⟨illas⟩ per gentis et minus g⟨lor⟩iae avidi imperio co⟨nti⟩nenda fuit. Praetere⟨a div⟩ersorum ordin⟨um⟩ . . . . As Levi has already pointed out (*op. cit.*, p. 85), Maurenbrecher's account of

the Aurelian palimpsest, from which this fragment
is derived, makes it plain that the event in question
was related by Sallust under the year 75. The
palimpsest contains five fragments, three of
which refer without doubt to this year. It is
true that the codex is in two pieces, but there
can be no question of the fragment which relates
to Cyrene (II, 43) belonging to the year 67, sinc
it is found on the same piece as II, 45, which
refers to Metellus' (Creticus) candidature for the
praetorship. Metellus was consul in 69 B.C.
A proper examination of the Sallust fragments
would therefore have saved Cuq from the statement that P. Lentulus Marcellinus of the Sallust
fragment is Pompeius' legate. The latter was
probably Cnaeus Lentulus Marcellinus (Dittenberger, Syll.³, 750), and we may suppose that
Pompeius appointed him to the command of the
Cyrenaic district owing to the connexion of his
family with the province. There was therefore
no king ruling in Cyrene in 75 B.C., and what
information we possess shows that there had been
no king since the death of Apion. The Romans
had at first delayed taking up their new inheritance
(cf. Livy, *Ep.*, LXX : Ptolemaeus, rex Cyrenarum
cui cognomentum Apioni fuit, mortuus haeredem
populum Romanum reliquit, et eius regni civitates
senatus liberas esse iussit), with the result that
the country had fallen into anarchy. During the
first Mithradatic war, Lucullus had found the
Cyrenaeans ἐκ τυραννίδων συνεχῶν καὶ πολέμων
ταραττομένους (Plutarch, *Lucullus*, 2), and further
information regarding the τύραννοι is given by
Plutarch and Polyaenus (Plutarch, *de Virt. Mul.*,

p. 255; Polyaenus, VIII, 38). It is therefore impossible to believe that there was a king reigning in Cyrene in 67 B.C., with whom the Romans could be said to be on terms of friendship and alliance.

The political circumstances of Cyprus, Egypt and Syria during the years 100-96 are in complete accord with what we find specified in the inscription. Cyprus was now ruled by Ptolemy Lathyrus, Egypt by Ptolemy Alexander (Niese, III, p. 310). The βασιλεῖς οἱ ἐν Συρίαι βασιλεύοντες are the half-brothers Antiochus Grypus and Antiochus Cyzicenus (Niese, III, p. 309). It is true, as Cary has pointed out (*Classical Review*, XXXVIII, p. 60), that Cicero speaks of reges Syriae shortly before the year 70 B.C. (*Verr.*, II, 4, 61), but Cary's argument that the sovereignty of Syria had again been put into commission is scarcely warranted. Syria at the time was held by Tigranes, and *reges Syriae*, as used by Cicero, does not mean more than the legitimate princes of Syria, the representatives of the royal house. After Tigranes' withdrawal we hear only of one ruler, Antiochus XIII Asiaticus (Appian, *Syr.*, 49, 70; Justin, XL, 2, 3).

A further point is raised by Cary, that in the phrase πολῖται Ῥωμαίων σ[ύμμαχοί] τε ἐκ τῆς Ἰταλίας Λατῖνοι the omission of all reference to the *Socii Italici*, whose interests were vitally concerned in a measure of this kind, which dealt with the safety of the seas, points to a date after the Social War. But the phrase σύμμαχοι ἐκ τῆς Ἰταλίας Λατῖνοι is a difficult one after 89 B.C., and to Levi at any rate (*op. cit.*, p. 85) would imply the existence of the Italian federation.

There is no reason why a law of this kind, which prescribes nothing more than the closing of the ports against the pirates, should be brought into direct connection with any of the known expeditions made by the Romans against them.   This is the error made by Cuq, when, by a process of exhaustion, he arrives at the conclusion that it must be the Gabinian law.   His argument that provisions of the kind specified in the law were unnecessary in the years which followed Antonius' expedition of 102 B.C. (p. 131), implies that Antonius was completely successful in exterminating the pirates, which was not the case. The law is simply a general police-measure, intended to supplement the first action undertaken bythe Romans against the pirates.

CHAPTER VII

THE EMPIRE

Pacatum Volitant per Mare Navitae

THE rapidity and thoroughness with which the reduction of the pirates had been achieved created a great impression among Pompeius' contemporaries ; there are indications also that he endeavoured to render his work permanently effective by arranging for the provision of a standing fleet to patrol the seas. Before his departure from the East he had given instructions that the maritime states should continue to supply their contingents of ships, and after he returned to Rome, it was at his suggestion that arrangements were made to patrol Italian waters.[1] Unfortunately, however, he still preserved the old system of dependence on the foreign states for the provision and maintenance of warships,[2] the inadequacy and dangers of which are illustrated by the sequel. One of the charges brought against Flaccus, the governor of Asia in the year 62, was that he had misused the powers which the system conferred on him to extort money from the provincials, on the plea of maintaining a fleet. Although there was no

1. Cicero, *Pro Flacco*, 29-30.

2. Discripsit (Flaccus) autem pecuniam ad Pompeii rationem, quae fuit accomodata L. Sullae discriptioni (*Ib.*, 32).

doubt that the fleet had cruised, Cicero's defence
of him on this point was prejudiced by the fact
that his own brother, who had succeeded Flaccus
in Asia, had decided that the maintenance of
a permanent squadron was unnecessary.[1] Cicero,
however, had no difficulty in glozing over the
extortions of Flaccus and in justifying the policy
of Pompeius, so far as the necessity of maintaining
a fleet was concerned. He could point to fresh
acts of piracy on the seas, in particular to the
murder of a prominent citizen of Adramyttium,
which had recently taken place.[2] The fault lay
rather with the Roman system of dependence
on the ships of the provincials, and with the
dishonesty of the governing class. Without
a permanent fleet the risks of occasional outbreaks
had still to be reckoned with. We hear of serious
piracy off the Syrian coast,[3] and in spite of the
measures taken by Pompeius to remove the
Cilician pirates from the temptation of falling
back into their old habits, there can be little doubt
that relapses occurred. Caesar mentions pirates
and brigands from Cilicia, Syria and the neighbouring districts as serving in the army of Achillas
at Alexandria,[4] and it is reasonable to suppose
that the people of Dyme, who according to
Cicero had been driven from their land and were
infesting the sea in 44 B.C.,[5] were not unconnected

1. Cicero, *op. cit.*, 33.

2. *Ib.*, 31.

3. Dio Cass., XXXIX, 59.

4. Caesar, *B. C.*, III, 110.

5. Cicero, *Ad Att.*, XVI, 1 : Dymaeos agro pulsos mare infestum habere
nil mirum. Ἐν ὁμοπλοίᾳ Bruti aliquid praesidi esse, sed opinor, minuta
navigia.

with the colony of Cilicians which Pompeius had settled there some twenty years earlier.

The conduct of the people of Dyme may be regarded as typical of much that was happening in the Mediterranean during the civil wars, when piracy again became serious and found its rallying point in the motley forces gathered by Sextus Pompeius. After his escape from Corduba in 45 B.C., Sextus had lived the life of a brigand in Spain,[1] and it is asserted by Appian that he was already practising piracy at sea before the death of Julius Caesar.[2] The ships at his disposal cannot, however, have been numerous until he was definitely appointed to the command of the naval forces of Rome in the year 43.[3] It is stated moreover by Dio Cassius, that he refrained from piracy even after his condemnation among the assassins of Julius Caesar, until he was proscribed by the Triumvirs.[4] His fleet then became a refuge not only for the proscribed but for all discontented elements, slaves and pirates from all quarters being enlisted in his forces.[5] Although he had become master of Sicily in the preceding year and his ships were manned by the most skilful sailors,[6] Sextus appears to have been able

1. Appian, *B. C.*, II, 106; V, 143.

2. *Ib.*, IV, 83.

3. *Ib.*, III, 4; IV, 84; Dio Cass., XLVI, 40; Velleius, II, 72.

4. Dio Cass., XLVIII, 17. Appian, however, says that he was already enlisting slaves after the occupation of Sicily in 43 (IV, 85). Cf. Livy, *Ep.*, CXXIII : sine ulla loci cuiusquam possessione praedatus in mari.

5. Dio Cass., XLVIII, 17. For the number of slaves see *Mon Anc.*, XXV where 30,000 are said to have been handed back to their masters by Augustus. Cf. Appian, *B. C.*, V, 131. According to Dio Cassius, XLIX, 12, the unclaimed were impaled.

6. Appian, *B. C.*, IV, 85.

to do little to interfere with the passage of Antony and Octavian to Greece in the year 42,[1] and all the serious work of interrupting their communications was done by the regular senatorial admirals, Murcus and Ahenobarbus.[2] Both now and after the campaign of Philippi, when his forces were increased by the addition of the squadron commanded by Murcus,[3] Sextus seems to have acted without any general plan of campaign, while his tactics differed little from those of the Cilician pirates of an earlier date. It is probable enough that his leading admirals were ex-pirates who had belonged to the Cilicians before their reduction. The most skilful of them, Menas and Menecrates, whose names suggest an Anatolian origin, are both said to have been freedmen of his father,[4] and may have been first enslaved in the war of 67 B.C. Beginning therefore, with Augustus himself,[5] our authorities are unanimous in regarding the war with Sextus as a pirate war,[6] a view which fairly certainly represents the opinion of contemporaries, when all the coasts of Italy were suffering from his raids and Rome itself was threatened with famine as in the days of the Cilicians.[7] Octavian had

1. Dio Cass., XLVII, 36-37.

2. *Ib.*, XLVII, 47; Appian, IV, 108, 115.

3. Appian, V, 2, 25; Dio Cass., XLVIII, 19.

4. Velleius, II, 73. On Menas (called by Appian, Menodorus) see also *B. C.*, V, 79. Demochares (*B. C.*, V, 83) and Apollophanes (*ib.* 84) are also said to have been freedmen.

5. *Mon. Anc., l.c.*: mare pacavi a praedonibus.

6. Strabo, V, 243; Velleius, II, 73; Lucan, VI, 421 (Siculus pirata); Florus, IV, 8 (o quam diversus a patre), etc.

7. Dio Cass., XLVIII, 46; Appian, *B. C.*, V, 67, 74; Florus, *l.c.*; Orosius, VI, 18, § 19.

realised from the first that there could be no peace
with Sextus. Although he was forced by popular
discontent into concluding the agreement of
Misenum in 38 B.C.,[1] the event showed that while
Sextus' forces maintained their present constitu-
tion, security at sea was impossible. By the terms
of the agreement, Sextus had been charged with
maintaining the police of the seas,[2] but it was
clear that, even had he so desired, he was incapable
of restraining the piracies which his own followers
were accustomed to practise. It may have been
an invention on the part of Octavian that
captured pirates had confessed under torture that
they had been instigated by Sextus[3]; but in any
case it was obvious that he could not hope to
keep his forces together, if he made any attempt
to check their depredations.

It was not until the conclusion of the war with
Sextus that Octavian was able to turn his attention
to the eastern shores of the Adriatic, where piracy
still flourished on the coasts, and disturbances
among the barbarian tribes of the interior
demanded vigorous action. Although Julius
Caesar, while governor of Gaul, had also held the
province of Illyricum, he had been able to devote
little attention to that district and had visited
it only on two occasions.[4] His second visit was
occasioned by the necessity of securing hostages

1. Dio Cass., XLVIII, 31; Appian, B. C., V, 67.

2. Dio Cass., XLVIII, 36; Plutarch, Antonius, 32.

3. Appian, B. C., V, 77, 80.

4. Caesar, B. G., II, 35; III, 7: Inita hieme (57-56) Illyricum profectus
est, quod eas quoque nationes adire et regiones cognoscere volebat.

from the Pirustae, a Pannonian tribe, which had made incursions into the Roman province.[1] A more serious invasion of the northern districts took place in the year 51, when the territory of Tergeste was over-run by barbarians, probably the Iapydes,[2] a tribe which had been nominally reduced in the year 129 but had revolted not long afterwards.[3] Moreover the Dalmatians, who had been engaged in war with the Romans in 78 B.C.,[4] had joined with other Illyrian tribes shortly before the outbreak of the civil war to raid the country of the Liburni, where they had captured the city of Promona. The force which Caesar sent to the support of the Liburni was totally destroyed, and a reverse almost as serious overtook the army of Gabinius not long after Pharsalus. A small detachment of Caesarian troops was already engaged in the defence of what remained of the Roman province, under Cornificius, who had achieved some measure of success in reducing a number of hill-castles and even in defeating the squadron of Pompeian ships commanded by Octavius. Gabinius, however, who had been despatched with fifteen cohorts of recruits in view of fresh dangers caused by the flight of many of the Pompeian refugees into Illyricum, was caught

1. Caesar, *B. G.*, V, 1. They had formerly been a part of the kingdom of Genthius, but having deserted him had been declared *liber i et immunes* (Livy, XLV, 26). Strabo, VII, 314, classifies them as Pannonian.

2. So Zippel, *op. cit.*, p. 202. Caesar, *B. G.*, VIII, 24. We hear of the Trans-Alpine Iapydes over-running Tergeste in 35 B.C. (Appian, *Illyr.*, 18).

3. Appian, *Illyr.*, 10.

4. See above, p. 185. The attitude of the Parthini also was doubtful in 48 (Dio Cass., XLII, 10).

by a Dalmatian force near Salona and suffered a crushing defeat.[1]

It is clear that as a result of these victories the power of the Dalmatians had been greatly increased,[2] the Roman hold on the province being practically limited to the settlements on the coast.[3] The coastal districts and the islands were themselves disturbed by the naval operations in this district during the civil war, and that this disturbance was accompanied by serious outbreaks of piracy is shown by the fact that Octavian found it necessary to depopulate the islands of Melita and Corcyra Nigra for the part which their inhabitants had played. The Liburnian pirates were at the same time deprived of their ships.[4]

It is unnecessary to examine in detail the long series of wars with the tribes of the Illyrian coast, which lasted almost continuously from the outbreak of the civil war to the battle of Actium.[5]

1. Caesar, *Bell. Alex.*, 42-43 (Appian, *Illyr.*, 12 ; *B. C.*, II, 59, puts the defeat of Gabinius before Pharsalus, on which see Rice-Holmes, III, p. 217.)

The Catilius, in whom Cicero was interested (see Vatinius' letter, *Ad Fam.*, V, 10 a), seems to have been a Pompeian refugee who was pirating on the Illyrian coast : hominem unum omnium crudelissimum, qui tot ingenuos, matres familias, civis Romanos occidit, abripuit, disperdidit.

2. Cf. Vatinius (Cicero, *l.c.*) : Viginti oppida sunt Dalmatiae antiqua, quae ipsi sibi asciverunt amplius sexaginta.

3. See Zippel, *op. cit.*, pp. 202, 208.

4. Appian, *Illyr.*, 16.

5. On Vatinius' campaigns of 45-44 B.C., see Appian, *Illyr.*, 13 ; Cicero, *Ad Fam.*, V, 9 ; 10 a and b. The operations were to have formed the prelude to an expedition against the Dacians (Velleius, II, 59 ; Suetonius, *Julius*, 44 ; Appian, *B. C.*, II, 110. See Rice-Holmes, III, pp. 325-326). In spite of Vatinius' indignation at Caesar's failure to appreciate the extent of his successes, it is clear from his letter to Cicero written in December, 45 (V, 10 b) that Dalmatia was still imperfectly subdued, and Appian, *Illyr.*, 13, shows that Vatinius suffered a heavy defeat after Caesar's death. He was still governor of Illyricum in 42 (Dio Cass., XLVIII, 21) and was awarded a triumph in that year (*C. I. L.*, I, p. 179).

The Parthini, who had favoured the cause of Brutus (Appian, *B. C.*, V. 75) and were also disturbed in 39, were reduced by Asinius Pollio in that year (Dio Cass., XLVIII, 41 ; Florus, IV, 12 ; *C. I. L.*, I, p. 180).

The campaigns organised by Julius Caesar and later by Octavian were alike intended to form the prelude to a wider scheme of conquest, which had for its object the rectification and extension of the whole of the northern frontier of the empire. Octavian himself was unable to give his personal attention to the task until after the defeat of Sextus, and his initial conquests on the Illyrian coast and in the Alps[1] were again interrupted by the war with Antony. It is clear, however, that the pacification of the Illyrian coast had been achieved by the time of the battle of Actium, and although the district was again disturbed during the Pannonian and Dalmatian revolt, the principal obstacles to peace had been removed by the disarmament of the tribes of the interior and by the gradual spread of civilisation from the trading stations on the coast.[2]

One other district demands a brief notice. There were still risks of piracy on the Cilician coast, and for this reason Augustus, after the death of Amyntas of Galatia in 25 B.C., put the greater part of the coast of Cilicia Tracheia under the rule of Archelaus of Cappadocia, who fixed his residence at Elaeussa. The motive for this arrangement is stated by Strabo to have been the prevalence of piracy and brigandage throughout the whole district.[3] At the same time, the

1. The principal authorities for the campaigns of 35-34 B.C. are Appian, *Illyr.*, 16 *seqq.*; Dio Cassius, XLIX, 34-38; Suetonius, *Augustus*, 20; Strabo, VII, 315; Velleius, II, 90; Florus, IV, 12; *Mon. Anc.*, XXIX; *C. I. L.*, I, p. 180.

2. See Mommsen, *Provinces*, I, pp. 201 *seqq.*

3. Strabo, XIV, 671. On the extent of Archelaus' kingdom, which included districts on both sides of Taurus, see Ramsay, *H. G.*, pp. 374-375. A great part of the interior of Western Tracheia remained, however, in the power of the Teucrids.

reduction of the robber tribes of the Northern
Taurus was vigorously proceeded with. Amyntas
had already made some progress in this direction,
having reduced Antipater of Derbe and Laranda,
but had lost his life in an expedition against the
Homanadeis.[1] The reduction of this tribe was,
however, completed by the war of 10-7 B.C.[2]

The insurrection of the Cilician Cietae in
36 A.D., and again in 52,[3] shows that the interior
of Tracheia was still far from pacified, and, as we
have seen, the whole of this section of the Taurus
range was still liable to outbreaks of brigandage.
Its northern face was, however, guarded by the
system of military colonies, based on the Pisidian
Antioch, which were planted by Augustus in 6 B.C.,
and which served to localise any disturbances that
might arise. We have no further mention of
piracy on the coast. No doubt the police
measures undertaken by Archelaus and his
successors[4] were sufficient to suppress petty
marauders, and behind them lay the strength of
the now fully organised Mediterranean fleets.

It was with the organisation of the standing
fleets maintained by the emperors at Misenum and
Ravenna, with auxiliary squadrons in Egypt,

1. Strabo, XII, p. 569.

2. See Ramsay, *J. R. S.*, VII, p. 253.

3. Tacitus, *Annals*, VI, 41 ; XII, 55.

4. Until 74 A.D., when most of Cilicia Tracheia was united by Vespasian
to the province of Cilicia.

For a full account of the history and organisation of this district
under the empire, to which it is impossible here to make more than a brief
allusion, see Mommsen, *Provinces*, I, p. 336 *seqq.* ; Marquardt, II (French
translation of 1892), pp. 317 *seqq.* ; Hill, *B. M. Cat. Lycaonia, etc.*,
pp. XXVIII *seqq.* ; and especially Ramsay, *H. G.*, pp. 371-375, and his
various articles quoted earlier.

Syria and the Cyrenaica,[1] that for the first time in history the whole of the Mediterranean was adequately patrolled, and the inhabitants of its coast obtained respite from marauders. With the reduction of the piratical communities, improved methods of government in the provinces, and the provision of an organised maritime police, piracy almost disappears from the Mediterranean during the first two centuries of our era. We hear, indeed, of an outbreak on the coast of Palestine during the Jewish war, but this, as we have seen, was merely the despairing effort of inexperienced refugees and was soon brought to an end.[2] The Pseudo-Nero, who in 69 A.D. established himself at the head of a band of slaves and deserters in the island of Cythnos, was speedily reduced by a detachment of the fleet at Misenum.[3] Such outbreaks were only occasional, and the general security of the seas is amply attested by our authorities. Both Strabo and the elder Pliny say definitely that there were no dangers from pirates and that the sea was safe for traders.[4]

While the Mediterranean was thus made secure, it is the more remarkable that the imperial government should have paid so little attention

1. Short accounts of the imperial fleets will be found in Stuart-Jones, *Companion to Roman History*, pp. 260-261, and the Cambridge *Companion to Latin Studies*, pp. 498-500; full references to literature and inscriptions by Fiebiger in Pauly-Wissowa *s.v. Classis*, and by Gauckler in Daremberg and Saglio, 3, 2, pp. 1328-37.

2. See above, p. 31. On Joppa, see Strabo, XVI, 759. The λῃσταί of Sardinia, mentioned by Dio Cassius (LV, 28) in A.D. 6, appear to have been brigands rather than pirates.

3. Tacitus, *Hist.*, II, 8; Zonaras, XI, 15.

4. Strabo, III, 144; Pliny, *N. H.*, II, 117. Cf. Horace, *Odes*, IV, 5, 19 (quoted at the head of this chapter); Suetonius, *Augustus*, 98 (The crew of the Alexandrian ship off Puteoli : per illum se vivere, per illum navigare).

to what was happening in the outer seas. The
Red Sea was infested by Arab pirates, who preyed
upon the shipping which followed the trade-route
from Myoshormos to India.[1]   Pliny tells us
that merchantmen were compelled to carry
detachments of archers on board owing to their
activities.[2]   The same difficulties had been
experienced by the Ptolemies in their endeavour
to open this route, when the Nabataeans, although
hitherto a law-abiding race, soon developed
a system of wrecking on their coasts, and like the
Tauri of the Black Sea, began to build small craft
to attack the merchant vessels.[3]   Attacks from
Arab pirates were the more dreaded owing to their
use of poisoned arrows.[4]

Great as were the commercial interests concerned in the Indian trade, the neglect of the
Black Sea coasts produced even more disastrous
consequences. We have already examined the
tactics of the pirates of the Caucasus,[5] and it is
obvious from Strabo's account that these piracies
were a common event in his own day.   Tacitus
also tells us that the wreckers of the Tauri were
still active in the first century after Christ.[6]

1. On the route, see Strabo, III, 18.

2. Pliny, *N. H.*, VI, 101.

3. Diod. Sic., III, 43.

4. Pliny, *N. H.*, VI, 176. In connection with piracy on this route
Lecrivain in Daremberg and Saglio quotes the ἄνδρες Πειραταί of Ptolemy,
VII, 1, 84, in India.

5. See above, p. 26.   The serious character of these piratical descents
is shown by an inscription of Tomi, which records the enrolment of a special
guard maintained by day and night against the repeated attacks of *Kares*.
The editor, however, regards the inscription as of pre-Roman date (*Arch.
Ep. Mitt.*, XIV, p. 34), and I am at a loss to understand who these Kares
may be. Pliny, *N. H.*, VI, 7, speaks of Cares in the Don Valley and Ptolemy
knows of Sarmatian Kariones (III, 5, 10).

6. Tacitus, *Annals,* XII, 17.

According to Strabo, some attempt was made by the native princes to check the Caucasian depredations, but in the districts controlled by the Romans little attention was paid to them by the governors,[1] in spite of the fact that even in the first century marauders from the Black Sea occasionally made their way into the Mediterranean. We find, for example, the people of Ilion honouring a certain Titus Velius Proculus for having cleared the Hellespont of pirates,[2] who may be regarded as marauders from the Black Sea extending their cruises into the Aegean. In the following century it is possible that the Costoboci, who were troubling Greece in the reign of Antoninus Pius or Marcus Aurelius, and were overthrown at Elateia in Phocis, were a band of Sarmatian robbers from the Black Sea, who thus anticipated the movements of the next century.[3] We have already seen that the Scythian and Gothic invaders of the third century obtained their ships and learnt their seamanship largely from the piratical tribes of the Black Sea coasts. Although it was not until the Mediterranean fleets had fallen into decay that these incursions became serious, it is probable that if the maritime police maintained during the first two centuries of the empire had been extended over the whole of the Black Sea, and the piratical tribes there exterminated, the confusion of the third century in the

---

1. Strabo, XI, 496.

2. *I. G. Rom.*, IV, 219.

3. Pausanias, X, 34, 5 (with Frazer's note); Dittenberger, *Syll.*³, 871. See Mommsen, *Provinces*, I, p. 242. Their home is variously given. Pliny, *N. H.*, VI, 19, may be right in placing them in the Don Valley, though Ptolemy, III, 8, locates them in Northern Dacia (cf. Dio Cassius, LXXI, 12).

Mediterranean would have been considerably diminished.

Here we may leave the pirate of history. The pirate of ancient fiction need not long detain us, although his character differs widely in different classes of literature. In the Homeric poems the pirate chieftain, as described by Odysseus, is, it is true, a fictitious character invented by Odysseus for his own purposes[1]; but although fictitious, the description is derived from reality, and its accuracy is corroborated by other evidence. The whole episode might well have been the actual experience of one of the Aegean rovers. The same can be said of other episodes of piracy in literature. In the Homeric hymn to Dionysus the tactics of the Tyrrhenians closely correspond with the known procedure of the ordinary pirate. A beautiful youth, whose value in the slave market would be great, or whose family be wealthy enough to provide an ample ransom, is seen on shore ; the crew of the pirate boat lands and carries him off.[2] The story told by the unjust steward in Pausanias, that the cattle which he has sold have been carried off by pirates, won credence owing to the inherent probability of his tale.[3] Events of this character were of frequent occurrence, and even when invented, carried conviction with them. There is an interesting example in the *Bacchides* of Plautus, where Chrysalus, in order to explain the disappearance of his master's money, tells an

1. *Od.*, XIV, 199 *seqq.*
2. *Hom. Hymn, Dionysus*, 1-31.
3. Pausanias, IV, 4.

elaborate story of a plot hatched in Ephesos between Archidemides, from whom the deposit had been received, and a gang of pirates, to intercept him and Mnesilochus, as they were conveying it homewards :

CHRYS. Postquam aurum abstulimus, in navem
      conscendimus,
    domi cupientes. forte ut adsedi in stega,
    dum circumspecto, atque lembum conspicor
    longum, strigorem maleficum exornarier.
NIC. Perii hercle, lembus ille mihi laedit latus.
CHRYS. Is erat communis cum hospite et praedonibus.

         *   *   *   *   *

    Is lembus nostrae navi insidias dabat.
    occepi ego observare eos quam rem gerant.
    interea e portu nostra navis solvitur.
    ubi portu eximus, homines remigio sequi,
    neque aves neque venti citius. quoniam sentio
    quae res gereretur, navem extemplo statuimus.
    quoniam vident nos stare, occeperunt ratem
    tardare in portu.
NIC.   Edepol mortalis malos.
    quid denique agitis ?
CHRYS.   Rursum in portum recepimus.[1]

The pirate's tactics are not unlike those which Strabo describes in his account of the Corycian trick, where the pirates discover on shore the cargo and destination of a ship and waylay her on the open sea.[2]

Although there is little mention of piracy in the fragments of the New Comedy that have actually

---

1. Plautus, *Bacchides*, 277 *seqq.*
2. See above, pp. 38, 205.

survived,[1] we are justified in regarding the numerous allusions to it in Plautus and Terence as derived from the Greek writers whom they imitated. In Messenio's denunciation of Erotium and her class (a passage which again recalls the Corycian trick), there can be little doubt that Plautus derives his vigorous comparison from a Greek original:

> Morem hunc meretrices habent:
> ad portum mittunt servolos, ancillulas ;
> si quae peregrina navis in portum advenit,
> rogitant cuiatis sit, quid si nomen siet,
> postilla extemplo se applicant, agglutinant.
> si pellexerunt, perditum amittunt domum.
> nunc in istoc portu (Erotium's house) stat navis
>   praedatoria,
> aps qua cavendum nobis sane censeo.[2]

---

1. In Menander, *Halieis*, fr. 15 (Kock) the situation is fairly obvious (see above, p. 25):

ὡς δὲ τὴν ἄκραν
κάμπτοντας ἡμᾶς εἶδον, ἐμβάντες ταχὺ
ἀνηγάγοντο.

In the *Citharistes* (Körte, p. 166) Col. II, 12-13 :

λογίζομαι πᾶν, μή τι κατὰ θάλατταν ᾖ
ἀτύχημα γεγονὸς ἢ περι . . . . . as,

Herwerden's restoration [ληστ]ὰς is convincing, and is adopted by van Leeuwen, p. 140. The sentiment is like that in the *Trinummus*, 1087 :

Ego miserrumeis periclis sum per maria maxuma
vectus, capitali periclo per praedones plurumos
me servavi, salvos redii.

2. Plautus, *Menaechmi*, 338 *seqq*. The metaphor is continued when Erotium draws Menaechmus inside :

Ducit lembum dierectum navis praedatoria (442).

Legrand, *The New Greek Comedy* (Trans. J. Loeb), pp. 526-527, compares *Anth. Pal.*, V. 161 :

Εὐφρὼ καὶ Θαῒς καὶ Βοίδιον, αἱ Διομήδους
γραῖαι, ναυκλήρων ὁλκάδες εἰκόσοροι,
*Ἄγιν καὶ Κλεοφῶντα καὶ Ἀνταγόρην ἔν'ἑκάστη
γυμνοὺς, ναυηγῶν ἥσσονας, ἐξέβαλον.
Ἀλλὰ σὺν αὐταῖς νηυσὶ τὰ ληστρικὰ τῆς Ἀφροδίτης
φεύγετε· Σειρήνων αἵδε γὰρ ἐχθρότεραι.

and notes that both this epigram and V, 181, are strongly reminiscent of the *New Comedy*.

The writers of the New Comedy owed much to the pirate and kidnapper in the construction of their plots. The child carried off by kidnappers in the town is a commonplace of the Latin comedy,[1] and with equal frequency the plot depends on the fact that one of the characters has been carried off by pirates and sold into slavery. This had been the fate of the daughter of Daemones in the *Rudens*,[2] and of the supposed sister of Thais in Terence's *Eunuchus*,[3] who was said to have been carried off as a child from Sunium. In the *Miles Gloriosus* Palaestrio, going in search of his master, whose mistress had been carried off, was captured at sea by pirates and presented to the soldier :

> Ubi sumus provecti in altum fit quod di volunt.
> capiunt praedones navem illam ubi vectus fui.[4]

Although these abductions are of a conventional character, and as a literary device are as old as Homer,[5] there can be little doubt that the writers of the New Comedy were familiar with piracy as one of the common dangers of contemporary life, and that their audiences were prepared to accept the situations depicted, without question as to their probability. The point has been dealt with by Legrand, whose arguments gain in force when it is remembered that our discussion has shown that it was precisely during the period

1. *Menaechmi*, 29 ; *Curculio*, 645 ; *Poenulus*, 84 ; *Captivi*, 7.
2. Plautus, *Rudens*, 39.
3. Terence, *Eun.*, 115.
4. Plautus, *Mil. Glor.*, 118-9.
5. *Od.*, XV, 427, 465.

of Menander's activity that piracy had entered upon one of its worst phases.[1] So far as he appears in the New Comedy, the pirate is still true to life ; where his tactics are described, they conform to the normal Mediterranean practice[2] ; he himself remains a sinister and detested figure,[3] and neither he nor his daughter has become the love-sick imbecile that we meet in later literature.

It is significant that we first meet with a change in a period when piracy was practically non-existent. Capture by pirates formed a part of the stock-in-trade of the schools of rhetoric, and as such may have been taken over wholesale from the New Comedy.[4] Some of the themes are straightforward enough : a man who has lost his wife buries her with her ornaments, and marries again. Later he is captured by pirates, and writes to his home for the ransom money. The wife opens the tomb of her predecessor and sends the ornaments. She is brought to trial by her stepson for violating the tomb of his mother, but the son is disinherited by the father on his return.[5] The letter sent by the victim to his

1. See above, p. 122. The evidence there collected renders Legrand's qualification (*op. cit.*, p. 207) " such proof as we have for this assertion dates from a period subsequent to that in which the prototypes of Plautus' and Terence's comedies were written " unnecessary. We have seen that the generation following Alexander's death was infinitely worse than the hundred years which preceded the rise of the Cilicians.

2. *Bacchides, Menaechmi, Halieis, ll. cc.*

3. Plautus, *Caecus vel Praedones*, fr. V:
   Ita sunt praedones : prorsum parcunt nemini.

4. Typical *controversiae* based on capture by pirates are : Seneca, *Controv.*, I, 2 ; I, 6 ; I, 7 ; VII, 1 ; VII, 4. Quintilian, *Declam.*, V, VI, IX ; *Decl. Min.*, CCLVII, CCCLXVII, CCCLXXIII.

5. Quintilian, CCCLXXIII.

relatives figures prominently in these cases,[1] and this feature was probably based on actual practice. How far the *vicarius* was accepted by the historical pirate is more doubtful.[2] In the inscription of Amorgos[3] it is true that two of the party carried off by Socleidas are retained as hostages, but in this case it was they who were to provide the ransom money. A *vicarius*, as we have seen, was not accepted by Stackelberg's captors. In one of the rhetorical themes[4] we hear that the pirates themselves write that the sister of the captive should be sent to take his place and become the wife of the *archipirata*. A maid servant is sent in her mistress' place, and she duly marries the pirate and inherits his wealth. It is obvious that in themes of this character we have a very close approach to the romance, the influence of which is still more noticeable in other cases. The pirate's daughter, whom we have already met in Suidas' story of the foundation of the temple on Cape Colias,[5] figures also in one of Seneca's *controversiae*,[6] where she falls in love with a captive, and enables him to escape after extracting an oath that he will marry her. The legal problem is created by the parental command that he should divorce his rescuer and marry a rich widow in her place. Themes of this character and those which

1. Seneca, I, 6; VII, 4. Quintilian, V, VI, IX, CCLVII.

2. As in Quintilian, VI. In IX, the *vicarius* is accepted after the captive has passed into the hands of the slave-dealer.

3. See above, p. 139.

4. Quintilian, CCCLXVII.

5. See above, p. 152.

6. Seneca, I, 6. For a variant of the " pirate's daughter," see Xenophon, *Ephes.*, II, 3.

depend on coincidences conceivable only by the professional story-teller, such as the wronged son who turns pirate and has the good fortune to capture his father,[1] raise an interesting problem as to their relationship to the later Greek romances. Seneca's second *controversia*, of the girl captured by pirates, who claims to have preserved her purity during this and subsequent adventures, appears to give us the lawyer's version of Leucippe's fortunes in Achilles Tatius.[2]

The pirate and brigand of the novelist is a hardworked individual, usually of an incurably romantic disposition, who in some cases is compelled to traverse wide tracts of land and sea in order to keep pace with the wanderings of the hero and heroine. Hippothous, the brigand and *deus ex machina* of the *Ephesiaca*, is thus brought through Asia Minor and Syria to Egypt, and thence is taken to Sicily, Italy and Rhodes in order to keep in touch with Habrocomes and Antheia.[3] Adventures with pirates are perhaps more closely packed in this romance than in any other. It is true that in all of them we can be sure of the consequences, if the hero and heroine are unwise enough to undertake a sea-voyage, or even to approach the shore,[4] but in none of them

1. Seneca, VII, 1.

2. Achilles Tatius, V, 7 *seqq.*; VI, 21-22. Compare the Apollonius romance, 30 *seqq.*

3. Xenophon, *Ephes.*

4. As in *Daphnis and Chloe*, I, 28. (Tyrian pirates in a Carian ἡμιολία). The rescue of Daphnis is very like Aelian's story of the pigs (see above, p. 160). On the resemblances between Longus and Aelian see Carin, *Studi Italiani*, 1909, pp. 455-6, to which Mr. R. M. Rattenbury drew my attention. It is difficult, however, to say how far similarity of incident can be taken as a proof of connexion. Many incidents of this type used by

does the pirate appear with such frequency as in the *Ephesiaca*. Phoenician pirates carry off the lovers on their voyage from Rhodes, and the usual complications arise owing to the passion with which their captors are inspired. Antheia falls into the hands of Hippothous' band in Cilicia. When she has been buried alive in Tarsus, robbers open the tomb[1] and carry her away to Alexandria. She is then sold to Psammis the Indian, but is again captured by Hippothous, who by this time has reached the borders of Aethiopia. Her fatal beauty once more inflames the robbers, and when, in self-defence, she has slain Anchialus, a member of the gang, she is sentenced to be shut up alive in a pit with two dogs. She escapes, however, through the effect which her beauty produces on Amphinomus, another of the gang, who has been left to guard her prison.

The adventures with pirates, which form so large a part of the romances, are not always handled with the same disregard of probability. One of the best episodes in Heliodorus is the long pursuit from Zacynthos to Africa. Although the motive of the arch-pirate is as much his passion for Charicleia as greed of the wealth on board the Phoenician ship, and the episode comes to an end with the interruption of his marriage festivities owing to a mutiny organised by the jealous mate, the rest is constructed with considerable skill and

the novelists and others were undoubtedly derived from popular stories. A case in point is Plutarch's story of the Ferryman and the Pirates (*Qu. Gr.*, 34), which is found in an earlier form in Heracleides Ponticus *F. H G.*, II, p. 223, No. 38).

1. In Charito, I, 7 *seqq.* Callirrhoe is similarly rescued from the grave by pirate tomb-robbers.

regard for probability. We see the pirate vessel lying under a promontory of Zacynthos, in wait for the Phoenician ship on which the lovers are voyaging. The fisherman Tyrrhenus, at whose house they are wintering, is the agent normally employed by the pirate on shore, so that word of the plot reaches them[1] early. The Phoenician captain endeavours to slip away before the winter has come to an end, but meets with bad weather and is compelled to put in to Crete for repairs. All this time he has been followed by the pirate, who does not, however, show himself until Crete has been left behind :

The spring gales were now blowing from the west, and as soon as we started we were driven on by them for a day and a night, our master steering his course for the coast of Africa. For he said that if the wind continued blowing and we kept a straight course we might get quite across the main sea, and that he was making all haste possible to reach the mainland or some harbour, insomuch as he suspected the barque astern to be a pirate. " Ever since we loosed from the promontory of Crete," said he, " he has been following us, and never declined one jot from our course, but pursues our ship as if he went our voyage with us. Indeed I have noticed, when I of purpose turned our ship from the right course, that he also did the same."

When he had said this, some were moved and exhorted the rest to make ready for defence, but some made light thereof saying that it was customary for a smaller ship at sea to follow a greater as being guided by their more experience. While these things were disputed on both sides, it was the time of day when the husbandman doth unyoke his oxen from the plough, and the vehement wind began to wax calm so that in a little while it was

1. Or rather their guardian, Calasiris.

almost down and blew softly to no purpose on our sails, rather shaking them together than making any way for our ship. At length it ceased quite, as if at the sun-setting it had appointed to cease blowing, or rather —that I may speak more truly—to do them which followed us a good turn. For those that were in the barque, as long as we had wind, were left far behind our merchant ship, our greater sails, as is natural, receiving more wind.[1] But when the sea grew calm and we were perforce compelled to row, the barque came on us quicker than I can describe, for every one on board her, I think, was at the oars, while she was a light boat and answered better to the rowers' efforts.

When they were now close to us, one of the men of Zacynthus who had come aboard with us cried ; " We are undone, comrades ; this is a pirate craft ; I recognise Trachinus and his barque." All our ship was moved at this news, and was filled with stormy tumult in calm weather. Everywhere was noise, lamenting, and running up and down.

* * * * *

The men on board our ship, as long as they were without danger and the battle without blood, were very stout and said plainly that they would not depart. But when one of the pirates bolder than the rest leapt aboard, and with his sword slew all he met, teaching them that wars are usually made with slaughter and death, and the rest leapt after him, then the Phoenicians repented of their ways and falling flat on their faces begged for mercy, for that they would do whatsoever they would have them. Although the pirates were now greedy to kill—for the sight of blood is a great incentive to fury—yet contrary to all hope, on command of Trachinus they spared them.[2]

However closely the episode agrees with the

1. See above, p. 16.

2. Heliodorus, *Aethiopica*, V, 23 *seqq*. (Underdowne's translation, ed. F. A. Wright).

actual practice of the pirate, we may nevertheless
be confident that Heliodorus relied on literary
sources rather than on first-hand information.
The case is clearer in his account of the Βουκόλοι
λῃσταί of the Delta.[1]   They play a part also in the
romance of Achilles Tatius,[2] and clearly formed
a standing menace to the safety of all persons in
the Romances who approached the Egyptian
coast.   Heliodorus' account is probably a compila-
tion from a variety of sources, one of the most
striking characteristics of the robbers' mode of life
being derived from Herodotus' description of the
lake-dwellers of Prasias.[3]   In the main, perhaps,
the Βουκόλοι of the novelists go back to
Eratosthenes,[4] and though the practice of human
sacrifice by robbers is found in other romances,[5]
its ascription to the Egyptian robbers may be
a reminiscence of the Busiris myth.   It is not to
be supposed, however, that Busiris was in the
habit of using a property sword to slay his
victims, like the robbers in Achilles Tatius.[6]

1.   *Ib.*, I, 5-6.

2.   Achilles Tat., III, 9 ; IV, 12.

3.   Hdt., V, 16.

4.   *Ap.* Strabo, XVII, 802, cf. 792 (I see that this is also suggested by
Rohde, *Griech. Roman*2, p. 420, note 1).

5.   Xenophon, *Ephes.*, II, 13.

6.   Achilles Tat., III, 20-22.

INDEX